Shakespeare's Shakespeare

Shakespeare's Shakespeare

How the Plays Were Made

JOHN C. MEAGHER

CONTINUUM · NEW YORK

1997

The Continuum Publishing Company
370 Lexington Avenue, New York, NY 10017

Copyright © 1997 by John C. Meagher

Printed in the United States of America

Library of Congress Cataloging-in-Publication Data

Meagher, John C.
    Shakespeare's Shakespeare : how the plays were made / John C.
Meagher.
        p.   cm.
    Includes bibliographical references.
    ISBN 0–8264–1007–3   (alk. paper)
    1. Shakespeare, William, 1564–1616—Dramatic production.
2. Shakespeare, William, 1564–1616—Stage history—To   1625.
3. Theater—England—History—16th century. 4. Theater—England–
History—17th century.   I.   Title.
PR3091.M43 1997
792.9'5—DC21   96–45474
                                                              CIP

This book is dedicated to

Allie Bertram Cannaday,
who gave me my first chance to teach Shakespeare when I was sixteen;

Gerald Eades Bentley and Alan S. Downer,
who helped me learn how to do so much more appropriately;

Alan Levitan,
who shared the learning with me then and still, refreshingly
and illuminatingly;

John Crow,
who gave me room (and some help) to do it still better;

and all the students with whom I shared Shakespeare,
especially *Ted McGee*, who ultimately helped me more than I helped him,
and *Marion O'Connor*, incomparable.

Contents

Preface 9

1   IF WE OFFEND, IT IS WITH OUR GOOD WILL
What this is about, and why it is needed 13

2   HOW LONG IS'T NOW SINCE LAST YOUR SELF
AND I WERE IN A MASQUE?
*How we lost, and may recover, Shakespeare's own
dramaturgy* 28

3   A LOCAL HABITATION, AND A NAME
A self-portrait of the artist as a dramaturge 38

4   IN SHORT SPACE, IT RAIN'D DOWN FORTUNE
Shakespeare's use of space and place 56

5   DEVISE THE FITTEST TIME, AND SAFEST WAY
Shakespeare's treatment of time and continuity 69

6   AND I MAY HIDE MY FACE, LET ME PLAY
THISBY TOO
The dramaturgy and dramatics of role-doubling 95

7   A GOOD PLOT, GOOD FRIENDS, AND FULL OF
EXPECTATION
*Shakespeare's plotting of plays and management of
sources* 116

8   STUFFED, AS THEY SAY, WITH HONORABLE PARTS
Shakespeare's dramaturgy of character 144

Contents

9 A TASTE OF YOUR QUALITY: COME, A PASSIONATE
   SPEECH
   *Shakespeare's language, especially his dramatic
   verse and prose* *171*

10 THE PURPOSE OF PLAYING . . . AT THE FIRST AND NOW
   The aims of Shakespearean dramaturgy *184*

   Notes *215*

Preface

Here's the overall scheme: my intent is to provide a general survey of the principles of Shakespearean dramaturgy, concretized and illustrated especially through reference to seven fairly well-known plays: the comedies *A Midsummer Night's Dream* and *As You Like It*, the histories *Richard II* and *Henry IV Part 1*, and the tragedies *Romeo and Juliet*, *Hamlet*, and *King Lear*. Other plays will come into view from time to time, but this arbitrary canon of seven will be the basis of the discussion. Readers who want to get the most out of this book would do well to refresh their memories of these seven plays; I will write as if you have at least a good basic recollection of them.

My quotations from Shakespeare will usually be adapted (though occasionally presented verbatim) from the primary collection of his plays, the First Folio edition of 1623. The Folio is not always the best text, and footnotes will occasionally supply a reading from an earlier Quarto edition (or admit that I have quoted a Quarto this time in the main text, and explain why as I give the Folio counterpart if there is one).[1] My primary reason for using the Folio is that the widely distributed Folio facsimiles by Yale and by Norton (and more recently by Doug Moston's wonderful edition published by Applause [New York and London]) make it the most readily accessible of early Shakespeare texts: my reasons for wanting to keep the reader in touch with the early texts in preference to still more accesssible modern editions will become obvious as the book unfolds, if they aren't already.

My reasons for taking the liberty of adapting Folio quotations (e.g., by modernizing the spelling and typography sometimes but not always, or supplying my own punctuation on occasion) is that while there are a few points where my argument requires, or at least authorizes, a rigorous reproduction of the original, most of the time a modernized or otherwise-adjusted version will be easier on the reader and not misleading, as long as you realize that I am not contracting to be true to the Folio other than in my fashion. (I see no merit in pedantically repeating something like the Folio's "vnueile" when the word is to be understood as "unveil," except to make the sort of point I am now making.) Though I may occasionally have blundered in these changes, I have been careful not to; and I generally warrant the reader that my quotations, varying from utterly literal to entirely modernized, will not be misleading. And yes, I am also taking refuge in the principles of Shakespearean dramaturgy in judging that the right way of handling a quotation is what makes best sense in the immediate context, even at the expense of uniform consistency.

Citations for the original locus of quotations or cited happenings will normally be given in the text merely in the form of the conventional act-scene indicators, in Arabic numerals (3.4 = act III, scene iv). This too is a substantial inconsistency all by itself, since it is potentially misleading to retain the act-scene divisions artificially imposed on Shakespeare's plays by their subsequent editors and additionally inconsistent in that sometimes the modern conventions of scene-division have overruled what explicitly appears in the Folio. This is a reluctant practical choice. Although act-scene references have close to zero value as indications of how Shakespeare designed his plays, they do assist us to locate quotations and citations. It is necessary to keep readers posted, and there is still no other widely distributed system for doing so. The Through Line Numbering (TLN) system developed by Charlton Hinman and used in his facsimile of the Folio (and in Doug Moston's) is superior but can be keyed only to those editions, so I use the conventional modern ways of locating specific scenes despite its lack of intrinsic appropriateness.

I do not use line numbers. The traditional 130-year-old Globe Edition line numbering is not regularly followed in recent editions, where lineation can vary considerably according to how the text is composed and the prose-margins set, so there is no exact way of specifying a line that will reliably hold true for the edition you may have at hand. I assume that readers will not often want to look up my references, and that when they do, a citation of the relevant scene—plus, in the case of especially long scenes, a hint of about how far along the citation may be found—will be generally sufficient, though inexact. If I could believe that all readers will have a First Folio facsimile beside them, I would perhaps use the TLN system, as it is both neutral and very efficient. But I have made what I think to be a fair and realistic compromise. I apologize to anyone who may be inconvenienced by this prudential decision, and hope that others will appreciate the reduction of what is really unnecessary clutter.

One final point. The notes to my text have up to now been signaled in the usual way, with a superscript numeral guiding the reader to a corresponding number in the notes section at the end of the book. From now on, there will be four types of notes, and the superscript signals that follow in this paragraph will direct the reader to samples of each kind. The bare superscript numeral indicates that I am supplying nothing but routine documentation in the notes section—an authoritative source for a quotation, the place where the argument referred to is worked out, some relevant readings on the subject at hand.[2] You may ignore these, unless you happen to be curious about my sources. Notes which involve further remarks that go beyond grounding what I have just said (i.e., parenthetical remarks that look up from my text to add something directly relevant to it, like supportive quotations or citations of opposing views) are signaled by a plus-sign after the numeral.[3+] These too may be ignored unless you are particularly interested in what is being discussed at that point. In cases where the note sets the text aside for a moment, to say something less directly relevant that I thought potentially worth your notice even though it be only obliquely related to the text, there will be an asterisk after the numeral.[4*] Try all of these for a chapter or two, and skip them thereafter if they aren't adequately rewarding. When the numeral is followed by an exclamation point, I am asking you please to check it out: this is something that I definitely want you to have a look at, even though it may be something of an aside.[5!]

I HAVE LOTS of thanks to sprinkle, inevitably. The staffs of various libraries, from Trinity College, Dublin (who put seven librarians on the job and managed to find their forty-odd volumes of *Shakespeare Survey* within three days), through the British Library (where *Shakespeare Survey* seems to be cataloged uniquely under the name of Allardyce Nicoll—why wasn't that obvious to me?), the Folger Shakespeare Library (where one can pluck the relevant volumes of *Shakespeare Survey* off the open shelves of the Reading Room), the Robarts Library of the University of Toronto, and the Kelly Library of St. Michael's College, to the Shakespeare Bibliothek in Munich, whence Ingeborg Boltz graciously allowed me to borrow books. The staffs of various hotels, restaurants, pubs, and cafes where much of the book was composed on my little IBM Thinkpad after it had been stuffed with gleanings from the aforementioned libraries. Friends and acquaintances who read parts of the MS and gave helpful advice and/or encouraging words: David Dixon, Teresa Gianfelice, Alan Levitan, a woman I met on a train who was curious, Marion O'Connor, Elena Lupas, a drama student in a Dublin pub, George Lawler, and especially Jane Barter. Also the inmates of ENG 2550, who worked valiantly through the *practicum* version of what I had been writing, with heartening results.

1

If We Offend, It Is with Our Good Will

What this is about, and why it is needed

There are as many legitimate ways of reading Shakespeare's plays as there are of having a conversation, making a meal, or rearing children. Not all of them are attempts to understand the plays themselves, though the most traditional ways of reading them are for some purpose of understanding what Shakespeare said, or why his work is a great artistic achievement, or what these plays actually *mean*.

There are various specialized styles of reading for what the plays actually mean—e.g., through a concentration on moral and religious values, or on principal themes, or on patterns of imagery. Most of them assume that such ways of reading will reveal what *Shakespeare* meant by them. But such ambitions have been steadily falling out of high-level fashion. Advanced readers of Shakespeare now often suppose one or both of two fairly modern notions about such a project. One is that a search for the author's intention is not a proper way to read a text; the other is that it is impossible to locate Shakespeare's intention in any case.

Hence we have other ways of reading Shakespeare's plays that stay agnostic or indifferent to Shakespeare's intent. Successive major waves of critical rereading have been undertaken from Marxist, structuralist, Freudian, or feminist analyses, and have disclosed features of the plays that may be considered significant whether or not Shakespeare was aware of them, whether or not they are even coherent with what he might have thought he was doing. An investigation of his representation of the lower classes might bypass all questions about his sympathies in order to register what is objectively present and absent in their portrayal within the plays, whatever may have been in Shakespeare's mind; the effect of a play's treatment of women may be evaluated as progressive, reactionary, perceptive, obtuse, or even subversive to the main drift, without the evaluator's having to decide what Shakespeare thought he was doing.

It is possible to approach the plays with the assumption that there is no reliable way of divining what Shakespeare intended, and still come up with helpful insights. A modern director may even mount a theatrically or cinematically successful production by deliberately overruling what she thinks Shakespeare intended, creatively transforming a comedy into a tragically dark experience (or *vice versa*), or changing the sense of setting from a somewhat Elizabethanized late-medieval Verona or a deliberately non-Elizabethanized Rome to an evocation of contemporary Manhattan or of the lives and machinations of modern supercorporation executives. The possible ways of reading Shakespeare's plays are nearly endless, and each may be thought valid within the limits of its own assumptions, goals, and questions.

There is no intrinsically illegitimate way to read Shakespeare's plays; there is no way that is uniquely valid. That does not mean, of course, that they are all equal. Just as some conversations are merely small talk and aimless weather-chat, and some meals are not very nourishing, some approaches to Shakespeare may be doomed from the outset to come up with trivial or idiosyncratic or generally unhelpful results. Some conversations are more searching, and those that take place among meteorologists may have results vital to saving crops and lives; and some meals are unusually various and tasty while remaining soundly nutritious and careful about guests' known preferences, possible allergic reactions, and dietary principles. If no single approach to Shakespeare can be ruled flatly wrong, or claim exclusive validity, that does not mean that there are not some that are more generally useful than others, or that it is impossible to devise a way that delivers superior results in understanding his plays.

The approach of this book is an investigation of Shakespeare's dramaturgy—i.e., his stagecraft, his repertoire of playwriting techniques, the strategies and schemes and tactics with which he put plays together. Its assumptions, goals, and questions will be gradually clarified and defended as it proceeds, but a quick sketch may be of help in your deciding whether you want to go further with it.

I will assume throughout that the early texts of Shakespeare's plays— from the single-play editions of the 1590s to the First Folio collection published in 1623—present a fairly authentic, even if not always reliable, version of what Shakespeare wrote, and comprise adequate evidence for inferring some of his own assumptions (some of which we no longer share) about the effective crafting of plays. I will further assume that Shakespeare designed his plays with considerable care, and that those early texts contain enough traces of his designs to allow us to reconstruct them to a considerable and useful extent, and that in fact the pursuit of the evidences of such designs can bring us to a more sound and well-grounded understanding of Shakespeare's plays than we have yet been able to achieve. I will, to put it more boldly and vulnerably, assume that it is possible to get closer to Shakespeare's deliberate designing of his plays and to his understanding of how they would work in the experience of his audiences.

My principal goals are two. One is the discovery and reconstruction of some of the important principles by which Shakespeare's plays were written and performed, including the implicit habits, assumptions, constraints, liberties, conventions, and practices of stagecraft that were aspects of the dramatic world he shared with his audiences—especially those aspects that are most neglected, undervalued, or misunderstood by modern readers. The other is the promotion of a way of rereading the plays that will incorporate an awareness of these principles, facilitate a more adequate recovery of Shakespeare's designs, and eventually convince readers that this approach, although not the only legitimate one, is finally more satisfying—and more appreciative of Shakespeare's accomplishment—than any other.

My principal questions will be qualified and finessed according to the nature of the specific problems, but they will mainly be variations on a common theme: Why did Shakespeare write this bit (this speech, this character, this stage direction, this scene)? What is its effect on the unfolding of the play, what function does it seem to have in a dramatic design, what is its value and contribution to the moment and the whole? What implicit features of his design can we reasonably infer from what is overtly presented in the text? What can all this tell us about Shakespeare's playwriting practices in general or his management of this play in particular or his value priorities in this specific artistic decision? And always latent will be a further question: How should the resulting discoveries and inferences invite us to change or adjust our ways of attempting to understand Shakespeare's plays?

The text of a Shakespearean play is significantly unlike the texts of Shakespeare's poems, or the texts of the stories, treatises, and chronicle books he may have used in writing the play. The latter were *meant* to be read. The play-text is significantly different in communicative intent: it was primarily a script composed for a company of actors rather than for book-buyers; it is designed to be staged rather than read; and the staging design is not always overtly presented by the text. Moreover, the play is designed in accordance with a dramatic style that is significantly different not only from novels and poems but also from the texts and productions of stage plays of the last 350 years, whose published texts accommodate to readers far more than Shakespeare's do. Ironically, we can read what Shakespeare read with far less difficulty than we can read what he wrote.

A Shakespearean play is, in short, an archaeological project rather than a finished public statement. It is the product of a set of happenstances that distance us doubly from what it was meant to be. On the one hand, it was primarily a privileged communication to his actors rather than an explication of what the public was to receive; and on the other hand, it was written in accordance with a dramaturgy that differs about as much from what we are used to as Shakespeare's language differs from contemporary English.

That is the dimension of reading Shakespeare in which modern readers are most in need of help, and get the least assistance from the editions they use. I would welcome changes in editorial policy and practice in this regard, but hitherto it has not been understood as part of the editors' task: it is appropriate to settle for their having done progressively well in presenting the texts, and venturing bravely (though not always adequately) into discussing dramaturgy from time to time. In the meantime, I offer this book.

Before going further in trying to describe, explain, or justify what I am trying to do in this book, I will plunge you directly into the project by visiting a minor scene in *As You Like It*. If you find this chapter convincingly and helpfully informative about how Shakespeare crafted a relatively marginal three minutes' worth of a play, the remaining chapters will take you much further in the same direction, amplifying the evidence and general argument for reading Shakespeare in accordance with his own dramaturgical principles and practices. What follows, in short, is a tiny and incomplete but representative swatch of what this book is about.

WHEN WHAT IS conventionally referred to as act 2, scene 5 of *As You Like It* begins, we have been provided with a preparatory understanding by what has gone before.

Since the opening scene of the play, we have known that the rightful Duke has been displaced by his usurping brother Frederick, and that he is now in exile in the forest of Arden, accompanied by his loyal lords. They have been described as living a pleasant and contented life, explicitly like that of a rather romanticized Robin Hood and his Merrie Men.

Shakespeare has already arranged for us to meet (in the first scene of act 2) the Duke himself, together with some of his followers. The Duke has there been presented as a patient and philosophical man who feels a bit out of place but is clearly making the best of the situation. His lords are generally supportive and admiring. But much of that scene is focused on the absent Jaques, another follower of the exiled Duke whose description makes him interestingly different from the generally sympathetic and loyal lords of 2.1. Jaques is established by the dialogue of 2.1 as being a valued member of the Duke's group, but something of an Odd Man In, a melancholy moralizer who does not share the others' positive attitudes but rather specializes in being cynically critical about the otherwise romanticized forest life, and about the life in courts and cities as well. Scene 2.1 ends with a general exit as the Duke, aided by the lords, goes to seek out Jaques in order to profit from his critical views. The play's action then abandons the Duke's forest world for scenes 2.2-4, which are dedicated to business elsewhere that is only marginally relevant to the scene we are about to address. After that, we are returned to Arden, and are given our first direct exposure to Jaques.

The following is a transcription of that scene (2.5) from the First Folio collection of Shakespeare's plays, published in 1623. This is the earliest and the only independently authoritative version we have, the text from which *all* modern editions of *As You Like It* must be ultimately derived. After quoting it in full, I will address the basic preoccupation of this book as it applies to this scene: What is the most illuminating and satisfying way to read this text? Or, to put it in a more practical way, What sort of editorial presentation would most adequately mediate this text to the understanding of a modern reader with little or no special training in the study of Shakespeare? If you are an experienced Shakespearean, you may enjoy formulating your own editorial policy before I offer mine; in any case, you are welcome to skip to the commentary and look back to the scene as I offer my own mediation of its unfolding.

SCENA QUINTA
Enter, Amyens, Iaques, & others.
Song.
Vnder the greeene wood tree,
who loues to lye with mee,
And turne his merrie Note,
vnto the ſweet Birds throte:
Come hither, come hither, come hither:
Heere ſhall he ſee no enemie,
But Winter and rough Weather.

Iaq. More, more, I pre thee more.
Amy. It will make you melancholly Monſieur *Iaques*
Iaq. I thanke it: More, I prethee more,
I can ſucke melancholly out of a ſong,
As a Weazel ſuckes egges: More, I pre'thee more.
Amy. My voice is ragged, I know I cannot pleaſe you.
Iaq. I do not deſire you to pleaſe me,
I do deſire you to ſing:
Come, more, another ſtanzo: Cal you 'em ſtanzo's?
Amy. What you wil Monſieur *Iaques* .
Iaq. Nay, I care not for their names, they owe mee nothing. Wil you ſing?
Amy. More at your requeſt, then to pleaſe my ſelfe.
Iaq. Well then, if euer I thanke any man, Ile thanke you: but that they cal complement is like th encounter of two dog-Apes. And when a man thankes me hartily, me thinkes I haue giuen him a penie, and he renders me the

beggerly thankes. Come ſing; and you that wil not hold your tongues.

    Amy. Wel, Ile end the ſong. Sirs, couer the while, the Duke wil drinke
vnder this tree; he hath bin all this day to looke you.

    Iaq. And I haue bin all this day to auoid him:
He is too diſputeable for my companie:
I thinke of as many matters as he, but I giue
Heauen thankes, and make no boaſt of them.
Come, warble, come.

Song. Altogether heere.
Who doth ambition ſhunne,
    and loues to liue i'th Sunne:
Seeking the food he eates,
    and pleas'd with what he gets:
Come hither, come hither, come hither,
    Heere ſhall he ſee. &c.

    Iaq. Ile giue you a verſe to this note,
That I made yeſterday in deſpight of my Inuention.

    Amy. And Ile ſing it.

    Amy. Thus it goes.

If it do come to paſſe, that any man turne Aſſe:
Leauing his wealth and eaſe,
A ſtubborne will to pleaſe,
Ducdame, ducdame, ducdame:
Heere ſhall he ſee, groſſe fooles as he,
And if he will come to me.

    Amy. What's that Ducdame?

    Iaq. 'Tis a Greeke inuocation, to call fools into a circle. Ile go ſleepe if I
can: if I cannot, Ile raile againſt all the firſt borne of Egypt.

    Amy. And Ile go ſeeke the Duke,
His banket is prepar'd.   *Exeunt*

This is the cue on which Shakespeare scholarship enters, to undertake the work of putting us in adequate touch with what has just happened, after the lapse of nearly four-hundred years.

The primary form of mediation falls to the editor of the play, who has the responsibility of presenting the text in such a way as to allow the modern reader convenient access to what Shakespeare has done in this brief and not particularly gripping scene. If we assume an editor with a fairly ambitious sense of mediational responsibility, there are four levels of problems that she must face.

First-level problems—finding comfortable modern ways of making the old text comfortably legible—are mainly superficial and readily solved by the substitution of modern equivalents. In the original text, in accordance with what was then routine practice, the letter *s* has two basic forms: when capitalized or at the end of a word, it has the familiar coiled shape, but in other positions we get the "long s (ſ or ſ)," which is like "f" or *f* except that the upright shank of the letter is not crossed through. The modern editor will simply replace long ſ's with short ones. The letters *u* and *v* were merely alternative versions of the same thing in 1623 and had not yet been specialized to indicate different sounds. The pointed form was used at the beginning of a word and the rounded one in any other position.[1*] The editor will switch these to modern habits, changing *vnto* and *vnder*, and *loue to liue*, into what we're more used to. Similarly, *j* was normally undistinguished from *i*; the editor will accordingly print the more familiar *Jaques* in place of *Iaques*. Spellings, which tended to be flexible four hundred years ago, will be regularized for the ease of modern readers: the editor will give *prithee* where the original text has three different spellings within five lines, and add the second *l* to *cal*, and drop the *e* from *thanke*. Since we no longer regularly italicize proper names, the editor will probably put them into the same typeface as the surrounding text.

Those are easy decisions. The punctuations and capitalizations of the text are slightly less easy, in that there are often no obvious modern equivalents. Early seventeenth-century practice was irregular enough to be of doubtful significance, and what shows up in a text is often the whim of the typesetter rather than the choice (or whim) of the original author: an editor may justifiably choose to treat the text according to informed judgment calls. Supplying a period at the end of Amiens' first line is appropriate (the sentence is apparently finished rather than interrupted, and a glance at the original text will suggest that there was simply no room for the period without creating another unnecessary line). It is not obvious how we should deal with the two colons in Jaques' third speech.[2] They may be significant of how the speech was to be delivered, or they may have no importance whatever. The editor knows that two colons in a sentence would be bad form in modern terms, and must decide what to do. Word changes are often just another step less easy. The last line's *banket* tells us how the word was then pronounced, but the editor is quite right to print modern *banquet*, since nothing hinges on the difference in spelling and pronunciation. (She may, however, wish to point out that the word then could mean a light repast rather than a substantial feast.) Similarly, we hit expressions that look superficially unfamiliar but may be translated readily (Jaques' "dog-apes" *could* be replaced by "baboons" but it is better to leave the original in place and to footnote the modern meaning; the word *complement* in Jaques' longest speech is trickier: the appropriate modern spelling is *compliment*, but the earlier maning—"ceremony" or "formality"—is no longer current, and a brief explanatory note is desirable if the meaning is to be safely conveyed). Most conspicuously, the opaque word *ducdame* will require an explanatory note (more on this presently). Finally, the expression "cover the while" deserves a comment, since its meaning is not entirely obvious (I will return to this as well). Among the standard editorial tools of adjusted typography, regularization of spelling, and the odd explanatory footnote, the first-level problems can usually be handled easily. But the toughest first-level problems take us to the brink of the second level of editorial decision.

The second level goes beyond the provision of modern-equivalent spellings and meanings to undertake *restorative improvements*. The accent here falls on *restorative*: the original printed texts of Shakespeare's plays were not very carefully proofread by modern standards, and editors must come to terms with typesetters' misreadings, accidental omissions of a word or a line, missing entrance and exit indications, and other corruptions and oddities of various kinds. The ideal is not to improve or correct Shakespeare, but only to correct and improve the defective text by restoring Shakespeare's design.

Some of the second-level decisions are relatively easy. But the editor must make some judgment calls about which level is in question, and what the appropriate solution may be.

The cautious editor always has the option of making the changes and then mentioning the original punctuation, or word or theoretical omission, or probably wrongly placed stage direction in a note rather than silently adjusting them, and at the second level this is an appropriate way of dealing with such matters and is regularly followed in the more careful and ambitious editions. Alternatively, though it is more troublesome for the nonscholarly reader, the editor may leave the original text as is and overload the notes with explanations of what the modern equivalent would be, why the stage direction should probably be located two lines later, and so on. Modern editions for the general reader are better served by the editor's imposing knowledgeable changes and annotating the decisions if they are potentially misleading.

Clarifications of such items as these will resolve the first- and second-level problems enough to make the text accessible to the modern reader. But some hidden problems still lurk as the second-level adjustments begin to impinge on Level 3.

Our scene offers two clear examples. The first is in the presentation of Jaques' speeches. The typesetter apparently did not realize that Jaques speaks consistently in prose: four of his speeches have been spaced and capitalized as if they were verse, and the editor will doubtless decide, quite appropriately, to present these as prose. The second is that near the end of the scene, three speeches in a row are headed *Amy*. Some corrective or explanatory intervention seems clearly in order. How was this supposed to read? Do the speeches in fact belong to Amiens (in which case an explanation for the repeated heading is in order) or is there something missing, or should the middle speech be reassigned in order to keep the dialogue rhythm that has existed so far throughout the scene? Something needs to be said or done or both. I would locate Jaques' accidental versification as a second-level problem, appropriately resolved by printing the modern edition in prose (ideally, with a note that acknowledges that they were, no doubt mistakenly, offered as if verse in the original text). But the matter of the three consecutive headings of *Amy* is of a different order. This is Level 3, where one must tread more delicately to understand Shakespeare's dramatic design, and a cleanup via an arbitrary changing of one or two of the speech headings will violate the limits of second-level editing.

At this point, exit the conventional editor—and enter this book.

The work done by good editors is indispensable to the appreciation of how Shakespeare's plays are designed and how they are meant to work. We want to have a text that is relatively free of correctable blunders by earlier editors, including those who set the original texts in type, one that comes as close as we can get to what Shakespeare originally wrote; we need to know what the speeches said, what their words and expressions meant at the time, and which characters spoke them. A good editor has ample work to do merely to arrive at that result, and deserves our gratitude if she does nothing more.

There is more to be done, but it does not necessarily fall to the task of editors. There are limits to what more can be expected of editors, and the limits are mainly of two distinguishable kinds.

The first is a limitation imposed on editors by the way the nature of the editorial task is normally understood.

Archaeologists who excavate an ancient building are expected to keep track of the kinds of material and the specific dimensions and placements of what they find in the various discriminable levels of the site. When engaged in that work, they are not held responsible for explaining what this room or that implement was designed to be used for: this kind of understanding comes later, and can compromise the descriptive stage if attempted too soon. Similarly, the editor's main job is to provide the basic materials for informed understanding, not a theory of the play or an explanation of why Shakespeare wrote this particular part of it or an evaluation of how well he did it. An editor who works within these boundaries is working appropriately enough, even though some problems in Levels 1 and 2 cannot be solved without reading Shakespeare at a third level—the level of dramaturgical design, which is where all the good things take place—though only if one has a text with which to work. The editor provides me with what I need to take you further, and gives you the text that will allow it to make sense.

Level 3 is where the reader moves from making basic sense of the archaeologically reconstructed text to understanding how it is designed to work dramatically. Careful attention at Level 2 may allow an editor or other reader to notice that Jaques speaks in prose in 2.5, without having to care how, or even whether, it matters; but by reading at Level 3 she will realize that this has some dramatic significance, assisting in his characterization and correlating with his disdainful remark about verse in 4.1.[3+] Similarly, the final *exeunt*, which is probably all that Shakespeare's original manuscript said, merely means that all characters leave the stage; but attention to the preceding speeches will indicate that Jaques does not go in the same direction as the others, and is evidently intended to leave through a different door. It is generous of an editor to take on this additional level of responsibility, but it is also dangerous. This is inadequately charted territory, and it is easy to be misled and misleading.

Attention to Level 3 can enhance the editor's capacity to improve the reader's grasp of the text at Level 2, as the last two examples show. In the first case, it would argue definitively that the original text would be restoratively improved by editorially correcting Jaques' apparent verse to a prose format, perhaps with the further help of a brief note on why the correction is apt. In the second case, it would allow the editor to indicate (normally in square brackets, the usual indication of an editorial intervention) that the final exeunt is at separate doors, thus assisting the reader to see the intended design more clearly and specifically than Shakespeare's laconic direction allows (albeit it would have been plain to his audience), to notice the way the lines imply it, and to perceive its relevance to the general separation of Jaques from the others and to his conspicuous absence when the Duke enters with Amiens two scenes later.

LET ME ILLUSTRATE the kind of gap this book attempts to fill, by returning to *As You Like It* 2.5 for a quick survey of its treatment in modern editions.

The scene is not particularly difficult for an untrained modern reader to follow, especially when readjusted into modern spelling and typography (though it is not hard to get used to the habits of the 1623 text). Most of what is said is clear enough, and what goes on falls neatly into place with what we already know by 2.5 about the greenwood life of the Duke and his men, and about the special differences in Jaques. It doesn't seem to be very ambitious, or to accomplish much. It introduces a song that carries something of the romantic air of the voluntary exiles; and it introduces Jaques in person in what we have already been warned is one of his usual sour moods, critically parodying politeness and romanticism and the song itself. Does it offer anything else?

In fact it does. But what it offers will emerge from the bare text only if one thinks in terms of purposeful dramatic design—and more precisely, a design according to the principles of Shakespearean dramaturgy and the peculiarities of the texts from which we must reconstruct it. The editorial habit of attending inadequately to the peculiarly dramatic character of the texts, and the consequent neglect of important clues to what Shakespeare was doing, result in deficiencies in editorial corrections and improvements, and often leave the editorial annotations misleading as well as insufficient. For instance:

1. In the middle of the scene, Amiens tells his companions (probably not including Jaques) to "cover the while" as the song is being concluded. What does this mean?—and more important, why does Shakespeare have Amiens say it? "Cover" is used later, in a brief exchange between other characters in 5.1, to mean "put your hat on," but here it goes rather with Amiens' accompanying statement, "the Duke will drink under this tree," and it means "set the table" (cf. French *couvert* and modern English "cover charge"). The final line of the scene tells us that the Duke's banquet is prepared. It has been prepared in the course of this scene by the "others" (i.e., other lords who, like Amiens and Jaques, are companions of the exiled Duke) in response to Amiens' spoken direction, perhaps assisted by Amiens himself as he leads them in song; and that in turn means that they must have brought the necessary supplies onstage. Shakespeare had two dramatic reasons for having the banquet set up here. One is that two scenes later, in 2.7, the Duke and his followers are about to enjoy this picnic (there is mention of a table, and of fruit, in addition to the drink alluded to in 2.5) when Orlando enters, sword drawn, to claim food for famished old Adam, and this occasions a dramatically important and revealing confrontation, to which I will return in another chapter. The other reason (which is also the reason why Shakespeare did not wait until the beginning of 2.7 to bring in the banquet that stays unused until then) is that in the intervening scene, 2.6, when Orlando and enfeebled Adam enter in desperate need of food, the banquet that will soon resolve their needs is on stage, quite visible to us but (according to dramaturgical conventions which I will discuss in a later chapter) understood to be at the moment too distant from Orlando and Adam to be seen by them: another nice dramatic touch. "Cover the while" is the textual surfacing of some significant activity that would have been clearly apparent in the original productions of the play—a luckily surviving clue to a dramatic design that can be adequately understood only through an awareness of Shakespeare's dramaturgy.

I consulted more than two dozen modern editions of the play in order to check on how the editors help their readers to understand the Shakespearean design. Virtually all of them gloss the expression "cover the while," and do so correctly. But only four of them help the reader recognize that this means the banquet is being set up in the course of the scene, and is therefore left on stage at the end of it; and not one offers an adequate explanation for why Shakespeare made this happen (one overtly confesses that there seems to be no reason why it wasn't done two scenes later instead, and another suggests that it must have been carried off with the general exit and brought back at the beginning of 2.7). None of the editions I consulted is adequate as a guide to how Shakespeare designed this aspect of the scene and the play.

2. The reader of this scene sees only a direction for a general entrance at the beginning and a general exit at the end. Reasonable attentiveness to the dialogue, however, clearly establishes that Jaques evidently leaves the scene through a different door from the rest of the group, heading for a nap while the others seek out the Duke—thus further underlining his differences from them as well as explaining why he isn't with them when they enter with the Duke two scenes later. Thoughtful reflection on the opening of the scene may suggest that Jaques also *enters* through a separate door (making the same dramatic point from the start) and catches Amiens by surprise partway through his song—hence Amiens' considerate and apologetic attempt to beg off when Jaques calls for more is not inconsistent with his having launched into the song in the first place without any apparent concern about feeding Jaques' melancholy. Strategic attention to exits and entrances can reveal that they are sometimes designed to convey more than mere traffic.

Of the editions I checked, not quite half draw the reader's attention to the fact that Jaques leaves separately, and none of them suggests what the point of that might be. Not a single one notices that there are grounds for supposing a separate initial entrance as well, let alone attends to the dramatic awkwardness that arises if there isn't one.

3. Everyone agrees that three *Amy* speech headings in a row is odd, but it is not altogether obvious how to deal with correcting (or explaining) the oddity. One way of dealing with it is to reassign the middle heading to Jaques. That is minimalist, economical, and restores the expected pattern of alternating speeches. The problem with that tactic is that it is quite unencouraged by the remaining textual clues. It is Amiens who says "And I'll sing it," which would be an odd line for Shakespeare to have him say if that's not the way it is about to happen. Morever, Jaques does not say that he will *sing* a verse, but that he will *give* one he made yesterday. Why "give" rather than "sing"? Probably because Shakespeare intended to have Amiens sing it (and had him say so), and considered it inappropriate to have Jaques do it instead. Confirmation that this is the design appears at the beginning of 2.7, where a Lord tells the Duke that Jaques was just now "hearing of a song," not singing one, and the Duke's reply characterizes Jaques as essentially discordant and unmusical, hardly a singer. His not singing his own verse is, like his speaking in prose (and like his saying to the singer in 4.2 "Sing it: 'tis no matter how it be in tune, so it make noise enough"), dramatically and characterizationally significant. So what happens toward the end of 2.5? Jaques doubtless "gives" Amiens his verse by handing him a paper on which he has written it down. How that matters dramatically goes further than keeping Jaques appropriately unmusical, as the next point will show, but in the meantime it solves the problem of allowing Amiens to sing a text he does not know.

Out of two dozen modern editions, only one recognizes that Shakespeare's having had Amiens say that he would sing the new stanza, added to the speech heading that assigns the words of the stanza to Amiens, probably means that this is how it worked. All but four reassign the words to Jaques as singer (or speaker), failing to notice that Shakespeare elsewhere gives clues confirming that Amiens did indeed sing it, and must. Not only do the modern editions not help us to grasp Shakespeare's design in this case, they positively obscure it by alterations in the text, usually left unmentioned as such. Their readers do not see what Shakespeare probably wrote, and can hardly imagine why Amiens is designed to say he will sing this new verse if in fact it does not happen. This drives assiduous interpretation into probing Amiens' eagerness as a performer, which is a misleading track (though intelligent in the editorially arbitrary circumstances) that takes us away from, rather than toward, Shakespeare's careful dramatic design.

4. The item that has drawn most annotative attention in this scene is the mysterious word *ducdame* in Jaques' new stanza. It must be pronounced as three syllables (since it replaces "come hither" in the rhythms of the melody[4]) but what does it mean? Editors, and writers of scholarly articles, have combed their linguistic resources to find out its origin. It is not literally Greek—in Shakespeare's day, "Greek" was used (as it still is) to mean something unintelligible. Various scholars have proposed that the word comes from Latin, or Romany, or Welsh: some six or seven languages have been formally offered in print. But such researches, however impressively learned, are nothing more than the chase of a wild goose by other wild geese, and miss the real dramatic point entirely. No useful purpose is served by discovering that this word may resemble something in some other tongue. On the contrary, it is, and is meant to be, flatly unintelligible to Amiens, and to us as well. Sung three times, it is indeed *conspicuously* unintelligible, and puzzles not only Amiens and us but the other characters as well. So what did Shakespeare have in mind in putting it in?

Just follow through with a bit of dramatic logic. Amiens sings a nonsense word from a paper he has just received as the text he is to sing. Jaques is the only one who is not curious about it, for what will eventually become obvious reasons. How do the others react? Baffled glances at one another would be in order, but Shakespeare's design seems to have taken them to a further degree of curiosity. Almost certainly, he intended (and directed) the other actors to gather around Amiens, trying to make out from Jaques' paper what the strange word is supposed to be—and then, when Amiens finishes the song and asks the question that is on everyone's mind, Jaques delivers the clincher: the meaningless word has in fact drawn the Duke's followers, characterized by Jaques's satirical stanza as fools, into a circle. Q.E.D. A nonsense word carefully choreographs a visible dramatic punch line—if we attend to the dramaturgy of design.

It is, however, important for the word to be sheer nonsense. The effectiveness of the design partly hinges on that. Less than a quarter of the consulted editions assure the reader that we are not to look for meaning, but only two even begin to glimpse the strategy of motivating a real circle cleverly called up on the spot as part of the prank.[5]

I HAVE FOCUSED on editors and editions not because I think that is where the most serious deficiency in Shakespeare studies lies, but only because that is the most convenient way to describe and diagnose it. Editors are not egregiously at fault: they are for the most part responsibly carrying out the mandate implicit in the way we have come to read Shakespeare. Their policies and practices are not the causes but rather the results of a widespread neglect of the understandings and attentions needed for the recovery of how Shakespeare designed his plays to be effective; they work as careful high-level civil servants carrying out the inadequate foreign policy of a misunderstanding government representing an ill-informed populace.

THIS BOOK IS, as I have warned you, about Shakespearean dramaturgy—the practical principles and strategies and devices used by Shakespeare in designing his plays for live performance. The table of contents indicates the main topics covered, but the ultimate purpose is to put Shakespeare in charge of the reading of his plays, and to assist readers to grasp, more intimately and accurately than seems to be the normal standard of even directors and scholars, what he was doing as a designer of drama and how he did it. This is about getting in touch with *Shakespeare's* Shakespeare, which I believe to be immeasurably better than that of anyone else. It is at a dramaturgically informed level of reading and understanding that the invested design is to be found, and there is far more stored there than the untrained modern eye can easily discern.

It is now more than four centuries since Shakespeare wrote his earliest plays. Much has changed in dramatic technique as well as in other respects, resulting in puzzlements that cannot be resolved by mere ingenuity. But enough has remained similar to cause a still greater difficulty: we can easily acquire the illusion that we're in tune with what Shakespeare is doing when in fact we aren't, and we fail to realize how much we don't really understand.

When LeBeau, near the end of the second scene of *As You Like It*, tells Orlando that the usurping Duke Frederick is "humorous," he does *not* mean that he is amusing, or amused. If we get that wrong by thinking that we know the word's meaning from our own regular vocabularies, we miss the point entirely. And so it is with more complex matters of stagecraft: what Shakespeare accomplishes through Jaques' *ducdame*, and what he sets up via Amiens' "cover the while," cannot be reconstructed merely by consulting a good dictionary. These are richer bits of dramatic design, far from obvious but recoverable if we approach them in specifically Shakespearean terms. For along with changes in the meanings of words and in the grammar through which they are expressed, there have been parallel changes in what might be called the vocabulary and grammar of dramatic representation—the practical principles of play design—and we cannot understand adequately or accurately how a Shakespearean play works if we look at it in terms of the nearest modern equivalents.

This book is an introduction to the principles of Shakespeare's dramaturgy and to a dramaturgical way of rereading Shakespeare's plays. The chapter that follows is an introduction to how that art of reading was lost, and what is unsatisfactory (for purposes of reading Shakespeare) about what generally replaced it. The remainder is an attempt to provide restorative improvements to the pursuit of understanding the most wonderful and accomplished works that were ever shaped in the English language.

2

HOW LONG IS'T NOW SINCE LAST YOUR SELF AND I WERE IN A MASQUE?

How we lost, and may recover,
Shakespeare's own dramaturgy

Shakespeare's plays are not poems. They are scripts for a stage production, put together by an extraordinarily gifted and successful man of the theater. Shakespeare was indeed also a poet, already respectfully noticed in print in 1598 for sonnets that were then still only circulating privately. He aspired to be recognized as a poet, and took considerable care with the publication of two major poems a few years later. He never showed equivalent interest in getting his plays into print. But it was his plays that inspired respect and fame from the beginning and eventually extended his reputation from the Globe in particular to the globe at large.

It was the playhouse that established his fortune as well. Shakespeare was in every way a theatrical professional. He was an accomplished actor before (and while) he was a playwright, he was a shareholding partner in a company of theatrical players, and he was a part-owner of the Globe Theater. He wrote plays neither for publishers nor for libraries, neither for patrons nor for posterity. He wrote them for his own stage.

In his own time, he was well recognized as an outstanding playwright. Frances Meres' 1598 testimony called him the best in England for both comedy and tragedy, and at this point he was still only halfway through his playwriting career. The writing of plays, however, was then (as it became again some two centuries later) regarded as only a secondary calling by comparison with the writing of poems, much as writing screenplays is still not thought as being as distinguished an accomplishment as writing novels. Shakespeare excelled at what was widely regarded as second-rate literature.

Two generations after his death, the picture had changed—and so had Shakespeare's reputation. A new literary respect for plays had grown up, along with a new conception of how they ought to be written. The kind of neoclassical conception of drama favored influentially by Sir Philip Sidney before Shakespeare began writing (and largely ignored by Shakespeare subsequently) had taken firm root, and a style of dramaturgy different from Shakespeare's took over the imaginations of playwrights and theatergoers—and readers of plays as literature.

The result was an enormous shift in the understanding of Shakespeare's plays, and a great irony settled in. When plays were regarded as inferior literature, Shakespeare was thought the best, by admirers who probably understood his work. Once the status of plays was elevated, he was no longer either so admired or so well understood. The shift of taste in the seventeenth century, consolidating a process that had already been under way in Europe two centuries earlier, began to put us out of touch with Shakespeare.

A few pages back, I glanced very briefly at some phenomena in the shifting history of language as an illustrative analogue to the problem (and necessity) of recovering the principles of Shakespearean dramaturgy. I would now like to look at some happenings in the history of art as symptoms of a major cultural shift that will help explain how and why we became alienated from Shakespeare's Shakespeare.

Native English drawings, paintings, and woodcuts from Shakespeare's time often strike modern viewers as rather primitive. This is largely because many of them were still being composed and executed according to principles that had already been superseded and rendered obsolete in Europe, and were about to be replaced in England as well.

Most strikingly, the sizes of images in popular English art were not consistently governed by their supposed distance from the viewer, and the angles of view are inconsistent with naturalistic observation. Distant but more important figures may be represented as larger than closer but less important ones; a building may be splayed out so that we see the front facade from straight on, the side wall as from an angle at the side, and the roof from an elevated viewpoint. Indeed, the artist was not even constrained to depict a single moment of seeing, but was free to build in a narrative dimension. A sketch by an amateur but competent artist who witnessed the execution of Mary Queen of Scots shows not only the typical distortions mentioned above but gives us three separate moments within the event: Mary entering the scene, Mary praying with her chaplain, Mary on the block for her beheading, all statically rendered in their different parts of the drawing like a multiple-exposure photograph.

This is not because the artists were unaware that this isn't the way we see things in real life. It is rather because art is different from nature, and permits the artists to take advantage of the difference in order to show more, or create special emphases, by manipulating form and space and time in ways that the natural eye cannot do.

In the meantime, Italian painters had developed perspective, as a way of rendering more truly how things look to a real human eye. By following strict geometrical rules, the artist could render an illusion of realistic spatial depth never achieved by medieval artists and deliver an image that was grounded in a specific vantage point, thus permitting them to combine a realism in the representation of the object with a coordinated realism in the representation of the act of seeing.

Perspective art rapidly became a fashion, and soon approached the condition of an ideology. Artists strained to depict a scene as it would be viewed by a particular person observing from a particular spot.

The fashion perdured. The rules of perspective became virtually the rules of painting itself, and perspectival faults were criticized much in the way that faults in psychological consistency were challenged (or intricately reinterpreted) in literature after the rise of modern psychologism. The painting now had a naturalistic order, defined from a rigorously consistent point of view; anything less rational was unsatisfactory. After the triumph of perspective, earlier styles that combined various points of view in order to bring out the object more fully, beyond what an eye can see from a single place, were thought crude and primitive. Having been born and bred in optical and geometrical correctness, the later viewers had to learn a seemingly odd style of representation in order to understand these pre-perspective offerings. Few bothered to do so. It was far easier to dismiss earlier work patronizingly and celebrate the perspectival advance in skill and taste.

"Artificial" was a commendatory adjective in Shakespeare's time, with about the same value as modern "artistic." To show three stages of a happening in a single image was artificial. That does not mean that it was false. The fact that the modern observer of the image assumes that time must be frozen in it, and that it *must* depict a single privileged moment, is a provincial bigotry that was fortunately absent in earlier days—notably, in the days when Shakespeare was crafting his plays. To read Shakespeare well, we must be willing to suspend our acculturated bias toward rationalized perspective.

That is because a similar change took place in drama. As the English republican movement, spurred by Puritan ideals, pressed toward the destruction of the monarchy and the institution of the Commonwealth, the drama industry was one of the early casualties. In 1642, the theaters were closed. The discontinuity between that moment and the restoration of the monarchy in 1660 is probably the only clean boundary in the history of English literature, not only because it represents a genuine substantial pause in activity, but because of what was lost in the meantime and what replaced it when the action resumed.

When 1660 arrived, it did not mean that 1641 sprang up again in full bloom. A new taste for the neoclassical, very advanced in Europe and already well developed in England before the theaters were closed, had been amplified by the experience of the court and aristocracy in their French exile, and dominated the restoration of theater in England. Shakespeare's plays were now perceived as somewhat crude and primitive when measured against the new norms, and critics gave readier approval to what the classicizing Ben Jonson had done in his plays than to Shakespeare,[1] whom John Milton characterized not as the Swan of Avon but as an unspecified bird of the forest, "warbling his native wood-notes wild."

Many of Shakespeare's plays were rewritten in order to rationalize and unify their time schemes, reduce their liberties in the handling of space, eliminate vulgarities in the comic parts, tone up speeches that seemed insufficiently smooth and elegant (or seemed too luxurious and redundant, or too metaphorical for strongly rational taste), and generally improve the standards of decorum and appropriateness that guided the action. Some of the rewritten versions, such as Dryden's remake of *Antony and Cleopatra* as *All for Love*, were presented as effectually new and better plays that merited new titles and new authorial credit, and others, such as in Nahum Tate's 1681 *King Lear*, as "Revised with Alterations," keeping Shakespeare's title and crediting his basic authorship, but giving us the reviser's version of what Shakespeare would have done had his taste been more refined.[2]

Shakespeare's Shakespeare was neither preserved nor sought after. Many of his subtleties were read as blunders; his strategies mystified readers; his apparent omissions and inconsistencies puzzled them; and although his readers were not so blinded as to fail to recognize the extraordinary accomplishments of his plays, they felt the need to apologize for their lack of finesse, and to improve them to the standards of a new taste.

His plays were no longer staged according to his designs, and would not have been well understood or appreciated if they had been. Instead, theater audiences heard reformed dialogue that had been deprived of much of Shakespeare's strength of language, wit, and color—and many of his speeches. They saw elaborate scenery that changed spectacularly between scenes (some of the plays' descriptive passages were cut accordingly), new characters to amplify the main plot (unaware or oblivious of Shakespeare's limitations in casting calls), and a different style of acting (that included women playing parts that Shakespeare had written for the talented boys of his troupe).

Nahum Tate's revised *King Lear* eliminated the Fool, introduced a romance between Edgar and Cordelia, and ended happily with Lear's restoration to the throne: for over 150 years it was this *King Lear*, in place of Shakespeare's own, that was offered to audiences. It was no longer possible to develop a sense of Shakespeare's dramaturgy from seeing his plays performed.

Students of Shakespeare might, of course, study his plays in published form, insisting on his own versions rather than Tate's or Dryden's or the still-earlier adaptations by William Davenant. Free from the distractions of artificial scenery and the interferences of substantial alterations in plot and cast and dialogue, there might be a chance to sustain or recover what Shakespeare had designed. But there too the cards were stacked against authentic understanding of what Shakespeare had been doing. Editors improved and tidied what they took to be irregularities and deficiencies in the original texts. In the name of restorative improvements, they "corrected" Shakespeare's grammar and phrasing, substituted more modern or more tasteful words here and there, emended difficult lines along with genuinely corrupted ones, created new scene divisions (changing original stage directions in order to do so), and labeled—usually arbitrarily and often misleadingly—the location of each scene. Studying these editorially adjusted texts rather than the originals, no one could possibly have reconstructed Shakespeare's dramaturgical management of space and location, and modern editions *still* continue to impose these misleading divisions and locations in the mistaken assumption that they are somehow appropriate.

And thus, with taste, style, values, and expectation much changed, with theatrical practice elaborately revised to accommodate these changes, with the very text itself readjusted and restructured to fit them better, with approximately no continuity left between Shakespeare's stage and the new stages that had totally replaced it, and with the judgment of Shakespeare's relatively primitive crudeness firmly in place, diplomatic relations with Shakespeare's Shakespeare broke down, without leaving behind any significant motivation, encouragement, or convenient opportunity to resume them. Readers, playgoers, even scholars lost the ability to understand Shakespeare on his own terms. Shakespearean dramaturgy had become not only a dead language but a language that had vanished with few remaining traces.

The reading, editing, and understanding of Shakespeare has never recovered from the breach in continuity from 1642 to 1660, or from the change in taste and the distortions in text that then took over. In later chapters, I will occasionally point out some of the damage that was done and the impediments that were imposed. For now, it is enough to say that the modern incapacity to understand instinctively how Shakespeare works is not especially a function of our trying to grasp him through what we know of cinema, television, modern drama, novels—none of these had been invented when the process of alienation from Shakespeare's Shakespeare began. The problem is now more than three centuries old, and it has given us three centuries of misinformation, misreading, and misconstruction as our heritage.

The First Step in learning Shakespearean dramaturgy is to recognize that Shakespeare was immersed in the theatrical world of his time. The second step is to surrender the illusion that we more or less already know how it works.

Modern readers' acculturated and spontaneous presuppositions when reading Shakespeare are, in fact, about as dysfunctional as the presuppositions of the Restoration. And we have extraordinary skill in forcing them on Shakespeare's plays, mainly for two reasons:

1. Each of us has a defective Bureau of Standards. We are not usually trained to read texts well and often wind up with a prospector's mentality when it comes to tackling classic literary (or dramatic) works: to pan through half a ton of rubble and come up with an ounce of gold is a good day's work.

If one feels a generally privileged superiority to the accomplishments of the past (as all twentieth century people are acculturated to do), one may fail to expect any more from past literary accomplishments than from past technology, and thus not be surprised when an uninformed reading ends with the judgment that this was a Very Good Try, For That Time. If one does not expect a great deal more, and lacks some of the equipment and awareness that are needed to recognize it, even the best may seem relatively unimpressive. Because of these impediments, most readers have not really *experienced* the best of the past, though they may have read through it: they therefore don't know what they can afford to hold out for, or the quality of the experience that waits to reward those who take the trouble to learn how to get there. If they themselves have never gotten there, being adequately entertained or mildly impressed may seem to be as far as they can expect to be taken.

2. Those who persist in the study of literature are usually clever, and often derive adequate satisfaction from their own ingenuity when a receptive attention to the text seems not to reward them enough on its own. The exhilarating activity of *interpretation*—finding more ingenious and intricate meanings than the text appears to invite—tends to dominate over the sometimes tedious labor of *understanding* how it is in fact designed to work. And once the text's own authority is overborne by the power of the reader's imagination, there is little chance of the reader's getting important self-correction by referring to it. There is even less chance of discovering its true secrets, because many of them are written in a dead (however rich and resourceful) language which many readers not only do not understand, but do not even know is there. Stuck in that place, they may understandably try to redeem the exercise by making something interesting happen through interpretive cleverness.

I am not here referring to students, but to the bulk of Shakespeare's readers at all levels. A 1981 survey of the previous year's contributions to "critical studies" of Shakespeare's work—i.e., by professional scholars and critics—remarked in general conclusion that "anyone attempting to survey recent critical studies of Shakespeare is bound to notice common problems," the first one being that "Given the richness of the plays and poems, it is easy to find in them confirmations that would seem to verify nearly every theory posited—that is, if one ignores all evidence that might refute it, as well as any alternative explanations for the same features of the works discussed.[3]

Interpretation can find whatever it wants, provided that the rules are slack enough. If we read Shakespeare without a grounding in Shakespearean dramaturgy, we are not constrained by the discipline that is built into the plays, and are therefore free to be pleasantly inventive rather than challenged to discover and understand. We tend to like it that way. And once we have confected an interpretive theory of the play, or created a meaning for it, all evidence bends (or is crushed) to cooperate, or retires from view.

Such an exercise in interpretive creativity, even when it is perverse or distorting, requires considerable imagination and mind power. It has produced some brilliant performances in the art of critical interpretation that deserve applause for their imagination, and often for an eloquence and grace that can bring us temporarily to suppose that the interpretation has been discovered in the text rather than embroidered upon it—but such accomplishments should not be mistaken for Shakespeare.

The talent that goes into "A New Reading of [name your play]" would be much more profitably invested in learning how to be disciplined by Shakespearean dramaturgy. But if you don't realize that Shakespearean dramaturgy is a different language, and mistake it for a rudimentary or quaint (or a clumsy and sometimes odd—or still worse, an arcane and labyrinthine) performance in a familiar one, you may not realize what can be done to improve the situation, and you may be accordingly thrust back upon pure ingenuity, which is a nearly impenetrable protection against learning what needs to be learned.

Let me give two examples, from *Hamlet.*

1. From the outside in: I regularly deal with university students who are persuaded that one of the major greatnesses of the play is its relentless consistency—everything in place, logical progression, deep psychological realism, and so forth. A little questioning readily establishes that they haven't even *noticed*, let alone explained away, counterevidence that such a hypothesis ought to have made vivid. Horatio is a schoolmate of Hamlet, something of a pal, and evidently is making his first visit to Elsinore. But he is chummy with the guards and has been around for a month without looking up his friend from school. He says that he *knew* King Hamlet; but he admits that he only saw him once. Young Hamlet speaks to him as if he were a foreigner, but Horatio refers to Hamlet Senior, as "Our last King," and continues to hang around Elsinore after Hamlet has been sent to England for an indefinite stay. Hamlet himself vows immediate revenge but is next seen strolling with a book. He professes a blighting depression but leaps to good cheer to hear that the players are coming and discusses the city's theatrical situation with obvious interest. He sets up a special play and arranges to insert a new speech, but his subsequent soliloquy concludes with what appears to be the first dawning of his idea of arranging for a play that will remind Claudius of his guilt. Any good reader of the play can multiply examples well beyond this: but this is enough to make the point that a commendation of *Hamlet* for deep and rigorous consistency is misplaced, clearly does not arise from a close reading of the text, is almost certainly a mere projection on the play of an irrelevant modern value, and (worst of all) can survive the most blatant counterevidence once the theory is in place. Revering Shakespeare, and their own notions of what his greatness consists in, my students are reluctant to deal with these problems, because they do not recognize that they are problems in their own address to shakespeare rather than deficiencies in what he wrote.

2. From the inside out: At the International Shakespeare Congress in Berlin, in 1984, an eminent Shakespearean scholar, rightly respected for fine work over more than thirty years, mentioned during a seminar that he was undertaking a study to show that the "To be or not to be" soliloquy was the interpretive heart of the play. That is not an uncommon opinion, though I have never seen it worked out in full. Perhaps one of the reasons why I have never seen it worked out in full is that it can't work very well. This soliloquy has almost nothing at all to do with the play—so little, in fact, that one can imagine Shakespeare's having written it before he thought of *Hamlet*, waiting for an opportunity to stuff it into some play where it would fit. Hamlet gives us a catalogue of general grievances, so general ("the whips and scorns of time") that most can be related vaguely to *Hamlet*'s plot, or to any other (though it's hard to squeeze "the law's delay" or "the poor man's contumely" into service for *Hamlet* in particular)—but there is not a word about his mother's hasty marriage, the murder of his father, incest, his charge to avenge: no concrete reference to what has obsessed him as long as we have known him. And then he characterizes death as "The undiscovered country, from whose bourne /

No traveler returns." There should be an obvious question here. If no traveler returns, whom does he think he was speaking with toward the end of act 1?[4] This soliloquy can scarcely be the key to a play to which it owes so little allegiance. A prepossession in interpretation can miss the obvious, even in seasoned scholars.

The essential problem in these cases seems to be the failure of readers to come to intimate terms with the text; and the principal cause of that failure is, I think, that their readings are insufficiently disciplined by an awareness of the nature of Shakespearean dramaturgy and substitute other (usually less demanding) kinds of dramaturgy for the only one that will finally make good sense. This is understandable and forgivable, but not acceptable. It is seriously faulty—but it is also remediable. The remedy has been variously, though not thoroughly, promoted by historical scholarship over the years, but has mainly been resisted. The resistence probably arises primarily from a parochial bias toward modern values (dramatic, critical, psychological, aesthetic, social, moral, poetic, and so forth) that leads readers either to assume naively that Shakespeare wrote in accordance with the reader's own value set, or to interpret his plays in a way that makes them look much more modern than they are—as if Shakespeare's greatness lies especially in his ability to transcend his time and think like us, and as if that would do him credit.

That is a common, but unfortunate, way of going about it.

Kiss Me, Kate, Cole Porter's takeoff on Shakespeare's *The Taming of the Shrew*, contains a song with an appropriate refrain: "I'm always true to you, darling, in my fashion; I'm always true to you, darling, in my way." Shakespeare's consistency is in his fashion, in his way, which was not the fashion or the way of subsequent drama, or of subsequent critical standards. It can be found authentically only if the reader will let go of modern provincialism enough to realize that Shakespeare's dramaturgy is significantly different from what is now expected, operates according to unusual rules and assumptions, has an unfamiliar kind of integrity and sophistication, pursues values that are in important ways unlike our own, and requires hospitable acceptance and respectful docility as a precondition of understanding. Neither interpretive ingenuity nor patronizing patience can bridge the historically established gulf between Shakespeare's Shakespeare and our unreconstructed selves. Our task is to learn how to read him on his turf and on his terms. It is *our* flaws, limitations, and oddities that need to be brought under control, not his.

We do not need rewritten versions of the plays, bringing them into respectable coherence by post-Restoration standards; we do not need to fancy that another hand has intervened, causing difficulties that Shakespeare would not himself have perpetrated; we do not need emendations or explanations dedicated to removing contradictions. What we need is a recognition that Shakespeare is almost always true in his fashion, even when inconsistent, and that inconsistency is for him a dramaturgical strategy, not a lapse. We need to learn the principles of Shakespearean dramaturgy, and that includes accepting his right to ignore our ideas about aesthetics and psychology and to embrace liberties like those of modern cinematic cartoons (where the steamrollered cat may rise again, and the un-catlike teeth that crack up and fall after the mouse's bash with the frying pan are in good working order by the next scene) and modern cinematic drama (where momentary flashbacks work effectively, and the zoom lens shifts us smoothly and swiftly from distanced objectivity to closeup intimacy) and children's "let's pretend" (where the rock may become a palace, and then a mountain that no one has ever succeeded in climbing, and then a dragon's cave, just by saying so).

Ben Jonson lamented that Shakespeare had been so careless of judgment as to permit himself the self-contradiction of having Caesar say "Caesar did never wrong, but with just cause."[5] This is an almost perfect emblem. Jonson, the classicist, the darling of the Restoration critics (who valued his works more than Shakespeare's because he had pioneered the new standards) was busy about exact consistency in his dramaturgy as well as in his logic, and disapproved of Shakespeare's apparent laxity in adopting the new mode. But Shakespeare wrote like Shakespeare, and in his plays he almost never does an un-Jonsonian thing but for the good of the play. Anyone can read Jonson's dramaturgy now, as they could in the Restoration. Reading Shakespeare's is another matter: it requires the recovery of a long-lost technique of understanding.

This book is dedicated to the proposition that we can no longer easily read Shakespeare on his own terms; and that we can, and should, learn how to do so; and that his earliest texts can teach us how; and that this is the only way we can get close enough to conserving, in relatively primeval and unpolluted form, one of our greatest natural resources.

3

A LOCAL HABITATION, AND A NAME

A self-portrait of the artist as a dramaturge

Shakespeare's earliest texts are, happily, not deeply defective. Most of them were derived from good manuscript copies. The ones that are not, like the First Quartos of *Romeo and Juliet* and *Hamlet*, remind us of what a nightmare it would have been to have only texts of such poor quality to go on: but in both these cases, fortunately, we have the plays in at least two other much better early editions.

"Better" does not in this case mean simply that they are more artistically respectable, as might have been claimed by proponents of Nahum Tate's remake of *King Lear*; it means "more authentic," and I believe it also means, in this case, closer to Shakespeare's own Shakespeare. The title page of the Second Quarto of *Romeo and Juliet* advertises it as "Newly corrected, augmented, and amended: As it hath bene sundry times publiquely acted, by the right Honourable the Lord Chamberlaine his Servants" i.e., brought into line with the play as Shakespeare's company actually produced it; and the Second Quarto of *Hamlet* assures the reader that its text is "according to the true and perfect Coppie."[1]* We are not told who did the correcting and amending, or just where the true and perfect copy was found, and we must make allowances for a publisher's blurb. At the very least, however, these notices indicate that the values underlying this book were recognized by those who were responsible for printing these improved texts—i.e., what we want is what they evidently thought their customers wanted: the version that hit Shakespeare's stage in accordance with his intent. At the most, Shakespeare may have intervened to drive an inferior text out of credit and circulation, but we have no evidence that he did so.

The bad news that poor texts got into print even during Shakespeare's lifetime is adequately compensated by the good news that the misleading versions were soon emphatically replaced by the real thing. The fact that the 1623 Folio collection was published under the auspices of friends and colleagues who had acted in them is a comforting reassurance that the texts it contains were regarded as essentially authentic by people who were in a position to know, and advertised as "truly set forth, according to their first original.[2] Again, publishers' rhetoric is both reassuring and suspect. "First original" is plainly hyperbolic, in that no serious scholar can conclude that the Folio texts are all antecedent to the Quarto versions that had already been published; but if it means "the true copy," i.e., the most authentic version that Heminge and Condell could lay their hands on, I do not think the claim can be seriously faulted.

The pre-1624 versions were apparently not compromised by the deep editorial interference and sheer rewriting to which the plays were subjected over the following century. The occasional misreadings, line-skippings, and casual alterations in spelling that took place in the printing-houses of Shakespeare's time leave us with unresolved puzzles but do not result in too much damage. Still, the results are inconveniently defective. This time the good news is that the defectiveness is not of the sort that leaves us helpless to correct it. That is, it is not primarily a matter of what was accidentally left out, or what was presumptuously added, or what was irremediably distorted, by others. It is rather the absence of what Shakespeare probably did not supply in the first place. The earliest texts are occasionally defective (in most cases, only trivially) in what they say; but they frustrate our curiosity far more often by what they *fail* to say.

They are, for instance, notoriously short on relevant stage directions. Especially for our dramaturgical purposes, this is a significant setback. There are what seem to be nearly countless (they have doubtless been counted) instances where the text fails to say that a given character has entered, providing us with our first clue only when he begins to speak. Similarly, exits must sometimes be inferred from the leave-taking nature of the character's last speech in the scene, or from a reference to him as no longer present. The stage directions that *are* provided are often skimpy at best: the bare *exeunt* at the end of *As You Like It* 2.5 tells us nothing about the arrangement for Jaques to leave by a separate door. Significant directional information is often omitted altogether. Amiens' "cover the while" is an implicit stage direction only if we study its implications; Shakespeare supplies no explicit description of what is meant to ensue. There is no overt way that we are let in on how he engineered the comic and satiric climax of the scene.

But the necessary clues are there, if we discover how to ferret them out. Consequently, learning Shakespearean dramaturgy from Shakespeare's texts may begin anywhere: the peculiar grammar and vocabulary of his stage practice are pervasive and may be found embedded almost everywhere in the surviving early editions of his plays. They are not often plainly on the surface of the texts and have not been thoroughly excavated by the modern editors whose notes attempt to guide our reading. Nevertheless, some of their fossil remains are present in the early texts, and they can often be inferred accordingly.

I acknowledge that this may seem to be a questionable claim. Granted that Shakespeare was not writing for readers who would need to be informed about actions they cannot see, but ultimately for audiences who neither have nor need stage directions, nevertheless his immediate target audience must have been the actors; and if he did not make it plain to them what they were to do in order to carry out the design, offering only oblique and obscure clues, then perhaps these putative implicit directions are at best unimportant and at worst fanciful and illusory.

This is a crucial issue. Anyone with even a touch of dramatic taste can think of interesting ways for a scene to be played, and modern directors and actors like to feel free to be inventive about it; there is considerable modern resistance to supposing that Shakespeare meant to restrict such inventiveness by imposing specific designs. My claim is that Shakespeare was not setting his texts free for creative improvisation but rather had firm ideas about how they were to be played out, and that his texts often allow these designs to be reconstructed if we take sufficient care about what they imply. But it is patently unreasonable to suppose that actors in a repertory company that included the author as one of the actors should be required to study the text for clues to the designs in the way that I am suggesting that *we* should do, when it is so obvious that if the author had particular designs in mind, he ought to have made them more plain to those who were to execute them.

There is indeed a link missing in my argument so far. I would like to supply it now. It is that the frustrating deficiency of overt directional information in the early texts is merely an abbreviational economy on Shakespeare's part, like the abbreviated forms of names in speech headings. *Iaq.* and *Amy.* are enough to tell us, and the actors, that Jaques and Amiens are meant. We know how to supply the rest of the names, because the initial stage direction has given them in full. Similarly, a hint in the text is adequate to cue us to a point of authentic design because Shakespeare provided for a way to expand it: the bare *exeunt* at the end of the scene does not overtly disclose that separate doors were to be used, but it is evident from the spoken lines that this is the case.

So how was this gap filled? For more concrete explanation and illustration, I appeal to Shakespeare's most revealing representation of what it was like to put a play together for performance: the mounting of the *Pyramus and Thisby* play in A *Midsummer Night's Dream*.

Shakespeare has here left us a caricature portrait of the sort of dramatic production in which he himself was engaged. A study of this portrait, making allowances for the element of caricature, can teach us some illuminating things about how he worked, and how to read what he wrote. I think that the most efficient way of beginning to get the hang of Shakespearean dramaturgy, and perhaps the most delightful way as well, is to explore A *Midsummer Night's Dream*. For in that play he not only sketched an invaluable comic self-portrait of a dramaturge at work but also played around revealingly with the overall subject of dramatic illusion and the relationship between reason and imagination, resulting in what very nearly amounts to an anticipatory manifesto against the trends that would eventually bury the principles of Shakespearean dramaturgy under an avalanche of rationalism and systematic correctness.

In the play's second scene, the Athenian mechanicals (i.e., manual laborers) gather to begin the process of submitting an entertainment for the wedding festivities of Theseus and Hippolyta, as they had been invited to do according to the invitation issued in the third speech of the previous scene. The situation is domestically normal for England (Shakespeare was not really concerned about what might have been normal for Athens). In Shakespeare's England, it was quite usual for the locals to offer entertainment to the higher-ups on special occasions: Theseus reminds us of this, from the higher-ups' point of view, in 5.1, as he tells Hippolyta how a ruler must be gracious in accepting the bumbling attempts of local amateurs to entertain the visiting court.[3+] If A *Midsummer Night's Dream* was itself an entertainment of an analogous kind (there is good reason, but inadequate evidence, to suppose that this play was commissioned for, and first played at, an aristocratic wedding feast), the fun of the *Pyramus and Thisby* project is of course redoubled; but its instructiveness does not depend on that.

Some of the usual problems of design pervade both the inner and outer play. In 3.1, the characters who prepare Pyramus and Thisby express concern about how to represent the chink in the wall that separates the title characters. When Bottom prescribes that Wall must "hold his fingers thus," we have apparently solved the problem for the inner play—but this introduces a new potential design problem in the outer one. We are left ignorant of just how Bottom holds his fingers, and we cannot be sure whether it matters. Will any gesture do, or is this another instance of a cagey design that will work only if an intended hand-position is got specifically right? All Shakespeare's audience could know at this point is that they see the actor who played Bottom holding his fingers in a specific way, and that the others seem satisfied that the playing of the chink is now settled. Later, I believe, they will discover that however arbitrary Bottom's specific suggestion may have seemed for *Pyramus and Thisby*, it was not in the long run optional for the purposes of *A Midsummer Night's Dream*, but was rather part of a clever long-range design. Bottom's proposal was the end of one matter of design, but it was also the beginning of a more important one, and I will argue that Shakespeare kept himself in charge of both.

So, for the most part, does his counterpart, Peter Quince.

Peter Quince is director and producer, and evidently author as well, of what is eventually performed as *A Tedious Brief Scene of Young Pyramus and His Love Thisby*. Shakespeare's company and their audiences could hardly avoid realizing that what Quince and his fellows do is a parodic version of what the players themselves had done in preparing *A Midsummer Night's Dream*, and were doing in performing it. It is easy to see that Shakespeare enjoyed toying dramatically with the parallel. It is not quite so easy to see, though I think equally true, that the representation of Quince & Company is potentially instructive about the conditions in which Shakespeare's dramaturgical designs were put in place.

In 1.2, Quince begins the process. He (impatiently anticipated by the eager Bottom) proceeds in a helpfully ordered fashion: he says what the play is, and assigns the roles, explaining their nature where necessary. When Snug gets the lion's role, he asks "Have you the Lion's part written? pray you, if it be, give it me; for I am slow of study."[4+] The Lion's part is, of course, nothing but roaring, but the practical meaning of the request emerges at the end of the scene, when Quince says "But masters here are your parts, and I am to intreat you, request you, and desire you to con them by tomorrow night . . ."

The "parts" are not the roles. They are what the modern theater calls *sides*, i.e., the scripts of the spoken lines belonging to the specific roles. This is the necessary second step in the production of a play, once the first step of writing the overall script has been accomplished. The actors must be given the wherewithal to learn their own lines. It was logistically impossible to give them copies of the entire play, since everything had to be copied by hand, but it was indispensable to give them their own parts.[5] It is obvious that to support what the lines say, Peter Quince must be provided with some paper to distribute at this point. Shakespeare, typically, does not bother to add a stage direction to confirm the action implicit in the design; but we can infer it from the text, and Shakespeare's actor colleagues could further infer it from their own experience—for they had been through such a routine many a time in their own production of plays.

Surviving "parts" from this theatrical era confirm that they normally contained not only the speeches for a given role but the last few words of the preceding dialogue as well, the speech's cue.[6] The parts distributed by Quince evidently followed suit, for during the rehearsal in 3.1 Quince chides Flute/Thisby for bungling the lines by failing to distinguish speech from cue and plunging on through consecutive speeches without pausing for the intervening speech of Bottom/Pyramus: "You speak all your part at once, cues and all."[7+] More important for the present purposes, the extant "parts" provide a very limited indication of relevant stage directions.

The provision of cues makes obvious sense. It is clearly useful for the actor not only to memorize his own lines but also to be alerted from the beginning to the signal that releases a given speech. But is it not equally necessary to indicate any designated stage business at the same time?

In fact, it is not. There are three reasons for saying so.

The first is that the speeches themselves often imply the intended business plainly enough for an experienced professional actor to see what must be done without explicit instruction. The second is that when such business is not indicated in an actor's own lines but rather in the lines spoken by another character, it would be cumbersome to spell out the action if there is ample opportunity to clarify it in the course of a rehearsal.[8+]

In 3.1, Quince remarks that "Pyramus and Thisby meet by moonlight," and his next speech is "Yes, it doth shine that night," spoken on Bottom's cue "Find out moon-shine!" With the whole text in hand, it is obvious that Bottom's call for an almanac earlier in his cueing speech is answered by someone handing a book to Quince, who consults it before giving his reply. Detailing this action in Quince's "part" would be far less efficient than setting it up when the pieces come together in rehearsal, when the design may be made fully intelligible and instantly learned.

The third reason is that Quince's example reminds us that there could be ample opportunity to handle designed but textually inexplicit stage directions in this more efficient way.

When Quince's men assemble for the rehearsal in 3.1, there is some discussion about how to represent the chink in the wall, followed by a digression on how to modify relations with the audience, and quite a lot of talk about the practicalities of representation—but that is another substantial point, which I will deal with later. I want now to call attention to Quince's directorial role. It includes telling his actors what to do apart from reciting their lines. He assumes that Bottom (whom he calls Pyramus, pushing him into his role like a good director) knows his speech, but needs to be informed about his actions: "Pyramus, you begin; when you have spoken your speech, enter into that brake, and so every one according to his cue," and then launches the enactment with "Speak, Pyramus; Thisby, stand forth." When Flute, as Thisby (Shakespeare gets into it, and the speech headings become *This.* and *Pir.* rather than the previous *Flut.* and *Bot.*) asks what comes next, Quince explains some of the continuity, and subsequently complains about Flute/Thisby's having mismemorized and having failed to wait for Pyramus' reentry before speaking the second of his run-on speeches.

Quince had another job as well. At the end of 1.2, after sketching the play, assigning the roles, and distributing the "parts," he announces that the actors are to learn their lines by the next night and gather for rehearsal—and "In the meantime, I will draw up a bill of properties, such as our play wants." It is, after all, Quince's play, and only he has the full script. Someone must eventually see to it that the necessary props are supplied, and Quince himself is clearly in the best position to draw up the list of what is needed.

What Quince does with his company of players, Shakespeare might have done, and probably did, with his. Shakespeare wrote for the company in which he acted. He knew what was necessary for prerehearsal preparation, and what could be supplied later as required. He was in the best position (and in some cases of inexplicit design, the only position) to realize what properties were needed. In the present case, an alert stage manager might recognize that a roll was required for Quince to read from at the beginning of 1.2, and parts for him to distribute at the end, and an almanac to consult midway; but it would be asking too much for a stage manager to infer that Jaques must have a paper to hand to Amiens at the end of *As You Like It* 2.5, so it is plausible that Shakespeare himself might ordinarily be in charge of compiling the list of properties for one of his own plays. And since he was the only one who knew the specifics of his design for the play's acting, who could better take on the task of instructing the players about it? There was no need for him to write all the features of his dramatic designs into the script he handed over to the playhouse book-holder to initiate a new production if he had access to a better way of getting them across. The deficiencies in dramaturgical explicitness that we experience in wrestling with Shakespeare's texts would not have been a substantial problem to those who originally acted them, if Shakespeare could simply tell the players what he had in mind.

What happens in the production of *Pyramus and Thisby* is entirely consistent with what we know about theatrical procedure at the time. But it is a parody, and only an oblique guide to Shakespeare's dramaturgical situation. He did not have to contend with the unruly enthusiasm of Bottom, or the incompetence of Flute, or wonder whether the moon would be shining on the night of the performance—but he did have to provide a text that could be copied into parts; and he probably did have to give some sort of preliminary description of the nature of the characters and actions that the actors were to present, in order to aid their preparation; and he likely was responsible for listing the required properties; and later it would make sense for him to direct movements that were not written into the script but apparently intended and potentially valuable for the performance, such as the circle gathered over "ducdame" and the separate exit of Jaques, or the way the chink in the wall was to be represented both in 3.1 and in the eventual performance in 5.1

The production of *Pyramus and Thisby* is accordingly (among other things) perhaps Shakespeare's parody of Shakespeare with his company—hugely incompetent by comparison with the real thing, but following a familiar pattern.[9+] Through it, Shakespeare has—and offers, both to us and to his own dramatic company—a bit of fun over the problems that can arise when the actors must rely on incomplete learning texts, and he hints about how practical designs may be made explicit and occasionally modified in the course of a play's rehearsal.

To this I would like to add one more item: Quince's justification of rehearsing in the forest. Shakespeare himself had other reasons for having the rehearsal there (he had to get the mechanicals, and especially Bottom, placed where Puck could conveniently stumble upon them and in the vicinity of the sleeping Titania), but Quince's explanation is revealing: "if we meete in the Citie, we shalbe dog'd with company, and our deuises knowne" (1.2).

This does not make good logical sense; the performance is to be for the court, who are unlikely to be snooping around the rehearsals no matter how accessible they are, and it doesn't matter whether other townsmen get a glimpse. But Quince's argument, in emphasizing the element of surprise, touches on a major value in Shakespearean dramaturgy, as the rest of the play will show: keep some things hidden, in the service of later special dramatic effects.

It would have been dramaturgically convenient for Shakespeare to supply more than the script to his company when he wrote a play. But can we say that he actually *did* take it some steps further?

There has been some question, in scholarly circles, about whether Shakespeare produced his own plays. Alfred Hart thought not when he first asked that question years ago, mainly on account of the legally complete transfer of rights that obtained when a playwright sold a play to a dramatic company.[10] David Klein answered (twenty-one years later, but well) with a revaluation of evidence dismissed by Hart and an assembly of a considerable amount of additional material.[11] I should think that any fair referee would award a clear victory to Klein and to the conclusion that authors were at least sometimes involved in the staging of their plays.

One interesting piece of evidence that Hart had already referred to and Klein subsequently pressed is an account by Johannes Rheinanus, a German visitor to England who had observed in 1611[12] that

> So far as the actors are concerned they, as I have noticed in England, are daily instructed, as it were in a school, so that even the most eminent actors have to allow themselves to be taught their places by the dramatists, and this gives life and ornament to a well-written play, so that it is no wonder that the English players (I speak of skilled ones) surpass others and have the advantage over them.[13]

Hart had dismissed this testimony rather breezily as either Rheinanus' misunderstanding or a prank played on his gullibility. Klein quite rightly insisted that it must be taken seriously.

Curiously, neither Hart nor Klein, though ostensibly contending over Shakespeare in particular, took adequate account of the peculiarity of Shakespeare's situation as an actor and shareholder, as distinguished from the bulk of his contemporary playwrights who had no such connections with the companies to whom they sold their works. I, of course, insist that this is the most important datum of all.[14*]

Did Shakespeare produce—or better, though still questionably, direct—his own plays?[15!] There is no completely compelling evidence either way, and the indirect evidence is both skimpy and hard to evaluate. Judgments about the matter must be provisional and based on plausibility. The question is significant enough to require at least a brief glance into what has been said about it, although the discussion is still too incomplete to resolve. It is important to my overall argument to establish a likelihood that Shakespeare's dramaturgical design was regularly communicated to his players in considerable detail, even if not through the scripts he submitted. Although Johannes Rheinanus' report can hardly be generalized across the entire theatrical spectrum (Klein mentions the obvious difficulties in mounting multiple-authorship plays in such a fashion), nothing whatever makes it impossible to suppose that Rheinanus may have witnessed a rehearsal of *The Tempest* at the Globe.

After Hart and Klein, the subsequent discussion has rarely joined the issue as directly as they did, but those who have touched on it have tended to concede the likelihood that Shakespeare had at least substantial influence in the production of his plays.[16]

For the opposition side, a recent book by a fine scholar questions whether new plays were carefully rehearsed at all: "Since the company was playing every afternoon, and probably spent part of each morning running through that day's play, the company cannot have had much free time for full rehearsals of new plays."[17] Andrew Gurr does not explain why he thinks that mornings were given over to rehearsals of *that day's* play, and I know of no evidence to support this notion. For a new play, it would be a reasonable way of spending the morning before the first performance; but after two or three more performances, surely the time might be better spent on getting new acquisitions ready.

Henslowe's *Diary*, the detailed records of the effectual producer for the dramatic company that was the major rival to that of Shakespeare (and about which there will be considerably more information later), shows that the Admiral's Men normally added a new play about every three weeks, and had about three weeks between the delivery of a new play-text and its first public showing. That might well argue both the importance and the opportunity of arranging some dense rehearsal time, but Gurr argues the opposite. The new play might not succeed. The company took chances on that. Henslowe bought around seventeen new plays each year in the company's early days,[18] and several of them appear only once in his performance records: the occasional flop was one of the system's risks. Gurr's conclusion is surprising:

> So the temptation must have been great not to put too much effort into a new play until its success on stage and its retention in the repertory were assured. Only then, perhaps, would much effort be put into polishing the production. With such large and rapidly changing repertoires of plays, no company could afford to spend much time on the niceties of staging.[19]

I suggest that Gurr has it backward this time. If the occasional turkey left the company at a financial loss, would this inspire them to offer inadequately rehearsed plays routinely, as a protective measure? That makes no sense. Surely the motivation would be the absolute contrary: do everything convenient, even if not everything possible, to make a good first impression and lengthen the run. Spend the mornings not on reviewing plays that have already been learned and have caught on, but on the still-untried new scripts, to get them maximally ready for public airing. Don't put "too much effort" into a new play, but be sure to put enough to give it a decent chance. How much is enough? With a company of accomplished actors who have worked together for years, a great deal can be accomplished in three days' worth of full mornings once the speeches have been learned. Three weeks can bring it to a state of considerable polish and finesse.

I think it much more plausible that considerable rehearsal time was budgeted before a play opened. In particular, we have the following considerations, in addition to Johannes Rheinanus' claim, which cannot be dismissed out of hand: (1) We know that rehearsals were regarded as an important part of an actor's duties: a surviving contract from Henslowe's lifetime (i.e., before 1616, and therefore within Shakespeare's lifetime as well) binds an actor

to attend rehearsals, or risk a substantial fine;[20] (2) Shakespeare would necessarily have been present at rehearsals anyway, since he was an actor in his
company, and had roles to play; (3) Shakespeare, as playwright, knew that he
would be there when the company confronted the elemental necessities of
staging, and that this would provide a convenient occasion to add clarifications, specifications, and enhancing byplay on the spot; and (4) there are so
many inadequate stage directions, specific actions inferrable from the assembled lines but hardly obvious from "parts," and other reconstructable dramaturgical niceties present in the early Shakespearean texts that it is difficult
to doubt that Shakespeare habitually skimped on stage directions because he
could afford to do so: he could rely on rehearsals for a chance to fill out his
intentions, this being much more efficient than writing extensive stage business details into the script.

To ask whether Shakespeare "directed" his own plays is probably to ask
an anachronistic and misleading question. But to ask whether Shakespeare
had interest in dramaturgical designs and strategies not overtly recorded in
the published texts and initially known to him alone, and had the opportunity
to make his plays happen in accordance with them, and made use of that advantage—well, that is a different matter. No other playwright in England was
in such a privileged position to do just that. I would also venture to say that
no other playwright in England has left us texts that are so obviously *in need*
of supplementary guidance to fill out the the designs that can, with informed
patience, be found lurking in the implications of the spoken lines. I conclude
that it is overwhelmingly probable that Shakespeare was in charge not only
(through the delivered text) of what the actors said on stage, but also (through
Peter Quincian on-the-spot instructions) of many of the further concretiza-
tions through which his designs could be dramatically realized and brought
effectively alive to audiences.

It is entirely possible that Shakespeare played the role of Peter Quince.
That would be delightfully appropriate. It is more than possible that Peter
Quince played the role of Shakespeare. But that performance is a parody, and
its most important disclosures for our purposes are not those about theatrical
practicalities, but the ones that bear on dramaturgical presuppositions.

The bulk of the discussion in the rehearsal scene, 3.1, attends to the problem of the communication between a dramatic company and an audience.
Scene 1.2 had anticipated the fine line that must be drawn. The Athenian amateurs realize that this is serious business. If the Lion is played too realistically, the ladies will be frightened, and they will all be in deep trouble: there
should be some very clear indication that it is not, in fact, a real lion but only
a theatrical illusion. Then they look at the other side of the coin. The play is
to take place by moonlight. Will the moon in fact be shining on the night of

the performance? An almanac establishes that they are safe on that score—but a better solution is to bring in Moon as a character, endowed with the folksy attributes of the Man in the Moon.[21+] And the wall? Another character, with some plaster or roughcast to identify him convincingly.

Shakespeare is spoofing the mechanicals' total misunderstanding of dramatic illusion, and their failure to understand that a sophisticated audience is neither fooled by a lion costume nor left at sea if asked to imagine moonlight or walls. He is, in the course of this, stuffing a couple of cards up his sleeve that he will play on us in act 5; but in the meantime, he is reminding us that one of the indispensable requirements of Shakespearean dramaturgy is the audience's cooperative and participating imagination.

The accomplishments of cinema and of dazzling theatrical sets, coupled with elaborate lighting and sound systems, do not prepare the modern reader to grasp the basic conditions of a Shakespearean play's production. There was no special lighting, only the steady ambient light from the open roof of the Globe, or the candles in the hall of a touring performance or a privileged playing at court. There was no scenery, as we know it. The stage for which Shakespeare designed his plays was usually a plain floor backed by a nonsignificant facade (with enough room behind it to serve for a tiring-house, i.e., dressing room), through which there were usually two entryways. Occasionally (but relatively rarely) a large prop, such as a bed or a throne, was employed. And that was roughly it. That design could work almost anywhere, including a hall in Gray's Inn or in a town visited on provincial tour. Some plays require another stage feature or two (more detail will be given in the next chapter)—a window above, a curtained enclosure, a trapdoor and a bit of room under the stage.[22+] But it was evidently Basic Bare: a simple and undefined stage, whose definition into specific places, scenery, spaces, and the like had to be made by the audience's imaginative cooperation with what the lines told them.

The mechanicals understand none of this. They are literalists of the imagination. Shakespeare drives these points home in a wonderfully ironic way with Quince's first speech in 3.1: "And here's a marvelous convenient place for our rehearsal. This green plot shall be our stage, this hawthorn brake our tiring-house, and we will do it in action, as we will do it before the Duke." What the audience witnesses, of course, is Quince pointing to the bare stage and calling it a green plot that will serve as a stage, and pointing to the tiring-house to say that it is a hawthorn brake that will do as a tiring-house. The playwright is in command, and has just subverted the Quince Theory of Dramaturgy by sifting it though his own—just as he will later subvert the Theseus Theory on Fairyland in a similar way.

The first and most pervasive principle of Shakespearean dramaturgy, and an indispensable condition for receiving its accomplishments, is that the audience (or, through more demanding discipline, the reader) must respond with participatory imagination. We must be ready to allow the play to define, mainly by what is said, just what sort of space the bare stage represents, just whom the actors are impersonating, just what the actions signify. This means that, within the broad limits of the time's conventional theatrical understanding, the playwright is always in charge. He makes the rules, and is in fact free to revise them as long as he gives sufficient guidance to take us with him. As Shakespeare has the Chorus say to the audience in *Henry V* 3.1, in a somewhat amusing (and uncharacteristic) self-effacing mode, he must depend on their generous imaginative participation to make it work: "Still be kind, And eke out our performance with your mind." Most of these considerations must obtain in any form of dramaturgy, if we are to retain an adequate distinction between the literal mechanics of play production and the unliteral dramatic illusion that they support as the play itself. And that leads us to the second principle.

The second principle of Shakespearean dramaturgy is less universal and much less well understood. It is that everything is provisional, and may be readjusted at any time. This will be elaborated in later chapters, but for the moment, it may be useful to give some examples.

What is the name of Orlando's beloved in *As You Like It*? Rosalind, the *Dramatis Personae* preface to your edition will say. But that is not the only way she is named. It is the name used in 1.1's reference to her, and in the initial stage direction and the first line of 1.2, her first entrance; but in her second entrance, at the beginning of the next scene, the stage direction and Celia's opening line call her Rosaline. She is referred to as Rosalinda in the middle of the poem (by Orlando) that Celia reads as she enters in 3.2.

This too is more a parable than an important dramaturgical point. Shakespeare can call her anything he wants, within intelligible limits, and if he sometimes picks "Rosalindÿ"] because it can be rhymed with *wind* and *Ind*, and sometimes varies the pronunciation to rhyme with *kind* and *find*, and one one occasion calls her "Rosalinda" because he needs three syllables to fill the verse's rhythm, whatever he chooses becomes the provisional truth. If he shifts occasionally to "Rosaline" by mere whim, he nevertheless gets his say.[23*] He is in charge. And he is not obliged to be consistent in this or in anything else.

Back to *A Midsummer Night's Dream*'s mechanicals. When Bottom enters the hawthorn brake (actually the tiring-house imagined as a hawthorn brake, to be mechanically literal), Puck is waiting with a prank: when Bottom emerges, the stage direction says "Enter Pyramus [Shakespeare is evidently still thinking in terms of the inner play, though it would be technically more appropriate to say that it is Bottom who enters] with the Ass head." The definite article may be

Shakespeare's shorthand for "the head that I have assigned him," or—perhaps more likely—for "the ass head that we have in our properties room." But in any case, it is apparent that this is the extent of Bottom's costume change. The subsequent lines confirm it, including Puck's later description to Oberon. But is he, as first seems, essentially Bottom with a transformed head, but unaware of any change? That is the way he behaves for the rest of the scene, and Shakespeare plays it for good comic effect. But Puck hints at a more thorough transformation as he tells Oberon that "Titania waked, and straightway loved an Ass," and Bottom seems to confirm the hint in 4.1, as he expresses a need to scratch, and an unaccountable appetite for oats, hay, dried peas.

Our accommodating Halloween imaginations allow us to accept a child as a mouse or a monkey on the basis of a mask alone. A full costume is not necessary for the representation of a full transformation. In the plays and entertainments of Shakespeare's time, animals were often represented similarly, the heads alone defining the meaning of the figure even though the rest of the body was left as usual. In *A Midsummer Night's Dream*, the literal dramaturgical fact is that the actor playing Bottom (and playing him as the traditional generic type of the *Clown*, which is the name given him in the entrance stage direction in 4.1 and in the speech headings for the rest of the scene) wears a prop ass's head. The more subtle dramaturgical truth is that Shakespeare sometimes asks us to imagine him as Bottom with an ass's head, and sometimes asks rather that we imagine him as quite metamorphosed into an ass who speaks like Bottom. Shakespeare can do as he pleases, according to what works best at the moment, so long as he keeps us informed. All definitions are provisional, and remain flexible.

If that seems too suspiciously subtle to establish the general dramaturgical point that blatant unrealism, apodictic redefinition, and creative inconsistency were all authorized in Shakespeare's dramatic license, let me add two more examples involving the mechanicals, and yet another involving the lovers, that are blatant enough to make it stick.

Mechanicals, part 1: after Bottom's transformation and Titania's abrupt falling-in-craziness, the two of them enter together and Titania calls upon her servants to attend to her new beloved. We have known about her fairy servants since 2.1, and before we have seen more than one of them, we have learned that when frightened by the quarreling of Titania and Oberon, they creep into acorn-cups; before the scene is over, we hear that a fairy can fit into a shed snakeskin; and in the meantime, her fairies have been associated with tiny tasks, like freckling and dewdropping cowslips. When we meet them by name in 4.1, not only are their chores diminutive—killing one bee and bringing the honeybag—but so are their names: Peaseblossom, Moth, Cobweb, Mustardseed. These are perhaps the smallest folks we've ever heard converse.

But wait! This isn't Walt Disney, whose form of dramaturgy permitted him to make fairies as tiny as he pleased. This is Shakespeare, whose fairies had to be presented by actors—and there is a certain limit to how small an adequate actor can be. We are asked to understand imaginatively that they are tiny, but our eyes see something different—or, to put that in better order, our eyes see actors of ordinary size, but Shakespeare's dramaturgical guidance brings us to imagine them tinier than Disney's Tinker Bell.[24*]

You are perhaps wondering why I am dealing with fairies when I promised a point about the mechanicals? I'll attend to that in a moment, but first I want to correct one more impression one might have about the fairies. They are not being played by the smallest competent boys Shakespeare could find, though something like that is often assumed because he succeeds in making us think small. Shakespeare could not afford to recruit additional actors lavishly whenever a play would be enhanced by an amplified cast, and he could not afford to write plays that would require that kind of extravagance. He was part of a repertory company, and it was good for all of them if they stayed within the budget. The proper dramaturgical strategy was to use the talent and resources he had at hand (including "the" ass head), and lead the audience to see them as he wanted. There will be a later chapter going into greater detail about how Shakespeare dealt with the need to have more characters than he had actors, but for the moment you can get a clearer idea about the *literal* size of the fairies by glancing at 1.2 or 3.1.

The fairies were, to the literal and physical eye, exactly the same size as the Athenian mechanicals, because they are played by the same actors, which gives us the additional fun of watching Bottom, much changed, bossing around the same fellows he been bossing around since we've know him—though they too are much changed. I will defend this claim more adequately in a later chapter; for the moment, I ask that you trust me, however provisionally.

Mechanicals, part 2: we have seen the *Pyramus and Thisby* play unfold from its inception. Its first rehearsal is interrupted and is not resumed. In 4.2, Bottom breaks in upon the dispirited company with the news (how did he get it?) that the Duke's dinner is over, and their play is "preferred," i.e., chosen for performance. Everyone must hie to the palace "presently," i.e., immediately.[25+] They eventually play it out with hilarious effect, but not because it has been inadequately rehearsed. The bunglings are not those of Flute's reciting cues along with his lines.[26+] The play goes forward as if it were just what they had hoped they would do after full rehearsal, because it is better comedy to handle it that way than to take advantage repetitiously of the actors' earlier failures. A sloppy rehearsal can be good comedy once; a ludicrous "polished" performance is far more amusing than a replaying of the inadequately rehearsed initial fumbling, and Shakespeare relies on our willingness to suppose that they have somehow arrived at their intended result, even though he has not provided means for them to do so.

But the main point is not how Bottom, of all people, found out that the Duke has dined and that their play is preferred, nor is it that the process of Theseus' choosing the play takes place before us in 5.1, *after* Bottom has told them that the decision has been made—though both of those facts are dramaturgically interesting and significant. It is rather that we get a *Pyramus and Thisby* play that is completely different from what we had seen in the rehearsal.

The cast of characters has changed. In 1.2, Peter Quince specifies Pyramus, Thisby, Thisby's mother, Pyramus' father, Thisby's father, and the Lion; the rehearsal in 3.1 makes an unresolved case for Moon and Wall; and when we get to the performance, all parents have disappeared and we have Pyramus, Thisby, Moonshine, Wall, and Lion. More importantly, *none* of the previously recited lines of the rehearsal appears in performance. It is a whole new ballgame. This change is absolutely unrealistic—but it is much more fun than the easy literalism of repeating the same text the rehearsal has already given us. And it allows Shakespeare to spring at least one silly surprise.

The surprise is the chink. In the rehearsal of 3.1, as they puzzle over how to present the wall, Bottom makes the creative suggestion "let him hold his fingers thus; and through that cranny, shall Pyramus and Thisby whisper." Quince evidently thinks that a good plan. We don't know what "thus" is, though Shakespeare doubtless told his players what he had in mind. But in 5.1, with a totally changed text and cast, we can hardly expect that he has made an unbreakable contract with our expectations. Pyramus asks Wall to "Shew me thy chink, to blink through with mine eyne." There is again no stage direction; but Shakespeare had a design nevertheless, disclosed by the surrounding language.

With a little help from the *Oxford English Dictionary*'s disclosures of sixteenth-century meanings, and a bit of imagination, we can fairly guess that lines like "Cursed be thy stones for thus deceiving me," and "My cherry lips have often kissed thy stones, / Thy stones with lime and hair knit up in thee," and "O kiss me through the hole of this vile wall," followed by "I kiss the wall's hole, not thy lips at all," indicate that the dramaturgical design no longer involves Wall's simply holding his fingers thus. He has probably opened his legs.[27*] The solemn and poignant encounter between Pyramus and Thisby through the chink has been rudely undermined (so rudely that it simply disappeared from stage tradition once such hearty vulgarity had become distastefully unfashionable, and appears to have disappeared from memory as well), and so brilliantly that it is not hard to understand why the story of Pyramus and Thisby, once as popular and moving as that of Romeo and Juliet, subsequently vanished from serious literature.

The final example involves the Athenian lovers. It is analogous to Shakespeare's having Bottom and his colleagues find out that their play has been chosen, and only afterward letting us watch the choice being made. Consider the state of information in the Athenian lovers when they are finally awakened, all relationships healed, at the end of act 4. We have seen the way in which Oberon and Puck have manipulated their fortunes, with a bit of bungling at first but finally putting things in order. They have seen none of this: they have interpreted all happenings in ordinary terms, and have shown no awareness that Puck and Oberon even exist, let alone that it is their intervention that has made things happen. The recovered Demetrius acknowledges that "I wot not by what power, (But by some power it is)" that he is no longer interested in Hermia and has returned to Helena as to good health. They express their general confusion after the Duke's departure: it was like a dream. Was it a dream that the Duke was here? But no: that was real. They proceed accordingly to the temple, to be married along with the Duke and Hippolyta, and will recount their dreams on the way.

There has been no hint that they have any knowledge of the antics of Puck. The dreams they recount offstage are apparently only their hazy memories of their own bizarre behavior. Yet 5.1, taking advantage of what Shakespeare knows we know, subtly changes their state of understanding. They have evidently debriefed (when? no matter) to Theseus and Hippolyta, with a story we thought, for good reason, that they didn't know. Hippolyta begins the scene with "'Tis strange, my Theseus, that these lovers speak of." We may at that point think she's talking of Demetrius' spontaneous reformation and Lysander's unaccountable temporary infatuation with Helena, but Theseus immediately steers us where we had not expected to go: "More strange than true. I never may believe / These anticke[28+] fables, nor these fairy toys." Now we know that the lovers have told them about the fairies, whom they hadn't known about a mere two scenes before, and that the situation is simply changed. Shakespeare has played another of his dramaturgical wild cards in order to create a new dramatic happening through this conversation, as Theseus (established long before in literature as the fair and thoroughly reasonable ruler) uses the lovers' new disclosure to explain away the fairies—who are in fact, to our dramatically imaginative eye, as real as he is, and who have come to bless his wedding, as they do in the closing of the play.

Who has the last laugh, or at least the last smile? Not reasonable and patronizing Theseus, who dismisses fairies and poets in a single breath, though he has been well taken care of by both. Not even Oberon and Titania, who dance the world back to harmony near the end of act 4 and jointly bestow their blessing on the ducal couple at the play's conclusion. It is Shakespeare, who has engineered the whole thing, showing that participatory imagination can be teased up to accepting a silly fairy machinery that may be sublated into a dramaturgical metaphor for the fact that young men are fickle and may temporarily defect yet come home again, and that a clown is an ass, and that even a powerful queen may fall foolishly in love—and that we, unlike Theseus on the one hand and the literalist mechanicals on the other, may hospitably entertain the accomplishments of dramatic illusion beyond the reach of limiting rationality, and enjoy the illuminating result without perplexity or disdain.

One of his biggest pranks on Theseus and Hippolyta, for all the former's skepticism, is one that appears neither in the direct lines nor in the stage directions but can be shown (and will be, in a later chapter) to be a part of his dramaturgical design that should not be missed: the actors playing Theseus and Hippolyta are the same as those who play Oberon and Titania. At the very least, that is a fairly decisive undermining of Theseus' views on the frivolity of imagination. His own validity as a presence in the play depends on our willingness to see that his confident conclusion is wrong, no matter how unimpeachably reasonable his argument may be. At least it is demonstrably wrong within the imaginative world Shakespeare has placed him in, just as what is rational is often wrong in the terms of Shakespearean dramaturgy—on which subject *A Midsummer Night's Dream* is an incomparably informative lesson.

4

IN SHORT SPACE,
IT RAIN'D DOWN FORTUNE
Shakespeare's use of space and place

Shakespeare's dramaturgical planning was as much conditioned by the theatrical space he worked in as is the work of modern directors by the possibilities of the camera or of the elaborate equipment available on advanced contemporary stages. Let me remind you of the basic physical particulars, and then go on to deal with the dramaturgical implications.

The regular theater of Shakespeare's day had an ample platform of about one thousand square feet—the surviving 1599 contract for the Fortune Theater, whose stage was expressly to copy the features of Shakespeare's company's recently constructed Globe,[1] provides for a stage of 43 by 27½ feet—and it was essentially bare. It projected out into the playhouse, so that spectators could stand or be seated on three sides (sometimes four, in theaters provided with a rear gallery that could be so used). It did not, and could not, have a general curtain that could close it to the audience.

Behind the stage platform was a façade that stood between the stage and the tiring-house, where properties were held ready and costume changes took place and actors waited to enter the stage. There were at least two entryways, at least one of them being large enough to permit the entrance and exit of a scaffold or a tomb or a throne[2+] when need be. (In some unusual cases, though not in any of our seven plays, a third entryway is evidently presupposed and required.)[3] The entryways were probably curtained so as not to show the backstage area when the action was on and only actors were moving through them, but in at least some cases it seems likely that there were also doors, making possible a concretization of the large dramatic gesture of sealing off Gloucester's castle against Lear and his followers at the end of act 2.

There were no backdrops (the façade would probably have standard architectural ornamentation, but nothing specific to the play), and no scenery (occasionally a prop bush, or even an arbor, might be brought on, and subsequently taken off; the same was true of a throne or a scaffold—token and temporary scenic hints, with no attempt at systematic decoration). The lighting was whatever was coming from the sky in the public theaters like the Globe (or from the omnipresent candles and torches in closed halls like the Blackfriars' Theater), supplemented only by token use of torches or candles on the stage platform, to remind the audience that the scene was taking place at night. A night scene required an imaginative adjustment like the one needed to grasp the classic Chinese playlet in which brightly lit actors pretend to be in total darkness as they flail out with their swords—witness the analogous imagined darkness as Lysander and Demetrius hunt for each other and are decoyed out of trouble by Puck at the end of *A Midsummer Night's Dream*, 3.2.

A few plays had special needs. One requires a window above through which Juliet could sigh into the night and Romeo could steal away from his nuptial bed into exile. In some non-Shakespearean plays, several people had to be presented in a location above the stage; but not even a window is needed in the other six plays of our canon, and a mere window is the most that was required by any play written for the first Globe Theater. Another play requires a trapdoor that could open as Ophelia's unfinished grave, with first a workman in it and then Ophelia's corpse and two struggling men. Earlier Shakespearean plays do not assume a trapdoor, but the Globe apparently had one of ample proportions that gave access to a below-stage space, which in turn could be used for the shifting voice of King Hamlet's voice in 1.5. A "discovery-space," capable of becoming Juliet's bed or the Capulet mausoleum, was provided with curtains that could be opened to reveal a sedated Juliet or closed to conceal the dead Romeo, Juliet, and Paris; but this was apparently a large prop rather than part of the stage architecture. Its construction may have permitted it to serve as the Flint Castle walls in *Richard II*, or as the frame of the arras through which Polonius is skewered in *Hamlet* (though the back wall of the stage may well have had such an arras, which was common enough in great halls for decorative and acoustical reasons).

Shakespeare did not use these optional features often, even when they were readily available. If he could count on an upper window for *Romeo and Juliet*, before the Globe was built, he presumably could make use of one for *Richard II* or *A Midsummer Night's Dream*, but he does not. The Globe evidently had such a window available, but neither Shakespeare nor the other playwrights who wrote for his company made much use of it. Two-thirds of the plays produced there have no need of any activity "above," and the remaining third deploy it as if only a limited area was available (it is usually treated as a window) and it was almost never used except in conjunction with action on the main platform.[4] This is all the more significant in that Shakespeare was in on the design of that theater and could presumably have installed a balcony or upper platform or some sort of elevated stage if he thought it dramaturgically convenient. Shakespeare used the trapdoor sparingly even when he could rely on its being there in the company's own theater (the grave in *Hamlet* is the only candidate in our seven-play canon, and *Macbeth* is the only highly memorable other exploitation of this feature). In general, he wrote for the basic platform. He wrote as if his plays might have to be staged in regular trapdoorless and upper-windowless halls at court or on tour (which was of course the case), or as if the bare platform was all that was really needed as the foundation of a solid play (which his ingenuity could make to be the case).

In any event, the stages of the time were relatively simple, and Shakespeare's needs tended to be even simpler. All he could expect when playing away from the usual home base was the platform; the most he normally had access to was a platform accessible through usually two (and perhaps, in a pinch, three) doors to the backstage tiring-house, an upper window, a trapdoor with an understage space, a curtainable enclosure of modest size for abrupt revealing and concealing of up to three persons (or one person and a bit of furniture), and stage properties that could be efficiently moved on and off by the cast in the course of playing.

And with that, we have a regular theater. Its space is almost entirely neutral, waiting to be defined not by elaborate sets, or stunning backdrops, or clever lighting, but by the shifting definitions and redefinitions imposed by the dramaturgical guidance given through speech and action. These shiftings and readjustments took place as the guiding cues of the text were received and registered though the participatory imagination of an audience that was used to being called upon to receive and register such hints. They knew how to share in the task of making it all work by accepting what they saw not with their eyes alone but as their mind's eyes imaginatively redefined it in accordance with established conventions and the playwright's guided designs.

While Orlando goes back and forth between the two areas we had seen simultaneously represented in 2.6, Jaques gives his most famous speech about the world as a stage. That covers the imagined time for Orlando to find Adam and carry him in—some thirty-three lines, plenty of time for Orlando's actor to go backstage and gather up Adam's actor, but the time is not to be taken at literal face value. It is not a realistic interval if we have adequately appreciated the psychological distance between starving Adam and the visible picnic.

Somewhere in the corners of our awareness, this sequence gives us the sense that the banquet was within Orlando's (though not Adam's) scouting range, but not at all near at hand. The literal proximity of the two Somewheres on the same stage is a visible fact, but not an actively dramatic one: the dramatic fact is that although we know that there is an accessible solution to Adam's plight, it takes Orlando's determined effort, the resolute bravery of his considerably increased desperation, and much more time than the literal hundred lines' worth of the opening of 2.7 (let alone half of the thirty-three lines' worth alloted to his round trip to bring the further-deteriorated Adam to the food) to find it.

Once it is found, of course, there is no dramatic need to delay much further, and the fetching of Adam is meant to be understood as taking place in a dramaturgically compressed time rather than what the audience could register with stopwatches. But we will examine Shakespeare's treatment of time in the next chapter: here it is enough to say that its foreshortening should not confuse us about how much space is being represented, any more than the artificial proximity of discrete locations in 2.6 should be allowed to mislead us about the imagined distance between the waiting banquet and the failing Adam.

The Somewhere in which Edgar resolves to transform himself to Mad Tom is also part of a highly complex spatial/dramatic construction. The stage is not bare when Edgar enters. It contains Kent, sleeping in the stocks that punish his assault on Oswald. As in Adam's sharing the stage with the banquet of *As You Like It*, the literal proximity between the actors playing Edgar and Kent does not compromise the independence of the spaces surrounding them, or imply that they are close together.

We know where Kent is, in the base court of Gloucester's castle, having been confined there by the stocks. But Edgar tells us that he has already heard himself proclaimed a criminal and has hidden for a while in a hollow tree: obviously, his old home is the most unlikely place in Britain for him to be at the moment, and the reference to the hollow tree suggests he is somewhere in the woods, the traditional hiding place for outlaws. His dramatic juxtaposition with his former home (as it is made marginally present by the sleeping Kent) enhances the poignancy of his new situation, just as the indignity of the stocks as an insult to both Kent and his kingly master is somewhat heightened by the simultaneous presence, albeit in another and unlocalized space, of the character who has been dragged farthest into the disgrace and danger that exiled and disguised Kent has pledged to undergo in service to Lear.

The two are in effect different versions of one another, and the spatial flexibility of Shakespeare's stage here allows a stunning effect that became impossible with the changes in theaters and dramaturgies only two generations later, when two quite different spaces could no longer be shown at once.

It is, of course, *possible* to rationalize these representations within the boundaries of the later rules. One *could* imagine that the density of the forest obscured from Orlando that he was approximately forty feet from rescue, and that it took him a hundred lines of wandering in the backstage area before he heard the voices and tracked down where they were coming from. But this is a silly tack, and it ignores the ways in which Shakespeare enforces a sense of greater distance and longer time. Edgar *could* have sneaked back from the hollow tree to a hiding place at home (he could even be credited with cleverness for hiding out in what his pursuers would consider the least likely place for him to be), and we *could* accordingly imagine him in Gloucester's courtyard, unaware of the stocked and sleeping Kent because of the darkness and his own urgent preoccupations.

But these modes of interpretation are simply ways of squeezing Shakespeare's careful design into another anachronistic box. Shakespeare gives adequate guidance to let us know that what is going on in the spatial dimension through dramatic imagination is quite different from the literalness of the physical eye, and the general tactics of Shakespearean dramaturgy, as familiar to his audiences as they were unfamiliar to audiences of a century and more later, allow him to accomplish much more through unconfusingly flexible strategies than the proscenium theater-box had room for. Instead of misreading through our inherited habits, we *can* learn to understand in the language of Shakespearean dramaturgy.

I pause to recapitulate. Shakespeare's stage was spatially neutral, until he defined it. Once defined, it did not have to remain spatially constant: it could be redefined so as to encompass more than one spatial locale, at indefinite (or, if he preferred, definite) distances from one another. The ratio could change to suit the flow of the play. All definitions are provisional, and subject to change on a line's notice. What counts is the coherent flow of the action; the coherence of imagined space is entirely subservient to that end, and has no intrinsic claim to stability.

Shakespeare could not only change the rules on space discontinuously and arbitrarily; he could also shift them more smoothly, in a way that had to frustrate post-Restoration editors who thought him obliged to stay where he had said he was, or seemed to be. Sometimes an awareness of Shakespeare's dramaturgical rights over space makes a crucial difference in the understanding of a decisive moment in a play. This is the case with *Richard II*, 3.3, the scene that shows, even more than the formal abdication scene 4.1, the shift of kingship from Richard to Henry Bolingbroke.

I have witnessed many a debate over whether Bolingbroke usurps the throne or Richard abdicates it in his favor. The majority of participants usually hold for the former, but often neither side can make a case on a basis stronger than overall impression, fortified with selected quotations. Shakespeare's management of space is a neglected key to resolving the question.

As the scene opens and the conversation begins, we soon learn that we are in Wales. Then we are informed that the place where Richard has taken refuge, Flint Castle, is "not far from hence." After twenty lines, there it is, at the back of the stage, and Bolingbroke is asking Harry Percy, "Will not this castle yield?"

The rate of spatial rediscovery and recognition is unrealistic and artificial, but full of dramatic good sense. Shakespeare gives us the sense of an indefinite but not brief period of journeying, but efficiently compresses it into twenty lines. It takes about a minute of actual playing time to go from Somewhere to Wales to "not far from hence" to Flint Castle itself—a change of place/perspective analogous to what film editors often do with their deft selection and joining of brief clips to effect transitions in space and time. But it is, unlike that sort of cinematic montage, a sequence of redefinitions of the overall visible space rather than a series of disjunct and visibly changed locales, and a progressive modulation of spatial meaning rather than a gradual discovery of where we really were from the start.

The conventional scene-heading, "Wales, before Flint Castle," bracketed or not, is accordingly misleading. To imagine that Flint Castle is there, visible in the background, from the beginning of the action and is only gradually discovered by those who enter it makes the entering group—the putative rebel-usurper and his closest advisers—seem amusingly incompetent to know only that Richard is "not far from hence" moments before they get around to noticing a castle looming yonder. More importantly for the appreciation of this form of dramaturgy, it obscures the way that Shakespeare has provided a process of spatial revision that takes place in separate redefinitional steps rather than in stages of noticing and identifying a fixed place.

When we get the spatial redefinition at Flint Castle, a vast meadow intervenes between the front of the stage and the back, because Shakespeare says so, whatever the literal eye may see. Near the end of the scene, the whole stage, which started as merely Somewhere, then Somewhere in Wales, then Near Flint Castle, then the Castle and the Large Meadow, is transformed into the base court of Flint Castle merely by Shakespeare's having Richard say so and having Bolingbroke advance, with a few token strides, into the new location—no shifting of scenery, no curtain-division into subscenes, just the manipulation of space through dramaturgical fiat.

The redefinitions and discontinuities are always made according to Shakespeare's guidance. Richard, standing on the castle walls, hears out Northumberland's embassy from Bolingbroke and then sends him back on a peaceful mission to tell Bolingbroke (who still waits in the distant meadow) that his demands will be met. Over the next fifteen lines, Richard begins to change his tune from accommodation to a confused medley of regret and defiance and, finally, submission (as he had previously changed from defiance to accommodation). Aumerle then announces that Northumberland is coming back, which obviously means that he has just finished his downstage consultation with Bolingbroke and has started, at an imagined considerable distance, to return with Bolingbroke's answer to Richard's reluctant acceptance of his modest but demanding terms. Shakespeare's audience could see Northumberland's movement as plainly as Aumerle, but to point it out enhances the illusion of distance as well as underlining Richard's present distraction and heightening the dramatic loading of this moment as crucial to Richard's fate.

If fifteen lines covered Northumberland's return embassy to Bolingbroke and a token mimed exchange of Northumberland's report and Bolingbroke's reply to it, it must have been clear to the original audience that Northumberland is still some distance from the castle walls when the demoralized king begins to buckle. The modern reader does not have that visual advantage, but we can calculate that according to the way space is defined at that point, Northumberland must still be on his way with the decisive response as Richard begins his frantic rhapsody on being an ex-king, and that he arrives at the castle at about the moment that Richard talks of giving his large kingdom for a little grave. The previous news from Bolingbroke was in fact relatively good news, though entailing an embarrassment to Richard. Bolingbroke has already respectfully (if forcefully) communicated that he will settle for his reinstatement and the return of his lands: no less, but no more. The only further development is that Richard has accepted these terms and sent Northumberland back to say so. We have no reason—and neither has Richard—to suppose that Northumberland will report anything other than that the deal is done.

But the expected final confirmation of this concession comes just a bit too late for Richard to be able to digest it. His earlier kingly composure has disintegrated under the pressure of helpless misgiving and apprehensive weakness by the time Northumberland arrives with what we have been led to expect is Bolingbroke's acceptance of his reinstatement, and is virtually complete before Northumberland gets a chance to speak. Shakespeare has arranged that we see Richard tumble into a demoralized virtual abdication just in time to prevent him from realizing that it was entirely unnecessary to do so.

After arriving, and waiting out the last lines of Richard's self-defeated lamentations, Northumberland shows the courteous deference he had withheld on his previous ambassadorial trip (and which had then earned him Richard's self-possessed and appropriate rebuke). But the King has already shown himself unable to assimilate it, having dismantled himself beyond personal recovery—a sad truth noted by his grieving followers as well as by a genuinely puzzled Northumberland.

There are, of course, more dramaturgical clues to support this reading, but a concentration on Shakespeare's use of space alone may be sufficient to establish that the scene's design is about Richard's unilateral collapse toward his disheartened abdication, and offers virtually no grounds for arguing that Bolingbroke intended to force it. Commentators on the play regularly evaluate Northumberland's return visit according to his later cruel attitudes and his earlier coldness in this scene, but a dramaturgical situation can be understood only by attending to what is immediate and local. Here we must take Northumberland's lines, their temporal/spatial context, and each moment's dramatic dynamics seriously. Whatever Northumberland had been earlier, and whatever he will become later, at this critical transitional moment he has been temporarily, if only provisionally, endowed with a relatively deferential and sympathetic stance, in order to highlight what Richard has done to himself. Shakespearean dramaturgical use of space is here an indispensable dimension of how the scene is designed, and therefore what happens, and as a result who is responsible for what. To misread space in this scene is to misread the play.

What Shakespeare's designs intend to *exhibit* in the theater is a set of costumed actors going through motions and speeches on a platform stage, sometimes with adjunct acting spaces. This is the literal dramaturgical mechanism that serves as the infrastructure of the dramatic enactment.

What this exhibit is meant to *represent* is a set of characters engaging in actions and conversations in various locational settings. This is the basic dramatic enactment itself, in which the exhibit is translated, by conventions and specific cues, into the elements of the governing fiction: at this still elementary level of imagination, four actors become four soldiers, and the stage becomes a piece of medieval Wales, and the speeches become Henry Bolingbroke's exchanges with Northumberland and York.

What this representative exhibit in turn *signifies* is the complete display of dramatic meaning that is aroused and guided by more intricate and integrated dramaturgical clues. At this most accomplished level of dramatic realization, a more ambitious form of deliteralization takes place: four actor-soldiers may be transformed imaginatively into an army, one thousand square feet into a large meadow before Flint Castle, and the recited speeches into the culmination of Bolingbroke's attempts to claim justice from Richard with the support of the wary York and the ambitious Northumberland.

Thus, according to these special uses of the words, *As You Like It* 2.6 *exhibits* a table set with food and two actors on another part of the platform, which *represents* a prepared banquet and two recognizable hungry and weary characters, which together *signifies* one part of the forest of Arden where the Duke's refreshment awaits his arrival and another part where fainting Adam and bravely kind Orlando confront their nearly desperate circumstances. The smooth transitions from what is exhibited through what is signified to what is represented depend on the audience's increasingly sophisticated imaginings within the conventions of dramaturgy, as guided by the author's invitations.

This takes us back to *Richard II.* In 3.3, at Flint Castle, Shakespeare intended to *represent* Bolingbroke's showdown with Richard by having him parade his unaggressive but ready and sizable army at the foot of the meadow in front of Richard's castle refuge, as the foredrop to his proposal of terms of peace and his concomitant warning that he will forcibly recover what is rightfully his if it is not given to him. No matter how many militarily equipped supers Shakespeare may have exhibited in this scene, the number of soldiers thus signified by the exhibited actors must have been relatively small by comparison with the sizable army that they are understood to represent. Of course the audience knew that it must be so, and was experienced enough to take this token band as representing a display of hundreds, perhaps thousands, of soldiers. The space must be accordingly expanded in the imagination; the steadily exhibited stage platform must therefore be taken to represent a considerable amount of land. It is a potential battlefield.

In *Henry IV, Part 1,* where the proffered peace is not made and the breakdown in negotiations leads to a real battle, Shakespeare handles the battlefield space differently. He assembles an army, all right—two of them, in fact, whom he sets into combat very convincingly. But he does so by a spatial selectivity that never attempts to represent the whole battlefield at once. He keeps the stage space small, and adjusts the armies to fit the stage, rather than *vice versa*—that is, he shows at a given time only as much of the action as can be fit into the literally exhibited thousand square feet of the platform, rather than asking our imaginations to enlarge the space in order to take in take in more of the battle simultaneously.

So we get the commanders discussing things in their headquarters; and we get excursions of warriors (exhibiting only two or three actors at a time, who both represent and signify two or three soldiers and no more) occupying the stage space for a while, and then yielding it to two or three more. Whether the space is to be imagined as representing a steady small locale, with a sequence of small battles conveniently happening into it, or (more likely) as a string of arbitrary small Somewheres on a battlefield far too large to glimpse all at once, does not matter very much. What does matter is that he is using space differently, demanding less of our ambient imagination and offering a more "realistic"—that is, a more perspectival—presentation of how wars appear to be planned or threatened or fought, from a viewpoint that settles for taking in only one thousand square feet at a time.

This was not new. The technique of representing wars by token excursions of realistic size, rather than attempting to represent a huge battle all at once through the collision of two skimpy token armies, was in Shakespeare's dramaturgical repertoire from the beginning, and may be found in his early *Henry VI* plays. By the time he wrote *Henry V*, he had gathered up a good fifteen years of experience in avoiding the direct representations of the vasty fields of France or of the whole battle of Agincourt, and knew how to give token glimpses of action that, taken together, would representatively suggest—i.e., signify—a great battle rather than attempting to show it. When he arrived at the great battle scene in *King Lear* 5.2, he used another dramaturgical trick he had known since his *Henry VI* days—placing the battle offstage, using only sound effects to exhibit and signify unseen what could not be conveniently represented.[5+]

It may look as if Shakespeare moved from the token army representation of *Richard II* into a new and more realistic mode of showing how armies collide in individual skirmishes that can easily fit within the space we literally see. But that is not quite so. There *were* large-scale shifts in Shakespeare's dramaturgy over the years, but few abrupt changes. Displaying battles by presenting selected small-scale excursions in spaces of about the size of the stage itself tends to be more characteristic of later plays, and the display of whole armies through token presentations in imaginatively enlarged space more characteristic of earlier ones. But it is not as if he abandoned one tactic in turning to the other.

In general, such shifts in his dramaturgical strategies were not all at once, and they were not dramaturgical adoptions of new ideologies, such as a conversion from traditional to classical modes of dramatic design. They were strategic selections from a large dramaturgical repertoire. Shakespeare did not, either gradually or swiftly, drop one type of military spatializing for another. He kept both modes going, no matter how inconsistent they might seem to be with each other if mistaken for philosophies of dramatic space. It might have been logical to give up the tokenizing of soldiers and the imaginative expansion of space, once he had mastered the technique of displaying battles effectively through a sequence of detokenized encounters in small spaces, but consistency was not a rule of Shakespearean dramaturgy. He apparently liked them both. He kept them both.

Thus *King Lear* 5.2 begins with the procession of Lear and Cordelia, with drum and colors, over the stage,[6+] on their way to the battle with which the scene concludes. It could be argued that we are merely seeing the leaders of Cordelia's army along with their immediate entourage, a sort of color guard in which the mode of signification is akin to the excursions of *Henry IV, Part 1* rather than to the token army of *Richard II* 3.3. A similar quasi-color-guard enters with Edmund and Regan at the start of 5.1, and yet another enters with Albany a few lines later; and one more accompanies Edmund and his prisoners Lear and Cordelia at the beginning of 5.3.

But there are two reasons why we are not entitled to think of these exhibits as more perspectivally realistic than the army in *Richard II*. One is that they look too much like the old familiar token army processions for the audience to read them otherwise without more guidance than is given. Shakespeare would know that our sense of what is being exhibited will not be automatically shrunk to the size of what is exhibited without his making a point of it. The other reason is that Shakespeare evidently thought of these presentations in accordance with the traditional token way of exhibiting enough of a token army to signify one.

In the Quarto version, the direction opening 5.1 is "Enter Edmund, Regan, and their powers," the answering entrance of Albany and Goneril a few lines later being "with Troupes." The Folio has Edmund and Regan enter "with drum and colours" as well as with "Gentlemen, and Soldiers," and repeats "drum and colours" and "soldiers" as accompaniment for Albany and Goneril on their entering.

Thus far, it is ambiguous whether the "soldiers" represent mere samplings or entire armies (though "their powers" appears to indicate the latter), but about halfway through the scene, when their business has been arranged, the Folio stage direction reads, tersely and significantly, "Exeunt both the Armies." When Lear and Cordelia enter at the beginning of 5.2, the Quarto direction begins "Enter the powers of France over the stage," and then adds Cordelia and Lear. The spoken texts never define these small groups of presenting actors. In the absence of instructions to hold our imaginings to modest sizes, established convention would lead us to suppose just what the stage directions seem to imply: that they represent armies. And that is apparently how Shakespeare meant us to receive them. They were to take up more space in the mind's eye than in the body's.

Sometimes Shakespeare used his spatial command in ways quite different from those we have just looked at. These other examples may seem at first less coherent, and less functional, than the ones just treated. Sometimes thay have seemed totally incoherent and downright dysfunctional, and editors whose respect for Shakespeare was filtered through an inflexibly different sense of dramaturgy have imposed corrections to free the plays from seemingly impossible awkwardnesses. There is a fine example in the last part of act 1 in *Romeo and Juliet*.

At the beginning of 1.4, the young gallants enter with "five or six [the indeterminacy is interesting in itself] other Maskers, Torch-bearers." The conversation begins with how they are to present the masque, turns to more teasing of Romeo, and takes off into new heights with Mercutio's cadenza on Queen Mab. But where are we?

That is a question that Shakespeare does not attempt to deal with, and the overall sense is simply "somewhere—and within striking distance of Capulet's home, if you *must* know." Benvolio's "Come knocke and enter" early in the scene may suggest that they have arrived at the house (or at least the outer gate), but by the end of the scene such a sense of spatial immediacy has faded and Shakespeare projects a distance still to be traversed. The usual editorial specification "The streets of Verona" may do, but it is more likely that Shakespeare supposed (and encouraged us to imagine) that we begin at Capulet's gate and need to march the masquers ceremoniously into the house that lies at some distance from it.[7+] We don't really need to know more than they are within striking distance but still away. A flexible and shifting "Somewhere," momentarily localized as just outside Capulet's mansion and then accepted as being within marching distance, is sufficient to house the content of the scene.

But at the end, a still stranger thing happens. Romeo bids them to carry on to Capulet's place, Benvolio calls for the drum to strike, and the stage direction reads "They march about the Stage, and Servingmen come forth with their napkins." After a little banter, the servingmen exit, and a new stage direction says "Enter all the Guests and Gentlewomen to the Maskers."

What is going on? If we were to rely on the original stage directions, and take them literally, the masquers would be marching about the stage all through the servants' chat (and their dramaturgically practical rearrangement of the furniture) and then would be joined by Capulet and his guests. The obvious incoherence of such a happening led post-Restoration editors to provide an exit for the masquers before the servants enter, mark a scene change, and then have the masquers reenter after Capulet is there to greet them. This is far more rational—and quite wrong.

Shakespeare's published texts, and probably the manuscripts he submitted to his company, frequently neglect to mention exits and entrances that we can infer from what the lines imply. But usually when we get a stage direction, it is really a stage direction, and is meant very literally. Bizarre as it may seem, especially to earlier editors, what is going on is precisely what Shakespeare has explicitly ordered.

The masquers march—not stroll: the drum-beats probably continue—about the stage, carrying with them the space of their passage to the great hall. As they thus define the part of the stage they happen to be on at any point, a simultaneous spatial redefinition takes place through the servants: we are now observing both the masquers covering the last distance to the feast *and* the main hall in Capulet's house, in a way analogous to our seeing at once the two different and spatially distant places of the Duke's picnic and the famished Adam with Orlando. When the servants exit from their redefined space and Capulet and company enter, the location at Capulet's house is reconfirmed and secured, and the greeting to the approaching masquers makes the outdoors of Verona vanish: the Montagues have arrived, and from now on the space is all Capulet's.

Is there a scene change? Yes and no. This happening exposes the limitations of the very idea. We have gone, in an uninterrupted continuum, from Somewhere to Before Capulet's House to En Route to En-Route-*and-chez*-Capulet to a point where *chez* Capulet takes over the whole stage. Drop the rationalistically restrictive assumptions that belong to quite another dramaturgy, and it works.

In fact, it works far better than the editors' alternative. Not just that it is interesting to witness this spatial *tour de force*, or that it secures a slightly tighter continuity in a play that partly depends on a sense of driving pace; something else has happened as well. Romeo closes the part where editors have traditionally drawn the scene change line with remarks about his sense that he is moving toward a destiny that will change his life, tonight. His approach to that destiny is before us as the completely different tone of the party begins to unfold with the bustling of the servants, but Romeo is still marching to the drum as he goes to meet it. It cannot be done according to the customs of later stages, but Shakespeare was working by a different rulebook, and used it to make a powerful dramatic point. The drumbeats take Romeo to the confluence of his unanticipated happiness with his eventual and foreglimpsed death.

Space, in Shakespearean dramaturgy, is a principal dimension of the matrix of dramatic action. The conventional permission granted him by the blank-check stage he used allowed him to shrink or expand the stage's spatial meaning—or to split it into spatially discrete dramatic places and happenings—in order to make the play work. He deployed space the way his actor had to play Northumberland: just enough to bring off what was dramatically desirable, without disallowing either a momentary alteration from the general norm or a progressive change to something quite different.

The accommodation of his scenes to a later stage that demanded a rigidly consistent place, bounded by the literal dimensions of the stage, is an understandable piece of history, but has no authority whatever in the recovery of what, and how, Shakespeare wrote, despite the fact that it continues to leave its footprints on the texts through which we struggle to read the most astonishing accomplishments of dramatic history.

It is only if we can understand his dramaturgical language that we will be able realize how, and how well, he gave his plays room to happen.

5

DEVISE THE FITTEST TIME, AND SAFEST WAY.

Shakespeare's treatment of time and continuity

In *As You Like It* 3.2, we have the first meeting between Orlando and Rosalind in her disguise as the boy Ganymede. Rosalind and Celia are already on stage when Orlando enters in somewhat unfriendly conversation with Jaques; Rosalind and Celia "slink by," out of Orlando's sight, to watch and listen. After Jaques' exit, Rosalind, protected by her boy's costume and affected masculine swagger, decides to open a conversation with a question that is still used for such purposes: "I pray you, what is't o'clock?" Orlando replies, playfully but appropriately enough, "You should ask me what time o'day: there's no clock in the forest."

This line catches critics' fancy. It is one of the most frequently cited lines in the play, and is usually presented as if it encapsulates the magical and leisurely atmosphere of the play's romance of the greenwood life, as distinguished from the pressures and bustle of the court—and perhaps of our own world.

If we look more carefully, however, we can see that the forest life is not all that casually timeless. The next scene begins with Touchstone's "Come apace [i.e., hurry up], good Audrey"; the following scene ends with Corin hustling Rosalind and Celia off to observe Silvius and Phebe, and the one after that ends with Phebe exiting to write a letter at once, with Silvius accompanying her so that he might bear it to Ganymede immediately; and the subsequent scene has Rosalind chide Orlando for being an hour late, while two scenes later, 4.3 opens with Rosalind's "How say you now, is it not past two o'clock?" In the meantime, a substantial passage of the scene we started with is dedicated to Rosalind's discourse on the lover's acute sense of time, and the ways in which time is experienced by others. If we want to pluck a characterizing catchword from 3.2, it is not the denial of forest clocks: the inhabitants can be urgent and time-conscious enough without them. It should rather be Rosalind's remark just a few lines later: "Time travels in divers paces, with divers persons."

The "somewhere" or "anywhere" that is the ground-level version of Shakespeare's representation of space is paralleled by a "sometime" or "anytime" that he starts with as the lowest grade of specificity in his representation of time.

In the overall temporal setting of his plays, he was of course constrained in the cases of relatively well-known situations. Thus all the plays drawn from the histories of England and Scotland and Rome usher us into an identifiable historical time frame and stay there—though without making many references to dates or taking much care to avoid anachronisms. *King Lear* and *Cymbeline* are, in a vaguer sense, history plays—they deal with the reigns of kings who are now taken to be fictitious but were accepted as authentic by many of Shakespeare's contemporaries, though perhaps not by Shakespeare himself.[1] At any rate the sense of history is vaguer in these cases, and Shakespeare stretches the properties of those times without nearly as much regard for historical verisimilitude as he puts into plays situated in better-known periods.

He did not use contemporary settings, either in his historical dramas or in his entirely fictional ones. Apart from *Othello*, his most recent time frame is that of *Henry VIII*, already beyond living memory. While Chapman dramatized recent events in France, and the anonymous author of *Arden of Feversham* wrote a tragedy built on a recent English scandal, Shakespeare seemed to prefer more temporal distance, perhaps because a distance and indefiniteness in time better suited the indefiniteness from which he liked to define the rest of his dramaturgy—i.e., provisionally, and as it suited dramatic needs.

One of his favorite temporal settings was a vague late-medieval/early-renaissance milieu, close enough to be readily understandable but distant enough to give a slight romantic air and a good deal of room for taking liberties. In plays like *Romeo and Juliet, Two Gentlemen of Verona, The Merchant of Venice, As You Like It, The Taming of the Shrew, Hamlet*: who could fix a confident date for when the action is meant to take place in any of these?—or, more to the point, produce evidence that Shakespeare had any interest in helping anyone do so, or even had one in mind? The indefiniteness was dramaturgically useful; he had no motivation for disturbing it.

And then there are the even more indefinite settings: the Illyria of *Twelfth Night* may or may not be meant to stand for the Illyricum that Paul claims to have visited in Romans 16:19, but even if it did, hardly anything is known yet (and less was known then) about it, at any period of its history. *A Midsummer Night's Dream* is situated in a very unhistorical Athens, a literary creation presided over by a literary Theseus, and owes far more to Chaucer's *Knight's Tale* than to any historians. One of the most wide-open of his temporal settings, this fictitious Athens affords Shakespeare room enough to import some suspiciously English-sounding workmen, not to mention some immortal and nearly timeless fairies.

The ability of *Hamlet* to incorporate into the fabric of the play a discussion of contemporary English theatrical problems under a veil so thin as to be transparent, *As You Like It*'s embrace of a highly topical discussion of the place of satire in a commonwealth as well as a minor controversy about the proper form of marriage,[2] even *Romeo and Juliet*'s assimilation of recent English importations of Italian developments in fencing, manners, and the *duello* code into a setting that feels much older, all these are anachronisms whose presence is softened by the relative indefiniteness of the overall temporal setting of those plays. It is not improbable that Shakespeare deliberately avoided specifying the temporal settings of his nonhistorical plays partly so that he could more easily get by with such an enriching mixture.

How aware was Shakespeare of his anachronisms? Critics are sometimes amused, for what I think to be the wrong reasons, by one that appears in *Troilus and Cressida*. No matter how legendary one may have supposed Hector to be, it was clearly out of historical order for him to quote Aristotle by name in 2.2. But if Shakespeare had blunderingly got history this wrong, surely there were enough reasonably learned people around to remind him that Aristotle, who was among other things renowned as the tutor of Alexander the Great, arrived a few centuries later. I suspect that Hector's foreknowledge here was really Shakespeare's playfulness with time, a joke made for those who could see that its blatantly incoherent juggling of ancient settings was deliberate fun rather than embarrassing ignorance. Perhaps not. But I daresay that no one will quarrel with my claim that he is doing just that sort of thing overtly at the end of *King Lear* 3.2, when the Fool ends a set of silly verses (imitative of putative ancient British oracles published shortly before the play was written)[3] with "This prophecy Merlin shall make, for I live before his time." I think both cases (and various others) should be understood s aspects of a general principle: Shakespeare had to deal with time in a play, as he had to deal with space—but once these were within his jurisdiction, he owned them both, and could do with them almost whatever he pleased.

Let me distinguish some different types of Shakespearean dramaturgical time.

The simplest is the one that may be called *normal time*, in which we are given, or invited by default, to understand that time is what it ordinarily is: the felt chronometry of the action. Three characters engage in a discussion that takes seven minutes, and we have the impression that about seven minutes of represented time have elapsed; two characters are deployed to set the Duke's picnic, and the task occupies as much imagined time as we see the actors take. Normal time requires no special adjustment on the part of the audience, and is accordingly the most comfortable and undemanding time scheme. That is the usual, and evidently the preferred, mode of time representation in Shakespearean dramaturgy—but it is far from being the only mode.

Normal time is, in drama as well as in life, sometimes inefficient for getting desirable things done. Normal time may entail an annoying amount of delay, or may be too short to allow the accomplishment of everything that ought to be taken care of. Shakespearean dramaturgy was not confined to normal time. It offered as many ways to manipulate time as it provided for redefining space and location. The business of the rest of this chapter will be to describe and illustrate a variety of Shakespearean dramaturgical deviations from normal time, and I would like to make it clear how I intend to proceed.

The basic question is the way in which the normal time in which we most literally experience the stage happening needs to be imaginatively adjusted or distorted to meet Shakespeare's design for what is represented as having taken place. I will refer to various disproportions between literal playing time and dramatically represented time accordingly: thus when we are told by the play's characters to understand that three or four hours have passed during a scene of 175 lines, I will refer to it as *expanded time*, because our instinctive sense of how long it has actually taken is imaginatively enlarged by explicit definition.[4+] Similarly, I will use the term *condensed time* when we encounter a foreshortening that covers in a relatively brief and unredefined playing-time a happening that we know would realistically take significantly longer. *Multiple time* is the use of two (or more) different and incommensurable operative time schemes to which Shakespeare may alternately appeal in the organization of the action; I will use this term for any instance in which a local happening within a play explicitly or implicitly revises the sense of time that we have otherwise been guided to accept.

Since the handling of time in Shakespearean dramaturgy is not exclusively concerned with its relation to naturalistic time (indeed, it is not nearly as concerned as these definitions imply: my labels are meant only to guide modern readers into a more malleable familiarity with what happens when naturalistic time is altogether suspended as a norm), there are further matters of temporal continuity that also must be addressed. I will use the term *displaced time* to refer to instances in which Shakespeare reverses a naturalistic sequence, presenting something as already having taken place and then following it by the scene in which it actually happens. And to highlight a major principle of Shakespearean dramaturgy, the illusion of a dense sense of continuity, I will deal with *linked time*, the enchainment of events by which Shakespeare encourages the illusion that there are no significant or unaccounted gaps in the overall temporal sequence of the action, and *intervening time*, the effect of an interposed scene or passage on the time sense that obtains between two stages of an interrupted action.

Natural time being the basic norm of Shakespearean temporal respresentation, I will number that **1**. The remainder, which are not necessarily exhaustive, will follow accordingly.

2. *Expanded time.* It is "near night" in *Romeo and Juliet* 4.2 when Capulet sends his wife to attend on Juliet, and resolves to stay up all night to see to the preparations for her wedding festivities. The next scene shift signals only a change of place: we are now in Juliet's chamber, and the continuity of time is assured by Lady Capulet's arrival to help, and Juliet's reference to tomorrow, reinforced by "And let the Nurse this night sit up with you." She is left alone, and finally takes the potion. It is probably best to treat her falling on her bed, drugged, as an effectual exit (she doubtless falls within the canopied bed's curtains), in which case the entry of Lady Capulet and the Nurse, talking about the need for more spices and a call for dates and quinces in the pantry, may be immediately afterward or indefinitely later. But then Capulet bustles in after their two brief speeches, with the news that it's three o'clock, fusses at the servants momentarily, and then, well within twenty lines of its having been three o'clock, announces that it's "day," that he hears Paris approaching, and that he will go chat with the bridegroom while the Nurse prepares Juliet. It all moves swiftly, and the references to time may get blurred within the general early-dawn-like busyness (not to mention their own literal incoherence), but somewhere along the way we have slid quickly through the last part of the night in only minutes of playing time, while being given the illusion that we haven't missed a beat since yesterday evening.

The first scene of *Hamlet* is not particularly long, but it begins with the bell having struck twelve, and ends with morning having arrived. The ghost has twice appeared before "just at this dead hour," says Marcellus, who has previously specified that the last time was on the stroke of one. About forty lines have been spoken between what is apparently just after midnight and what is evidently one o'clock. The ghost vanishes at the cock-crow (Capulet has heard the second cock at three, in *Romeo and Juliet* 4.5), and in about twenty-three lines the morn walks over the eastern hill in russet mantle. The nature of the scene makes it appropriate to begin at midnight (conventional ghost time) and end at dawn (now they can seek out Hamlet immediately, instead of waiting until a more distant morning), but it can hardly be denied that Shakespeare has pushed the process along through expanded time, having inserted at least some three or four hours of continuous represented time into some 175 lines.

3. *Condensed time.* The peculiarities of condensed time arise not from Shakespeare's direct manipulation of the clock (I have noticed no cases in which he asks us to suppose that the represented time is *less* than the stage-time), but from his squeezing more into an admittedly brief period than is naturalistically plausible. That is, he sometimes foreshortens an action so as to make it fit into less clock time than it would realistically take. In expanded time, the characters seem unaware that more time is passing than we are eventually asked to suppose; he simply has them tell us that it is later than we thought. In condensed time, he allows characters to seem unaware of their unrealistic foreshortening of the action, but he usually puts them in charge of deliberately foreshortening it nonetheless.

Shakespeare uses condensed time in order to let us witness the beginning of a rounded action (rather than fill us in through flashbacks), or to wrap up an action that has run its course and has no more to offer, or to reduce delays in developments in the midst of an action.

All three forms of condensed time are involved in Shakespeare's presentation of Capulet's feast. In *Romeo and Juliet* 1.2 Capulet announces to Paris that his "old accustomed feast" takes place tonight, invites Paris as "One more, most welcome," and then hands his servant the list of the invitees, giving him the mission to bid them to come. Some of us are not above doing things that way, but it is hardly realistic to have one of the most substantial citizens of Verona send out his invitations right on the brink of the occasion, just after informing his daughter's noble suitor that he had not been on the guest list.[5+]

It works dramatically, if we are able to relax our realism. Once we have accepted not only the dramaturgical possibility of condensed time but the additional adjustment of allowing characters to participate deliberately in it, Shakespeare's strategy is effective. It puts us there at the start of the eventfully decisive happenings of 1.5, acknowledging that Capulet's feast is a major annual social occasion for Verona as well as the Capulets but placing us at the beginning of this year's version while simultaneously promising a minimal delay before it actually happens; and incidentally allowing Paris to be, in a way, the honored first invitee (rather than being a mere afterthought, as he comes close to being).

The foreshortening of the feast's beginning is fairly extreme; but the part of the celebrations that we see is hardly less condensed. The routine for masquers was to perform their costumed dance, then take ladies from the assembled company to dance with them. After that, they may depart or stay through the "revels," the general ball. It is not likely that Shakespeare allowed enough time for more than a token masque-dance and a token "commoning" of the masquers with the lady guests: although the dancing might be entertaining in itself (in later plays, Shakespeare appears to have given such a spectacle more room in less dramatically pressured circumstances),[6] there is important business to attend to. However long the masquers' dance was designed to take (if indeed it was separately presented: Shakespeare may have skipped this usual preliminary and proceeded directly to the commoning, but that in itself would be a condensation), the text allows only some seventy-five lines of dialogue between the beginning and the end of the common dancing. The masquing episode is condensed.

Once we get near the end of Capulet's party in 1.5, and the necessary central business has been accomplished between Romeo and Juliet, the time is even more condensed. Benvolio says that it's time for the masquers to go. In this feast, they are not among the regularly invited, but have merely taken advantage of the most socially acceptable way of crashing a party (Capulet's greeting to them and his reminiscences with his cousin confirm within the play the ample external evidence that such a custom was well accepted). They *should* leave before it's over; masquers regularly did so with some sort of flourish, parting as openly and mysteriously as they had arrived. Shakespeare can take the Montagues away without breaking up the party. But then what dramatic interest will the remainder have?

When Capulet, genial host that he is, pleads with the masquers to stay for the customary buffet after the dancing, we are to understand that the general dancing is almost over, which is a further condensation; but when he realizes that they are determined to part, and thanks them for their masquing contribution, Shakespeare speeds up the temporal condensation about as far as it can be pushed. Naturalistically, we would now expect Capulet to return to his invited guests and lead them to the banquet—but Shakespeare, having already accomplished almost everything that is dramatically necessary, has Capulet break up the party and head for his sleep, in a single line! ("More Torches here: come on, then let's to bed"). This is *very* condensed time, but Shakespeare was done with Capulet and his festivities; and his cooperative cast, along with his understanding audience, probably made it rather easy to dismiss the remaining guests and the weary host with so little ceremony and so little verisimilitude. The time at the end of the feast is even more compressed than at the beginning. It then relaxes enough to allow for the execution of some more straggling Juliet-and-Romeo business, and thus is made sufficient to contain the central dramatic agenda. That final shift in pace underlines the way in which Shakespeare dramaturgically tailored the overall time, mainly through compression, to fit the form of his dramatic design.

4. *Multiple time.* A digital clock, like a post-Restoration dramaturgy, displays only one consistent time-scheme in its visible changes. An analogue clock can track three time-schemes simultaneously through one type of movement: a complete circuit around the dial registers a minute if one attends to the second hand, an hour if the minute hand, and half a day by way of the hour hand. The temporal meaning of a movement through any given arc of the circle depends entirely on which of the three hands is in question. Shakespearean dramaturgy is more like the latter: the time covered by any particular scene, or even a segment of a scene, may be a matter of minutes or seconds in playing time, but it may (as in the case of expanded time) represent hours—and can simultaneously project days' worth, or even months' worth, of happenings.

The most common variety of multiple time in Shakespeare's plays is the type that has been labeled "double time"—the imaginative projection of two concurrent but noncoherent (or, more exactly, nonintegrated) time schemes, one operative in the foreground and another unfolding, or projected, at a recognizably different rate in the background. *Othello*, the play through which the phenomenon of double time was apparently first appreciated and analyzed, gives us a rather swift pace of action (which we follow closely) in what is in fact represented on stage as covering a few days, but in the meantime a series of hints by Iago, not directly confronted but effectually insinuated, creates another, more expansive, time frame behind it.

At the play's beginning, Othello and Desdemona have just been married: we are almost witnesses. But Iago subsequently treats Desdemona's putative adultery as a matter of long standing, and Othello never questions the alternative time scheme this must imply. How much time is imaginatively embraced by the three hours' traffic on the stage? A briskly paced few days, if we focus on what is happening; weeks or even months, if we take our bearings from what Iago suggests—and *Othello* comes to believe—has been happening offstage in the meantime. The critical discovery of double time in Othello has been justly celebrated as an important breakthrough in the understanding of how the play works, and is a significant landmark in the recovery of Shakespeare's dramaturgy. It allowed readers to confront what had otherwise seemed to be inconsistencies, incoherences, and psychological implausibilities in Shakespeare's design, and to appreciate that they can be intelligibly resolved into deliberate, though unfamiliar, strategies of dramatic management.

Othello seems still to be the only play that is well recognized for its use of "double" time. The recognition *is* important, insofar as it has alerted fairly advanced modern readers of Shakespeare to one of the ways in which his dramaturgical techniques can be mistaken for carelessness or blundering if approached with inappropriate modern assumptions. But it is still not widely recognized that "double" time is more than a curious trick in the construction of *Othello*. It is a particular variety of a standard Shakespearean employment of what I am calling multiple time, and Shakespeare often used it, and other varieties, in his other plays.

The multiple (alias double) time in *Othello* involves two competing and unreconciled time schemes that are imaginatively *projected by* the action rather than *concurrently represented within* it—i.e., a given segment of natural-time happening may imply either the longer or the shorter time frame but does not itself embrace two different lengths of time. In many cases, Shakespeare more boldly presents us not with alternative overall time frames but with immediate double standards of represented time. A striking example occurs in a small but important scene near the end of *King Lear*.

King Lear 5.2[71] contains less than a dozen lines, but it also contains the decisive battle between the predominantly French forces of Lear and Cordelia and the British troops led by Albany, Goneril, Regan, and Edmund. It begins with the parade of Cordelia and Lear, with their army, over the stage, after which Edgar enters with Gloucester, places him in a secure place that is apparently visible to the audience, and exits. We then get one stage direction: "Alarum and retreat within," followed by Edgar's reentry with the news that Lear's side has lost.

What sort of time sense is projected by the Edgar–Gloucester sequence? The procession itself is apparently a token representation of the movement of an entire army, and thus stands for a longer time than the group literally requires to move across the stage: effectually expanded time. There is a clearing of the stage between the procession and the entrance of Edgar and Gloucester, so we may not assume a continuity of place and therefore cannot know, as Edgar stations Gloucester in a brief segment of normal time, how much more expanded time the pageantically silent army is taking offstage before joining battle. Gloucester remains visible but apparently unresponsive, offering no time cues as the whole battle is conveyed to us by background sound effects. Is it conveyed to Gloucester as well? We cannot tell. He may fall asleep as Kent did in the stocks, or merely sit in stoic silence—either of these would leave the foreground time indeterminate as the background time of the battle takes over.

The fact that the sound effects can be indicated by a mere four-word stage direction does not mean that they were perfunctory: it is plausible that there were multiple sounds of battle—clashing of swords, cries, possibly hoofbeats, interspersed with trumpet calls for charge and ending with the recognizable trumpeting of the retreat signal. But it is hardly imaginable that Shakespeare devoted a great deal of playing time to this offstage rumor. A minute might be tolerable; anything more would enter the margins of tedium for any audience. And indeed, the terse and sparse wording of the stage direction may well express Shakespeare's intention literally: the sounds may have been restricted to the barest token abstraction of a battle, pushing the artificial condensation to its extreme and using the continued presence of Gloucester to insure that we receive the sound effects as a very unliteral signification of a represented full battle of indefinite duration.

Edgar's retrieval of Gloucester brings us back into normal time alone. The transition is abrupt, but unconfusing. Gloucester's "A man may rot even here" may remind us how long he has waited beyond how long we *saw* him wait— but in any case, we have experienced some deft modulations and overlappings of differing time schemes through this brief episode of playing time.

A still more intricate use of multiple time occurs in *Richard II*, in a crucial sequence that is at least as important for evaluating Bolingbroke's intentions as the spatial dramaturgical strategies of 3.3.

Shakespeare has Richard send Bolingbroke into exile in 1.3, arranges for Richard to receive Aumerle's up-to-date report of Bolingbroke's journey partway to the coast in 1.4, and concludes that scene with the news of John of Gaunt's illness, whereupon Richard scrambles to get to his uncle's bedside as quickly as possible. The next scene opens with moribund John, includes Richard's arrival and John's death and Richard's confiscation of the inheritance of Bolingbroke—and concludes with the dangerous and secret news that Bolingbroke is about to land in Yorkshire with powerful support.

What do we learn from this about Bolingbroke's aspiration to the crown? Many commentators have concluded that he is crafty, already designing an organized invasion before his exile, and thus invalidating his earlier pose of submissive humility by showing that he was even then planning treason and already organizing his military strike. Few commentators remark on the temporal incoherences projected by this sequence, but they are a crucial consideration for understanding the design.

It is impossible for these events to have come about according to the time scheme implied by the earlier part of the sequence, which gives us discrete segments of action that evidently occur as close together as possible and cover a minimum of normal time. The gap between Aumerle's reported parting from the exile-bound Bolingbroke at "the next highway" and his debriefing to Richard at the start of 1.4 is at most a matter of a few hours; the gap between Richard's eager departure at the end of 1.4 and his arrival at Gaunt's deathbed (which is defined as being at Ely House) adds less than an hour.[8+] If we stay with this schedule, Bolingbroke must be, when 2.1 ends, at best somewhere in the English Channel, en route to exile: it is utterly impossible for him to be off the coast of Yorkshire with a supporting army. If we credit

Northumberland's disclosure about the impending invasion (which of course we must do),[9*] then the dramatic time must necessarily have been warped. While a few hours have passed in the life of Richard, months have gone by in Bolingbroke's. Shakespeare has contrived a remarkable multiple-time transmutation: a continuous scene that began half a day after Bolingbroke set off for exile ends something like half a year later.

York has in fact been mediating the shift to this secondary time scheme by talking of things that must, by their nature, be long subsequent to Bolingbroke's departure and substantially motivating to an unauthorized return. He observes that Bolingbroke has attempted to sue for the recognition of his title (inherited only partway through this scene, at Gaunt's death) and for the return of his lands (which were confiscated only moments before on the natural-time surface), and has been denied. These are things that the chronicles attest to, as Bolingbroke's honorable attempt to rectify things from his awkward place in exile—and those who do not know the chronicles may nevertheless perceive that York is dipping into the future as if it were already the past. The foreground action of the scene has been continuous, and has—even making allowance for some expansions, as in the brief playing-time interval between Gaunt's exit and the report of his demise—apparently been encompassed by not more than an afternoon's time. But the restructuring of the background time has been signaled clearly enough, most of all by the ludicrousness of supposing that Bolingbroke's movements (starting alone toward Dover and ending with an army on the Yorkshire coast) could have been contained within the approximate day into which they would otherwise have to be crammed.

Anyone who approaches this sequence with an unyielding insistence on naturalistic time must be misled if reading carelessly and entirely baffled if more careful; but an awareness of the multiple-time options of Shakespearean dramaturgy puts it all in place. Shakespeare has manipulated what are evidently dramatic flexibilities that his audience could follow comfortably, and has rather neatly accomplished a transition in the play's developing action that modern playwrights would be unlikely to attempt and unretrained modern audiences and readers find nearly impossible to follow.

But if we miss the independence of Bolingbroke's eventually projected timetable from the movement of the scene in which it is disclosed, we must misevaluate the significance of his return. The way we size up the main action of the play can be deformed if we fail to grasp the dramaturgy of time that is really operative. Once we get hold of it, Bolingbroke the sly plotting opportunist, doubtless bent on usurpation, must give way to Bolingbroke the abused and thwarted victim of Richard's illegal takeover, frustrated in his attempts to secure justice and eventually summoning ready anti-Richard support in order to reclaim his denied rights of inheritance. With a little dramaturgical sophistication (in the modern sense) about time, it becomes a very different play—and makes far more sense of what ensues.

   5. *Displaced time*. This fifth species of dramaturgical time is in some ways the most daring and demanding of the lot. *Displaced time* is a reversal of normal, logical, sequence in which a scene or passage is inserted before, rather than after, an event or scene to which it must be chronologically subsequent. I have already mentioned, in chapter 3, the curious way in which Shakespeare handles the process of getting Peter Quince's *Pyramus and Thisby* chosen as the central entertainment at the Duke's wedding festivities. At the end of act 4, Bottom bursts in with the news that their play has been selected; but in the early part of act 5, we see the selection being made: Theseus runs through the list of possibilities and finally settles on "A tedious brief Scene of young *Pyramus*, / And his love *Thisby*; very tragical mirth."

   Why this glaringly incoherent transposition? My speculation is that Shakespeare simply recognized that it is significantly better drama to move, without a break, through the whole sequence that ensues: from the general amusement at the very idea of wedding party's spending the evening with such an unlikely entertainment (in case the absurd title is not enough to discourage its candidacy, the review offered by Egeus/Philostrate should be definitive), through Theseus' unencouraged preferment of the play and his thoughtful argument that a generous attitude on the audience's part can appreciate even bungled entertainment, right into the performance itself with minimal delay.

   Realistically, this requires that Bottom be already rejoined with his fellows and the mechanicals' troupe be already mobilized to perform. But why Shakespeare chose to justify their readiness by having Bottom know Theseus' decision in advance of his making it is less important than the recognition that Shakespeare evidently knew he could get by with doing so. An audience used to cooperating with manipulations of time could apparently be expected to adjust to this literal impossibility as it adjusts to others, and the result is in fact dramatically more effective than an observance of sane chronology would permit.[10+]

   The opening of *King Lear* apparently displaces time in a similar way. Gloucester and Kent discuss the division of the kingdom as if it has just been published (comparing the shares of Cornwall and Albany, and conveniently leaving Cordelia out of the question), but it is yet to come, later in the scene. The enacted division, of course, has to do with Lear's responses to Goneril and Regan rather than their husbands: establishing the dukes' place in the scheme in this initial conversation is dramatically useful, but it could have been done without reference to the land grants. Still, there it is—and the rather gratuitous way in which it competes and conflicts with the main business of the scene may at least be taken to suggest that Shakespeare did not suppose that such a transposition of events was difficult for his audience to handle. It may have been his way of setting up the traditional conflict between the dukes, referred to at the start of 2.2, or a way of defusing the oddity of Lear's division of the kingdom by having it so casually accepted by leading nobles from the start. Whatever the purpose, this opening reverses the order of events.

The first scene of *Henry IV, Part 1* uses a similar transposition, but less blatantly. It begins with relief at the conclusion of civil warring and organizes the new united crusade to the Holy Land; but at the end of the scene, we learn not only that Hotspur is insubordinately withholding his prisoners but also that King Henry has sent for him to answer to the matter, and the crusade must be accordingly delayed. The logical sequence might be better secured by a post-Restoration rewriter of Shakespeare through having the initial relief followed by news of Hotspur's disobedience, requiring a change of the initial plans. But no messenger has entered to add this complicating factor, and Henry tells us that he has already acted on it.

That might seem to be a problem, but this is Shakespearean dramaturgy, not the later dramaturgy that replaced it. If we do *not* allow for the possibility of displaced time, this scene as Shakespeare wrote it must seem to imply that Henry's initial expressions of relief and new purpose are disingenuous—that he already knew both that the troubles were not over and that the Jerusalem expedition must be indefinitely delayed. But this would be dramatically pointless, since no such deception is otherwise even hinted at, let alone used to make a dramatic point. The only way to make *dramatic* sense is to acknowledge another instance of displaced time, and adjust our imaginations accordingly. Again, it appears that Shakespeare thought that such a displacement of time would not be much of a problem. His dramaturgy had its own ways of accomplishing Aristotle's notion of plausible impossibility in a play.

6. *Linked time and intervening time.* There are two more topics that need to be dealt with, and they are closely related. *Linked time* is not quite a separate variety of dramatic time but rather a mode of establishing temporal continuity between one passage of action and a subsequent one that does not immediately follow it in the same scene—not so much a species of dramaturgical time as it is of continuity control tactics. *Intervening time* is a secondary temporal property of a passage that separates two stages of development in a given action (e.g., a scene that presents a development in a subplot)—that is, it is the implications of duration not according to the way in which that intervening passage is time-defined for its own purposes, but rather as it affects the time sense of the action that is suspended meanwhile. Both of these are

features of a general Shakespearean tendency to foster the illusion of a relatively uninterrupted temporal continuity in the play.

Shakespeare apparently did not like leaving temporal gaps of the sort
that later plays might register in an opening note to the reader (and often
specify in the distributed program), to the effect that while scene 4 takes
place in the drawing room of the mansion, or in the cottage on the coast, the
setting of scene 5 is "The same, one week later." Shakespeare evidently much
preferred to offer a sense of steady and unbroken pace, and thus makes use of
what may be called *linked time*, which is the overt or strongly implicit binding together of successive stages of an action in such a way as to encourage
the illusion that the time flow is fairly constant, without obtrusive gaps.

In its most elementary form, linked time is nothing but an extension of
the expectations of normal time, in that it rests on the assumption that the
usual pace of time-flow continues when we pass from scene to scene unless
we are given clues to the contrary: the entrance that begins scene B is thus
felt to occur as immediately as possible after the exit that closes scene A.
Scene B may be in quite a different place from scene A, but seems to be following the same clock; the shift in locale is accompanied by a sense of
"meanwhile. . . ," as in standard cinema cuts between two places that relate to
the same overall action.

At the end of Lady Capulet's conference with Juliet in 1.3, a servant enters with the news that the guests have arrived and the feast has begun; the
next scene begins, in some unspecified Elsewhere, with the final arrangements for the Montague party-crashing masque, and its time frame is accordingly confirmed, without requiring overt time cues, as having begun
approximately a moment after Lady Capulet and Juliet leave to join the
guests. After his moonlight interview with Juliet in 2.2, Romeo resolves to go
to Friar Laurence; after his exit, 2.3 begins with a lengthy soliloquy by the
Friar, whereupon Romeo enters to him. The sense of time is clearly that the
Friar's entrance follows immediately upon Romeo's exit, and that his musings cover the time needed for Romeo's arrival.[11] In the first example, the
linkage is apparently assumed, and is confirmed by the content of the subsequent scene; in the second example, the linkage is explicitly made by
Romeo's final words in 2.2 and the assumed immediacy of the transition is
supported by the intervening time taken by the Friar's opening soliloquy.

Shakespeare seems to have assumed that two contiguous scenes will normally be perceived, unless he has instructed us otherwise, as being immediately continuous in time, or at least as closely related as imaginable (with
nothing significant having happened in the meantime), and he appears to
have customarily designed scene sequences in such a way as to avoid interrupting this assumption.

The Friar's soliloquy protects such an assumption by allowing time for Romeo to cover the distance to the monastery. Shakespeare deals similarly with the linkage between the first two scenes of *Hamlet*. Scene 1.1 is designed to take place in expanded time, which allows it to extend until dawn. That is artificial, but not arbitrary. The scene ends with its three characters exiting in search of Hamlet, and their subsequent entry to him, partway through 1.2, allows the imagined time frame to remain continuous and unbroken: Shakespeare has evidently lengthened 1.1 and pointed its ending toward this entry in 1.2 in order to encourage and sustain that assumption. Richard II leaves 1.4 with the intent of getting to Ely House as soon as possible; the following scene opens with "Will the King come . . .?" and the supposition that this is spoken almost immediately after Richard's exit is protected by the sixty-seven lines of dialogue that intervene before he enters 2.1.

It is not difficult to multiply examples. The importance of time linkage in Shakespeare's dramaturgical values is generally evident from the number of instances in which he emphasizes, beyond the call of duty, the continuity between the end of one scene and the beginning of the next; but it is especially evident in the transition between the third and fourth scenes of *King Lear*.

In the midst of the brief exchange about Lear that constitutes 1.3, Oswald tells Goneril "He's coming, Madam; I hear him," whereupon Goneril gives orders for the household servants to be more negligent in attending to Lear so that Goneril may force a showdown with him, concluding with "prepare for dinner." After their exit, Kent enters with a seven-line speech, whereupon the direction reads "Horns within. Enter Lear and Attendants."

What was it that Oswald heard? Probably an earlier winding of the horns that are expressly sounded as Lear enters (plausibly dressed as if from hunting). Lear's first line, "Let me not stay a jot for dinner—go, get it ready" echoes Goneril's last words in the previous scene, and links the two scenes further as nearly overlapping. I proposed long ago, in an article that seems to have had no effect on subsequent editions of the play,[12*] that the response to Lear's command is probably a conspicuous nonresponse, in keeping with Goneril's instructions that her servants be inattentive to Lear's orders. Lear calls again for dinner a few lines later, with no more success and probably for the same reason: Goneril's demand for Lear to be neglected is being dutifully carried out, at Lear's expense. Lear calls unsuccessfully for his Fool to be fetched. Oswald enters briefly, snubbing Lear as he exits again. One of Lear's knights diplomatically remarks that he has perceived that the servants seem to be less responsive recently, and Lear acknowledges that he has had a similar sense. If we heard the terms set out in 1.3, we can hardly fail to make the connection.

The fact that the temporal linkage between 1.3 and 1.4 allows virtually no time for the new policy to be promulgated among Goneril's staff (seven lines by Kent, with Lear already within hearing distance) need not matter to those who are used to Shakespeare's other manipulations of time. It is not, in Shakespearean terms, rude or irregular for Lear's Knight (or Gentleman) to notice the recent effect of a policy that was (in literal, normal time) introduced only seconds before.

The important point here is that Shakespeare could easily have allowed Oswald to accept Goneril's instructions without hearing Lear's approach, and could have had Goneril conclude the scene without specifying *dinner* as the occasion of Oswald's exit, and then we could imagine at least a little more time for making the arrangements for Goneril's orders to be carried out. Shakespeare chose instead to link the two scenes so closely together that they virtually overlap (thus purchasing a more intense dramatic continuum at the cost of verisimilitude) and at least partially displaced the time so that Oswald's insolence in 1.4 apparently climaxes, rather than initiates, the show of disregard for Lear set up in 1.3. Shakespeare evidently thought tight time continuity important.

The time linkage of juxtaposed scenes involving a shared character almost always includes the provision of pre-reentry business that provides, as one of its incidental but dramaturgically important by-products, a token allowance for traveling time, thus supporting the sense of unbroken temporal continuity. The most conspicuous case, and the best evidence for this practice as a point of Shakespearean dramaturgical principle, is the exit of John of Gaunt ten lines before the end of the opening scene of *Richard II*. Shakespeare usually provides at least a token motivation for exits, but in this case not only is there no explanation given, Gaunt's exit is almost spectacularly countermotivated by the situation itself. His beloved son is in the midst of a crisis of extraordinary proportions when Gaunt walks out for unknown reasons, toward an unknown destination.

It has long been recognized that there is no use trying to account for Gaunt's departure at a motivational level: it is a dramaturgical decision by Shakespeare, not a personal one by Gaunt. The usual explanation appeals to a "Law of Reentry," an imaginary rule dictating that a character cannot leave at the end of a scene and then return immediately to start a new one: ergo, in order to begin the next scene, Gaunt must leave this one before the end. Shakespeare's practice is almost always like that,[13+] but not because of dramatic legislation or dramatic inexorability. The restriction on immediate reentry is a function of Shakespeare's dramaturgy of time, which normally avoids a gap in continuity by providing that a character who enters in a setting different from his location in the previous scene must have a passage of absence (no matter how small) as token offstage traveling time, in order to keep up the illusion that the flow of continuity has not been unnecessarily interrupted.

Shakespeare's rather awkward provision of intervening transition time for Gaunt in this case reminds us that the direct linking of contiguous scenes may entail difficult problems of design. That is probably one of Shakespeare's motivations (though hardly the most important) for incorporating more than one major process of action in his plays. *Richard II* and *Romeo and Juliet* are relatively single-minded about their focus on the title characters (although the former includes the activities of Bolingbroke during Richard's absence and the plotting against him after he assumes the crown, while the latter engages the two principals with their friends and families as well as with one another), but *A Midsummer Night's Dream* and *As You Like It* contain multiple subplot actions—and Shakespeare's incorporation of the Gloucester/Edmund/Edgar story into *King Lear* was apparently the first time the traditional Lear story had ever been combined with another. Providing multiplicity and diversity in the action not only offers the virtue of variety, but also makes it considerably easier to sustain a tight continuity in the play's time line through intervening scenes, which make it more convenient to develop the action in the normal time that Shakespeare seems to have preferred, without having to appeal to special dramaturgical privileges.

In terms of general dramaturgical practice, what would be the most convenient way of avoiding the awkward early departure of John of Gaunt to meet the Duchess of Gloucester? The obvious answer appears later in *Richard II* and is found repeatedly in the other plays: insert another scene between two stages of a particular action. That takes care of covering either traveling time to another location or further developments at the same place, or both. The graceful "Garden Scene" that forms 3.4 of *Richard II* covers a multitude of dramaturgical purposes, and one of them is that it covers the necessary geographical transition from Flint Castle in the previous scene to Westminster in the following one, without making a discernible break in the continuity of time.[14]

A scene, or even a part of a scene, that intervenes between two segments of an action may have a timetable of its own, but that is not necessarily definitive for the sense of how much development may be supposed to have taken place in the interrupted action during the interval. Shakespeare quite regularly returns to the next part of the interrupted action to pick it up at a more advanced stage than its own time frame could allow. The Garden Scene of *Richard II* takes 111 lines of normal time, but gets intervening-time treatment as if this is sufficient to allow for the transition from the previous scene's Wales to the following scene's London. One may, of course, argue that the continuity of time is simply broken, and that the Garden Scene takes place indefinitely long after the Flint Castle confrontation and concludes indefinitely long before the Parliamentary assembly of the scene that follows. But I would like to point out grounds for thinking otherwise.

Gaunt's early exit is apparently a truncated version of a standard Shake-spearean dramaturgical practice: providing enough intervening matter to cover the imagined time between a character's exit from one place and reappearance in another. The truncation in this case calls the "enough" deeply into question, but takes us more adequately into the heart of the matter. If this is really what Shakespeare was doing, how much is enough?

Do sixty-seven lines of dialogue in normal time consitute a sufficient interval to allow Richard to travel from his palace to Ely House? Certainly not in any literal sense. Intervening time is often treated as a temporal wild-card with respect to what it bridges, however it may be treated in itself. Orlando's fetching of Adam in the course of thirty-one lines of offstage time in *As You Like It* 2.7, Edgar's burying of Oswald's body in less than six lines of Gloucester's musings at the end of *King Lear* 4.6, and the swift arrival of the Capulets and Montagues at the scene of trouble in *Romeo and Juliet* 1.1, 3.1, and 5.3 are all instances in which what is projected as having happened offstage must require more time than the onstage interval represents. Intervening time as such is token time and represents, for the action that takes place unseen, simply as much time as is needed for its completion. A passage's imagined duration as intervening time is almost always longer than its duration as overtly represented time, and there is no principle of commensurability between the two values. Just as we can deal with expanded time and condensed time when the onstage happening employs them, so we can deal with token intervening time when the offstage happening requires it. Gaunt's early exit is a clumsy version of a principle that makes time management sense.

An intervening *scene* has a significant advantage over intervening *passages* like those just cited. An enclosed passage has only its wild-card variability as a token for offstage developments. A full scene has all those advantages plus the additional wild-card possibilities of a stage-clearing at both ends. Scene contiguity is generally understood to relate two scenes as closely as need be for continuity, if not otherwise defined; but a scene break without an explicit linkage relaxes the urgency and specificity of the need without eliminating the connection. *Richard II* 3.3 (at Flint Castle) and the subsequent 3.4 Garden Scene are not explicitly time-linked. The casts of the two scenes have no characters in common, 3.3 does not point ahead to 3.4, and 3.4's information about the happenings of 3.3 is vaguely based on a combination of general rumor and ambiguous letters from a marginal figure. That is, the scene break between 3.3 and 3.4 blurs time rather than redefining it, leaving the Garden Scene in a generalized continuity with the previous scene. And how did Shakespeare intend 3.4 to relate temporally to the following grand deposition scene, 4.1? The Gardener apologetically suggests that the Queen might confirm the truth of what she has just overheard by posting to

London, and the indignant Queen resolves to go to London to meet Richard. The linkage is thus established. Scene 3.4 effectually fills in the gap between 3.3 and 4.1, rather than merely marking a minor patch of time somewhere in between. Its normal time of five or six minutes is sufficient, especially given the content of its dialogue, to function as an intervening time bridge on which Richard and Bolingbroke may cross efficiently from Wales to London.

A different form of time linkage takes place in *A Midsummer Night's Dream* in the movement from the next-to-last scene of act 4 to the opening of act 5. This involves not the explicit linkage of individual segments of action but rather the illusion, the *feel*, of smooth unbroken continuity despite unsuppressed indications of a literal lapse of time.

At the end of 4.1, the Athenian lovers exit, having accepted Theseus' invitation to join their marriages with his, musing on the strange events of the blurred night and agreeing to recount their dreams on the journey home. Act 5 opens with Theseus and Hippolyta talking about the lovers' stories. We *know* that their dramatized encounter with the lovers started near dawn, and we *know* that act 5 must take place in the evening, but Shakespeare creates the illusion of direct continuity between the two scenes, through several maneuvers that not only bridge but virtually eliminate the gap between dawn and evening.

1. First, he has Theseus bid the lovers to meet him in the Temple "by and by" (which then meant "right away"), to be married; then, a dozen lines later, he has the lovers close the scene by reminding us: "Do you not think / The Duke was here, and bid us follow him? . . . And he bid us follow to the Temple. . . . Why then we are awake; let's follow him, / And by the way let us recount our dreams."

2. Bottom awakens as they exit, is puzzled by the absence of his fellows, and talks about his own dream, proposing to present it at the end of their play before the Duke, in the form of a ballad to be written by Peter Quince, whereupon he exits.

3. Shakespeare immediately brings in Quince and the others, talking about Bottom and their play, and after seven brief speeches, he has Snug enter to announce that "The Duke is coming from the Temple, and there is two or three Lords and Ladies more married," followed some ten lines later by Bottom's entry to announce that "the Duke hath dined" and that their play has been chosen.

4. Another ten lines later, Theseus and Hippolyta enter discussing the lovers' dreams, which was of course the subject of discussion as 4.1 closed, after which Theseus turns to the subject of the after-supper entertainment— and this leads directly into the performance of *Pyramus and Thisby*, which begins some twenty-five lines after Theseus selects it from the list of possibilities.

There are no discernible time gaps in this sequence. The flow seems continuous and smooth. It also seems relatively brief. The whole movement from the Duke's invitation to the lovers to his first inquiry about the evening's entertainment (well under ten minutes' worth of natural-time segments) takes only twice as many lines as the process of his choosing *Pyramus and Thisby*, and can easily be thought to represent only an hour or two of passing time. But that is a deftly contrived illusion, built from a variety of time styles, linkages, and manipulations of sequence, duration, and pace. Through dramaturgical sleight-of-hand, the time is shifted smoothly and swiftly not over the hour or so that seems to have elapsed, but from morning to evening, in just over one hundred lines. In this case, as in many others, it is only in retrospect that we can see how long it has been since just a little while ago.

It is difficult (and pointless) to resist the conclusion that the avoidance of felt time gaps, even at the expense of a flagrant temporary abandonment of the ordinary rules of time, was a higher value in Shakespearean dramaturgy than an imitation of more naturalistic time or even a graceful admission that some hours are unaccounted for. Continuity and the sense of unbroken momentum that it supports were evidently important in establishing the sort of dynamic movement Shakespeare generally seems to have preferred.

Shakespeare is dramaturgically expert in cutting corners to make this happen; but he is not recklessly cavalier about a naturalistic sense of time. In setting his major time frames, he takes some trouble to establish the illusion that a reasonable overall period of time has been allotted for the main action—dense, usually, but in tune with his audience's normal expectations about how long a complex sequence of happenings takes to develop. Once he had made a basic accommodation to ordinary time in the central action, he could then finesse this schedule with other tactics, in order to keep up a strong pace without seeming too unrealistic. *Romeo and Juliet* and *A Midsummer Night's Dream* afford us two interesting alternative ways in which he handled the kind of problem in time continuity that arose from this policy.

In both plays, there is concentrated action that is dramatically enhanced by a sense of swift and relentless unfolding. But in both plays, there are realistic constraints that discourage overcompression of the principal scheme of action. Capulet may get by with sending the invitations to his feast on the morning of the event (that being a minor eddy in the dramatic flow), but the arrangement of Juliet's marriage to Paris cannot be dealt with in quite so bold a fashion. Theseus and Hippolyta could enter the stage the day before their wedding, or even the morning before, but if we are to fit in the resolution of the Athenian lovers' problems *and* make adequate provision for the mechanicals to put together the conspicuous act 5 entertainment, the initial allowance of four days is hardly expansive. In both cases, a four-day budget is about the least that could be decently negotiated. (Shakespeare's narrative source for *Romeo and Juliet* spread the story over some months.)

Capulet recognizes this when the establishment of a major deadline first enters the play, in 3.4. Concerned about Juliet's mourning, and its interference with Paris' wooing (and implicitly keen not to lose Paris as a candidate in the midst of these unexpected mishaps), Capulet decides[15+] to make an audacious commitment on Juliet's behalf, instructing his wife to "bid her, mark you me, on Wednesday next— / But soft, what day is this? . . . Monday, ha ha: well, Wednesday is too soon. / A Thursday let it be: a Thursday, tell her, / She shall be married to this noble earl."

Thus clipped down to the minimum delay (but after the recognition that anything less would be decidedly indecorous, and that even Thursday is a bit hasty), the wedding plans develop, with reminders about the time. In 4.1, which clearly takes place the next day, Paris (who has already supported Capulet's foreshortening by saying that he "would that Thursday were tomorrow") begins the scene explaining to Friar Laurence why Thursday is a good choice, and later greets Juliet with a reference to Thursday. Laurence then composes his new plan, observing that Wednesday is tomorrow and telling Juliet to contrive to spend Wednesday night alone. In 4.2, Juliet asks the Nurse to help her select "such needful ornaments / As you think fit to furnish me tomorrow," but her mother counters with "No, not till Thursday, there's time enough."[16+] And then Capulet sends off the Nurse along with Juliet, saying "We'll to church tomorrow."

However casually Capulet's line may seem to be tossed off, it means that he has just moved the wedding from Thursday to Wednesday. Lady Capulet objects that this doesn't allow enough preparation time, but Capulet is firm and leaves to inform Paris of the change. Meanwhile, notice that Juliet had *already* spoken in terms of tomorrow, and that although she has left the scene without comment, almost as if she hadn't heard or hadn't understood what her father had said, we next see her a dozen lines later, finishing the selection of "attires" for "our state tomorrow," clearly aware that her wedding day is now to be Wednesday. She has not only accepted the shift in schedule, she has in effect anticipated it. She is helping Shakespeare speed up the time.

Capulet had originally named Wednesday, but recognized that it was too soon. Paris can hardly wait. From their side, a reduction in time has already been established as a viable—and even desirable—possibility. Juliet's earlier total reluctance in 3.5 has now been replaced by a new plan with Friar Laurence, and she can afford to seem cooperative. Capulet's delight at this apparent repentance, combined with his and Paris' eagerness, make a shift to Wednesday seem in order, except for the difficulties in getting provisions ready, which is the only ground advanced by Lady Capulet for resisting the change. But Capulet has already mentioned in 4.1 that the guest list will be small, on account of Tybalt's recent demise, and now overcomes his wife's objection by volunteering to stay up all night getting things ready. Shakespeare makes it fall into place.

But why did he bother?

The general dramaturgical answer, I think, is that speeding up the action is dramatically typical of this play, fostering a sense of urgency and intensity that helps drive the plot to its explosive conclusion. The specific dramaturgical answer is that Juliet has nothing more to do. Her plans are all prepared, and can take place as easily on Tuesday night as Wednesday—and that spares the play a lull in her engagement with her own fate that would have somehow to be dealt with if she were given another twenty-four hours to make her next move. It is, quite simply, dramatically more effective to take her directly from her arrangements with Friar Laurence into their execution than to have her wait out another day: the focus can then stay with her, where it is most appropriate, until she has followed her new scheme through its first major phase. Constricting it by a day adds to the impetus of the action, and the uncomplaining way in which she meets this alteration underlines her resolution. It works well, and somewhat more effectively than simply having planned for Wednesday in the first place, which could have been done at some slight but affordable cost to realism and good sense. The dramaturgical manipulation of time is on the table, negotiated within the play, and dramatically successful.

If we accept that it is appropriate for Theseus to allow four days for Hermia to make up her mind and for the Athenians to devise entertainments (and it is, in much the same way that it is appropriate for Capulet to decide initially that Wednesday is "too soon"), then we have a parallel situation in *A Midsummer Night's Dream*, but one that cannot be as conveniently altered by setting up the elimination of a dramatically unnecessary day. Instead, the official timetable remains constant in this play, and it is in the illusion of time that the desirable sense of density is accomplished.

Shakespeare might have projected a four-day action in order to provide for what needed to take place, and then quietly condensed the time, as he often does on a smaller scale in the subactions of his plays. But in *A Midsummer Night's Dream*, as in *Romeo and Juliet*, he keeps faith with his original framing of the schedule, and gives us time-markers to show that he is sticking to it.

The first of these is issued with firm emphasis before the first scene is over: "If thou lov'st me," says Lysander to the beleaguered Hermia, "then / Steal forth thy father's house tomorrow night . . ." Hermia swears by Cupid's bow and best arrow, by Dido's pyre and men's broken vows "In that same place thou hast appointed me, / Tomorrow truly will I meet with thee."

Suddenly, they encounter Helena. Lysander confides in her that they plan to steal away "tomorrow night"; Hermia tells her where they are to meet, and takes her leave with "Keep word, Lysander; we must starve our sight / From lovers' food till morrow deep midnight." Helena soliloquizes on love's blindness, and then resolves to blab to Demetrius: "Then to the wood will he, tomorrow night, / Pursue her."

If the most spectacular oddity in the passage is Helena's decision to tell Demetrius of Hermia's flight (it seems obvious that the smart thing for her to do is to keep totally mum about it until Hermia is safely out of Demetrius' grasp and life), the best candidate for second place is perhaps this repeated insistence on *tomorrow night*. Not only is it mentioned unnecessarily often, it is a queer choice to begin with. Why not tonight? We are given no motivation for waiting (especially if they cannot see one another in the meantime), and they have every reason to strike out as soon as possible.

The next scene, the organizational meeting for *Pyramus and Thisby*, is very unspecific about its own place in time (leaving us with the default inference that it is is some sort of temporal continuity with the scene before) but clear about the time frame for the group's next meeting: they are to learn their parts "by tomorrow night, and meet me in the palace wood, a mile without the town, by moonlight." The reason for choosing the wood is given, and the need to memorize their lines may be taken as sufficient explanation for why they are to meet tomorrow night rather than tonight—and besides, it is easy enough to see that this will bring both groups into the woods simultaneously, a convergence that we are ready to assume will turn out to be a good idea, no questions asked.

So far, the schedule is entirely straightforward, however puzzling it may be in the case of Hermia and Lysander. Neither of the first two scenes is placed clearly in a specific time of day, but we have learned that when we next see the lovers and the mechanicals, in the forest, it must be more than a day later, late at night. And in the third scene of the play, we meet the fairies and the beginnings of some Shakespearean temporal sleight of hand.

Fairies are generally associated with night. The two who open 2.1 talk about distributing dew (a nighttime occupation), characterize Puck as a wanderer of the night, and mention the starlight encounters of Oberon and Titania—whose fresh encounter within the scene is initiated by the memorable "Ill-met by moonlight." We are obviously deep in nighttime, and given the normal Shakespearean habits of default continuity, we naturally suppose that the night in question is the one following the conference with Theseus and the first meeting of the mechanicals. Nothing interrupts this supposition for nearly two hundred lines, and then Demetrius runs onto the stage, chafing about Lysander and Hermia, with Helena in warm pursuit.

Suddenly, we are not (according to the firmly established schedule) at the end of Day 1 or the beginning of Day 2, but twenty-four hours later, at the end of Day 2 or beginning of Day 3. A full day has dropped out of view.

Or, to be more exact, a full day has failed to come into view at all. We knew that a space for it had been provided, but we somehow arrived at the other side of it without perceiving anything other than smooth continuity from the beginning. Nothing had been planned for it; being without anticipated content, its failure to appear had no effect other than diminishing delay. There was nothing lost but mere empty time, and that vanished without a trace, like a canceled reservation.

Shakespeare sustains close connections in the action through the rest of act 2, all of act 3, and up to the brink of act 5. Before we see Demetrius and Helena, and realize that we've skipped a day, Oberon sends Puck for the magic flower to use on Titania; Puck promises to return promptly, and when he does he is given the task of fixing Demetrius and then meeting Oberon again before the first cock-crow. By the end of act 2, Titania and Lysander have both been daubed, Lysander is pursuing Helena, and Hermia is in search of Lysander; it is apparently still, at least officially, the night between Days 2 and 3, and the mechanicals begin act 3 right on schedule. Before Puck and Oberon are rejoined—that is, before the night is over—Bottom has been translated, and doting Titania has taken him off to her bower; shortly thereafter, Puck's bungling of Demetrius' transformation is discovered, and Oberon charges him to put everything right before daylight, whereupon Oberon goes to Titania's bower while Puck shepherds the lovers into solitary sleep, overwhelmed by what Helena understandably calls "O weary night, O long and tedious night," muttering about the hostilities, and looking forward to day. In 4.1, Oberon, referring to the time of the whole set of adventures as "this night," releases Titania, Puck restores Bottom, and together they work a final charm to secure the lovers, until the morning lark announces the arrival of Day 3's dawn. The fairies then depart, succeeded directly by the hunting-party of Theseus and Hippolyta. The lovers awaken, all is in order, and Theseus abandons the hunt (the morning being no longer in its early stage), inviting the lovers to join him and his bride at the Temple soon, for a triple wedding followed by a feast. Before act 4 is over, the mechanicals have been reunited, their play has been "preferred," and they are off to the Palace to perform it. Everything is set up.

But another day has been set aside in the meantime. If we concede that the lost Day 2 still counts, we are put back on schedule for the initial four-day plan; but we now find ourselves late in Day 3, and everything will be over shortly after midnight. There is no temporal reference that reaffirms the original scheme, but none that revises it, either—nothing equivalent to Capulet's pushing the wedding back from his hasty choice of Wednesday to a more decorous Thursday, and then pulling it back to Wednesday with considerable ado. The official timetable, with departure on Day 1 at an unspecified hour and arrival after midnight on Day 4, remains unaltered but it is decidedly overshadowed by a smooth temporal continuity that we would naturally take to encompass only one full night, were it not for the overt references to four days and "tomorrow night." Our dramatic experience of time is that the initial interview took place sometime on Day A, with forest adventures that night, resolution achieved by dawn on Day B, weddings and festivities concluding just after midnight on Day B—something well short of forty-eight hours.

If it can be done smoothly in less than two days' time, why did Shakespeare insist on four, inserting an unexplained and countermotivational delay until "tomorrow night" as if he had to lengthen the time artificially, and then quietly losing track as the action seems to reach its natural temporal level within two days? I cannot provide a satisfactory answer. My best unsatisfactory answer is that in addition to four days being a fairer allotment than two for Hermia's life-determining decision, and a more reasonable length of time for putting together a courtly wedding entertainment, the unexplained delay until "tomorrow night" is another instance of the course of true love having to face unsmoothness, and the sudden appearance of the lovers in the forest well before we expected them is dramatically welcome and helps us participate in the sense of rush and urgency that drives them.

Whatever the true answer may be, it is not the main point of this pair of examples. What these are meant to illustrate is not the effects of foreshortening time, but the differing means that Shakespeare could call upon in doing so. In *Romeo and Juliet*, he arranges situations and character responses so as to bring about decisions that change the scheme within the terms of the action. In *A Midsummer Night's Dream*, he bypasses literal and internally dramatized changes in schedule and instead works with our sense of the continuity and illusion of time through a manipulation and guidance of the action's apparent implications. Or, to put it shorthandedly, in *Romeo and Juliet*, he handles a problem in time readjustment as Capulet might; in *A Midsummer Night's Dream*, he pulls off a similar alteration more in the manner of Oberon. Dramaturgy, in the hands of a master, has just such a range of possibilities, from the practicality and hard-headedness to the finesse of effective illusion.

For Shakespearean dramaturgy, time, like space, is an independent variable that the playwright may control. It may be sped up, slowed down, overstuffed, split into incommensurable but commutable alternatives, artificially linked—whatever will make the play work more smoothly, or coherently, or effectively. The seemingly careless and primitive chronological blemishes that post-Restoration critics winced at, and sometimes attempted to correct, were (more often than not) well-calculated and highly accomplished strategies in the service of a more flexible dramaturgical idiom than the critics were prepared to recognize. The botherment experienced by editors and interpreters and "correctors" was caused not by Shakespeare's being careless or deficient in verisimiltude, but by his later critics' valuing chronological realism too highly, and failing to appreciate that there was disciplined method in Shakespeare's seeming temporal madness. It is not unfair to argue that Shakespeare valued dense continuity too highly, though that is not an argument that I would support. It is decidedly unfair to suppose that he just didn't know how to handle time.

The Tudor proverb was *veritas temporis filia*—truth is the daughter of time. The Tudor playwright could arrange time in order to assist the birthing of dramatic truth. By the latter half of the Stuart era, this sense of relationship had been reversed, and time was treated as if it were a direct function of truth, of reality itself, and thus stable, regular, uniform, as reality itself was assumed to be. There was no longer room for either fairies or unnaturalistic temporal flexibilities. The tactful art of understanding Shakespeare's handling of time was gradually lost, along with other elements dependent on a versatility in cooperative imagination. But Shakespeare's texts can still teach us how to recover it, and to see once again that time travels in divers paces, with divers persons, especially if the dramaturge will have it so.

6

AND I MAY HIDE MY FACE, LET ME PLAY THISBY TOO

The dramaturgy and dramatics of role-doubling

Shakespeare could rely on his actors because he knew that they were professionals in their craft. For some dramaturgical maneuvers, they gave him important additional opportunity in his shaping of plays: he knew *them*, personally as well as professionally; he knew what they could do best, what they looked like, and what resources they offered for the designing of a dramatic scheme.

As previously noted, most of his plays were written for the company in which he was an actor as well as a financial shareholder. This was the Lord Chamberlain's Men, which first appears in the records in 1594, at the beginning of Shakespeare's playwriting career. It was reconstituted, with the same actors, as the King's Men after the accession of James to the throne in 1603 and continued to play well beyond Shakespeare's retirement and death, closing down along with the theaters in 1642. I have already, in earlier chapters, glanced at minor ways in which the stability of a single acting company seems to have affected the way Shakespeare conceived and wrote plays. A brief inventory of evidence here may be helpful in indicating how he took particular advantage of his familiarity with the cast, and how our understanding of how he designed his plays may be helped by bearing his peculiar situation in mind.

Many of Shakespeare's plays require a strong male lead. Among them are two obvious examples in our seven-play canon, the title roles of *Hamlet* and *King Lear*. We know from contemporary evidence that these parts were carried originally by Richard Burbage, a regular member of Shakespeare's company from the beginning and one of the two most outstanding actors of the time (the other being Edward Alleyn of the rival Admiral's Men). Similar

evidence establishes that Burbage also played the parts of Richard III and
Othello, and the pattern doubtless extended to the chief strong roles of most
of the other plays. Shakespeare, knowing that Burbage could carry what are
still among the most demanding parts in all of dramatic literature, could write
them accordingly.

There are no comparable female leads in Shakespeare's plays. This too
was a matter of practical adaptation. Female actors did not appear on regular
English stages until the Restoration, long after Shakespeare's death, and it is
possible that his company did not contain an actor who could do a comparable job in a mature woman's role.

Younger women's parts were another matter. Juliet, Rosalind, Helena
and Hermia, Ophelia: these were evidently parts that he could assign to the
boys of the company, who were evidently strong enough to carry them (probably with some instructional assistance from the older actors to whom they
were vaguely apprenticed). More precisely, Shakespeare seems to have been
able to count on two boys in particular, and Shakespeare often wrote young
women's parts in pairs. Helena and Hermia are presented as like sisters in *A
Midsummer Night's Dream*; Rosalind and Celia are cousins in *As You Like It*
(and so are Beatrice and Hero in *Much Ado about Nothing*), but the parallels
go still further. There is considerable fun stirred up about blonde Helena's
height and the shortness and darkness of Hermia; Rosalind describes herself
as "more than common tall;" speeches in *Much Ado* tell us that Hero is dark
and short. These specifications might cause some casting problems on the
modern stage, but Shakespeare knew they would be accurate for his audiences. A few years later than the cited plays, he has Lear's fool remark (in
1.5) that Goneril is as like, or unlike, Regan as an apple is to a crabapple: it is
not unreasonable to guess that the same two boys, now a little older, are playing the sisters.

The last part of *Romeo and Juliet* 4.5, after the grieving family and Paris
have been ushered out from the bedside of the supposedly dead Juliet, is a
bit of fun initiated by the entrance of the clownish Peter. That, at least is how
the Folio text reads, but the Second Quarto has a different stage direction:
Enter Will Kemp. This, rather than *Peter*, is probably what Shakespeare originally wrote. Will Kemp was another of Shakespeare's colleagues, and the
most celebrated comic actor in England at the time. His name appears similarly in some of the speech headings of *Much Ado about Nothing*, silent testimony to Shakespeare's having written the part of Dogberry with Kemp
explicitly in mind. He probably played Bottom as well, along with the various other clown parts that appear regularly in early Shakespeare plays.

Roles of this latter type are mainly confined to the first half of Shakespeare's writings. Their disappearance probably has much less to do with a

shift in public taste than with the fact that Kemp left the Lord Chamberlain's Men in 1598. Subsequently, Shakespeare generated comic effects in a different way, with less call for the bawdy and boisterous style in which Kemp evidently excelled. Robert Armin, who joined the company shortly after Kemp's departure, was a singer as well as a witty actor; Lear's Fool is too, probably much for that reason.

Shakespeare could enlist minor members of the playhouse staff (e.g., the gatherers who collected money from the audience as they entered, and became dispensable once the play was well under way) to swell crowds on the stage, or even to take swords and chase each other through brief battle excursions. But the skilled fencing that must take place in all of our small canon's tragedies and histories had to be part of the accomplishments of major actors—and since they were, Shakespeare could build in the scenes in which these skills are needed. The restrictions of his repertory company also provided abilities that he could count on, and he wrote accordingly.

I do not mean to suggest that Shakespeare thought his actors had limited versatility and accommodated the parts to them accordingly. I mean merely that he knew (or decided) in advance, at least in many cases, who would be playing which role, and occasionally built that knowledge into his script, availing himself of particular talents and perhaps catering to what he knew from experience would work well with audiences.

Versatility was not in question. It was not in question for two main reasons. One is that this was possibly the most accomplished group of actors in all of Europe: an unusual versatility was part of their professionalism. The more compelling and practical reason is that both the basic conditions of a repertory company and the specific conditions of Shakespearean dramaturgy required them to be versatile. They had to play many different parts.

Burbage had to play Richard III, Hamlet, Othello, and Lear, but he also had to play other roles in a given season's repertoire, most of which were not written by Shakespeare. All the actors had to be able to adapt to parts that had not been designed with them in mind. And if Shakespeare's own writings sometimes give them roles for which they were especially suited, it posed some additional challenges for them as well. Within a specific play, some actors—occasionally several actors—had to play more than one part.

The roles in a Shakespearean play regularly outnumber the cast that was to enact it. Shakespeare's dramaturgy had to deal with the problem of building a full play on the foundation of a restricted number of actors. Our attempts to understand what guided his structuring of a drama must always keep this unfamiliar limitation in mind.

This was a common phenomenon in Shakespeare's time, and the limitations were even more demanding in earlier sixteenth-century plays. It was routine for playwrights to design things so that the actor who plays the role of A in the first half can also play B later on, after A disappears from the text; and it was not uncommon to require an actor to alternate between roles C and D as the action develops among different groups of characters (in the course of which the same actor may occasionally have to pick up the roles of E here and F there, while C and D are offstage).

Pre-Shakespearean playwrights sometimes give explicit instructions about which roles can be thus doubled, or otherwise multipled. *King Darius* (1565), *Like Will to Like* (ca. 1568), and *The Tide Tarrieth No Man* (1576), for instance, declare on their title pages that they can be produced with six, five, and four actors, respectively, listing the specific roles which the play's design permits each individual actor to play (two of the actors in *The Tide Tarrieth No Man* have to carry six parts each).[1+] Thus an acting company with limited staff need not be intimidated by the number of roles in the *dramatis personae* list and will know how to deploy the available actors so as to fill out the drama manageably and efficiently. Nor was this custom of providing a casting menu confined to pre-Shakespearean plays. The examples above appeared during Shakespeare's boyhood, but *The Fair Maid of the Exchange* (published in 1607 and probably written later than *Hamlet*) follows the same pattern, claiming that the twenty-one characters may be portrayed by eleven actors and specifying the division of labor.

Needless to say, practical playwrights wrote with such companies in mind, and added characters with an eye to the logistics of filling the roles with available actors who could retire from one part in adequate time to assume another. Shakespeare stepped into this tradition, and made good use of it.

How many actors are required to produce *A Midsummer Night's Dream*, *Richard II*, *Henry IV, Part 1*, *Romeo and Juliet*, *King Lear*, *Hamlet*, and *As You Like It*? Count the cast of characters, and you get seven different answers, which are the answers normally honored by modern Shakespearean productions: one actor per character. Count according to the principles of Shakespearean dramaturgy and you get very different answers.

The Swiss traveler Thomas Platter, visiting England in 1599, saw *Julius Caesar* at the brand-new Globe Theater, and estimated that it was acted by "about fifteen persons."[2] William A. Ringler, Jr., in a remarkably fine study of the question,[3] concludes that Shakespeare's pre-Globe plays (which include the first four named above) require sixteen actors, though he includes the "mutes" who have no speaking parts. My own analysis, based on the obvious and simple-minded technique of tallying the on-times and off-times of the various roles and calculating which combinations could be taken on by a given actor (allowing time for costume changes), tells me that all seven of our plays can actually be produced with as few as thirteen speaking actors.

This chapter is mainly concerned with the ways in which Shakespeare was constrained by the need for doubling, the effect that these constraints had on his designs and techniques, the strategies he occasionally used to turn them to dramatic advantage, and in general the importance of taking account of doubling in our attempts to understand what, and how, Shakespeare wrote. Before proceeding, let me add four cautionary notes:

1. There is no doubt that Shakespeare's plays could be produced more comfortably (except perhaps in financial terms) with fifteen or sixteen actors than with thirteen. I do not intend to argue that Shakespeare employed thirteen speaking actors and no more. I merely claim that, in a pinch, all seven of our plays *can* be delivered by thirteen speakers, and that there is reason to think that Shakespeare designed a large number of his plays with this minimum in mind. Why he would do so is unclear (though it probably had to do with the number of actors that he thought he could always count on), but this number computes so consistently that it is difficult to suppose that it was not deliberately aimed for.

It would, of course, be convenient to have a minimum staff when the company went on provincial tour, which happened occasionally when the plague or some other cause resulted in a temporary suspension of playing privileges in London.[4+] While extras, supers, might be hired on the spot in the provinces to fill out those dimensions of a play, speaking actors were another matter: they had to be trained regulars, and it would be economically efficient to be able to make do with relatively few of them. Moreover, the company's shareholders, supplemented by two or three indispensable boy actors, were for obvious financial and other reasons bound to be the essential pool from which the cast would be normally drawn. Thirteen speaking actors as a norm would be almost exactly the right number to keep everyone busy with an occasional day off. Whether or not Shakespeare's plays were regularly produced with thirteen speakers, it made sense to design plays so that a constant number of minimum staff could always do the job, even if in relatively easy times hirelings were added to the available pool.

2. There is also no doubt that the plays can be produced still more comfortably (apart from the budget) by double and sometimes triple a lower limit of thirteen. But if the question is why the plays were written as they were, we must accept the practical constraints that mattered to Shakespeare as a company shareholder—and only then can we see some of the less obvious subtleties in how his plays are organized. If we read them as if we can easily and regularly have a different actor for every role, we miss some of the elements of Shakespearean design. That design had to include the possibility of doubling some roles, and thus the job of steering around the impossibility of doubled roles appearing on stage simultaneously. It also had to consider the need to provide time for costume changes between the stage appearances of doubled roles, and to offer occasional official explanations for the conspicuous absence of a character who cannot be present because its actor is otherwise employed, and to make sure that the viewers are not confused into supposing that the presence of the same actor means that he is still in the same role as before, or supposing that a costume change necessarily means a different character. Moreover, we would also miss some positive values built into the design in the light of Shakespeare's awareness that the audience could recognize the same actors in differing roles, about which I will say more presently.

3. This is one of several areas of Shakespearean dramaturgy in which we are at a disadvantage if we do not return to the original texts, since their irregularities contain clues, especially in stage directions and speech headings, that modern editors tend to smooth away by a tidy regularization. If you occasionally consult modern editions of the plays as this chapter proceeds, please bear in mind that I am not using them: some of the evidence I cite will not appear in them. Ideally—both for my credibility and for your discovery—you would have a facsimile of the First Folio by your side as you work through this chapter, though by now it should be clear that this would also be an advantageous companion to all the other chapters.

4. In our return to original texts, it is important to appreciate Folio and Quarto versions separately, in the case of plays for which both types of text are extant (six of our seven plays are of this type, *As You Like It* being the lone exception). Modern editors are expected to deliver one final text per play, and normally proceed by identifying which of the early versions seems, on rigorous critical grounds, to be closest to an original highest-grade Shakespearean manuscript, correcting the result by adjusting apparent corruptions through comparison with other versions.[5+] But as our task is different, we need not be constrained by a need for a single final text, and can learn more if we give independent, but comparative, attention to alternative early versions. We are accordingly more free to notice that Capulet's feast in 1.5 is designed both in the Folio of 1623 and in the Second Quarto (1599) to be playable by twelve speakers plus one responsive but silent boy, but that they are *differently deployed* in the two versions (F provides three servants for the opening business, and two kinsmen for Capulet to chat with about masquing, while Q2 gives us four servants and only one kinsman). Other examples will emerge as the chapter moves on, and will suggest that the phenomenon of doubling can be best observed through *all* of the original versions, and will sometimes help to disclose evidence of Shakespeare's revisions of his plays.

The investigation of this matter is, in short, a bit more complicated than the tallying of roles on which it is based. But it produces results that make the complications worth struggling with.

Ben Jonson's play *Every Man in His Humour*, originally staged in 1598 and first printed in 1601, was published again in Jonson's first collection of his *Works* in 1616, and this time he added a list of the principal actors who originally played the roles almost twenty years before. They are all members of the Lord Chamberlain's Men, and William Shakespeare is one of them (along with Richard Burbage, and Will Kemp, and the John Heminge and Henry Condell who put together the First Folio in Shakespeare's memory). Jonson lists only ten actors. He presumably left the boys in the company unmentioned (they were in fact not needed for that particular play), and may have omitted actors of very minor roles. Jonson also lists the principal actors who staged *The Alchemist* in 1610 and *Catiline* in 1611—again, there are ten names (with one variation in the two lists), still including Burbage, Heminge, and Condell.

Ten good men and true sufficed for these plays, the largest cast lists given for Jonson's performances; the same number, plus a small allowance of apprenticed boys, could probably produce any Shakespearean play from *The Two Gentlemen of Verona* to *The Tempest*, given a willingness of actors to play more than one role.[6+] Nonspeaking parts, such as soldiers, members of a mob, even silent servants pretending to tidy up as they change the stage furniture, could easily be taken care of by throwing costumes on some of the company's stagehands or money-collectors (or, when on tour, some of the locals hired to do those jobs)—hence Shakespeare's occasional indefiniteness when dealing with nonspeaking roles, e.g., "Enter three or foure Citizens with Clubs," "Enter Romeo, Mercutio, Benvolio, with five or sixe other Maskers, Torch-bearers," "Enter Father Capulet, Mother, Nurse, and Seruing men, two or three" (*Romeo and Juliet* 1.1, 1.4, 4.2), "Enter old Polonius, with his man or two" (Q2 version of *Hamlet* 2.1), "After them, Titus Andronicus, and then Tamara the Queene of Gothes, & her two Sonnes Chiron and Demetrius, with Aaron the Moore, and others, as many as can be" (*Titus Andronicus* 1.1).

We may well feel entitled to take more than a grain of salt at directions such as are offered in *Henry VI, Part 2*: "Enter Cade . . . with infinite numbers" (4.2) and "Enter Multitudes with Halters about their neckes" (4.9), but they still indicate that Shakespeare, in these cases, wanted as many nonspeakers as he could get, and was aware that they did not need either freelance actor wages or special costumes: for a fifteenth-century mob scene, a brief appearance by theater functionaries in ordinary sixteenth-century knockabout clothes would suffice.

The evidence suggests that Shakespeare's fellow players were more than accommodating to a scheme that often required them to play two or more roles. I have already mentioned the economic convenience of their doing so;

but this is not all that counts, and it has been suggested that doubling would be too great a burden on the cast. There are three counterarguments that cumulatively seem to me decisive. Earlier sixteenth-century plays, as I have pointed out, sometimes required an actor to do six parts: by comparison, two or three need not be too onerous. Furthermore, some actors enjoy acting, and would not feel necessarily abused by being asked to do more of it. Most importantly, there is clear textual evidence that Shakespeare wrote doubled roles into his plays, and that is enough to authorize looking for hints of doublings that are not so obvious.

What this means in terms of reading Shakespearean dramaturgy is mainly the need for a sensitivity to the practical considerations of a play produced through a group of actors that was distinctly smaller than the cast of characters, and therefore required the doubling (or even tripling) of roles, and therefore required a design that would make this logistically possible, and therefore offered Shakespeare not only severe constraints in the deployment of his actors (which gives us a chance to appreciate how he does it, as well as explanations for why certain things do or do not happen) but also some interesting opportunities to play around with the audience's awareness that this actor, now in this role, also played—or continues to play—that one as well.

On the one hand, understanding the dramaturgy of doubling includes knowing how to accept a Shakespearean dramatic maneuver that arises sheerly from the limited number of his actors, whether or not it is rationalized in the text of the play. In the last scene of *Romeo and Juliet*, Lady Montague's conspicuous absence is explained by the sad report that she has just died of grief over Romeo's exile: "Alas, my Liege, my wife is dead tonight, / Grief of my son's exile hath stopped her breath." The scene nearly cries out for her lamenting presence, not only to add to the number of the bereaved and grieving but also to complete the symmetry previously employed in the parallel largescale and accumulating scenes 1.1 and 3.1, where the last entries before the Prince's are given to the two couples who head the feuding factions. All this considered, it is downright awkward for Lady Montague to be absent.

Shakespeare's withholding of her is almost certainly because she was simply not available: her actor was being deployed in another role within the same scene (which in fact needs thirteen speaking parts as it stands). As the occasion was far too important to permit her casual absence, Shakespeare signs her death certificate into the play, thus simultaneously accounting for her failure to appear and adding another tragic touch. This is not an altogether satisfactory solution, but was perhaps the best Shakespeare could do if he was to be able to supply all of the more indispensable characters.

But Benvolio is also absent. His faithful friendship with Romeo makes this slightly odd, not to mention that it reduces the Montague component in the scene to the barest minimum. Nevertheless, his absence is less conspicuous than Lady Montague's, especially since we have not seen him since the end of 3.1. Lady Montague is a dramatically less important and a vastly less memorable character than Benvolio, but her failure to appear at the end of the play is simply more obvious than his, and cannot pass unnoticed. Some excuse, however limp, is required.

If Shakespeare does not bother explaining why Benvolio is not there, neither does he deal with the absence of Juliet's Nurse, whose devotion to Juliet might be thought to have earned her a place in the final scene (not to mention that it could give her occasion for a new level of histrionics). But having severed the Nurse from Juliet's confidence at the end of act 3, Shakespeare may be assuming that we won't particularly miss her if she isn't mentioned, just as we may not consciously miss Benvolio, whose position as Romeo's *confidant* has been fully taken over by Friar Laurence, making Benvolio rather redundant (does anyone miss him in act 4?). In the First Quarto edition of the play, his death is announced along with Lady Montague's, but the effect is more ludicrous than tragic, since it gives—and not altogether misleadingly—the impression that Shakespeare is conveniently slaughtering, offstage, everyone who can't be on and might be missed. It was less awkward, however unsatisfactory, just to let him be quietly absent.

We see that Lady Montague is not there; if we look for them, we see that Benvolio and the Nurse are absent as well. But the relative conspicuousness of specific characters' absences is only half of the practical dramaturgical question. The other half mitigates his need to keep us from expecting them: it is that Shakespeare knew that his audiences could see the corresponding actors on stage in other roles, and therefore *knew* that neither the Nurse nor Benvolio could show up. Providing or not providing an explanation was more a matter of diplomacy and continuity than of intelligibility. The death of Lady Montague was required not because *we* notice her absence, but because the other characters on stage must expect her, even when we are aware that they must expect in vain. And that brings us to the other hand.

The other hand is that Shakespearean dramaturgy, while being embedded in staffing constraints, *takes advantage* of what happens when he has to double roles.

I certainly cannot prove, though I believe I can defend rather persuasively, the proposition that just such a thing takes place in *Romeo and Juliet* 5.1 when the exiled Romeo, galvanized by the bad news of Juliet's death, decides to join her. On his first falling in love with her, he had visited Friar Laurence, whom we first meet in 2.3, just before Romeo's entry, as he gathers herbs from the monastic garden and philosophizes on the divers properties of various plants, including how the medicinal can be poisonous if misapplied, and how human willfulness can choose death over grace. This characterization of the Friar establishes his credentials for concocting the potion by which Juliet later attempts to feign death in order to get out of her otherwise impossible position, as well as his right to be considered the center of gravity in the play's occasional appeals to a wisdom more comprehensive than Capulet's intermittent flashes of good sense and the Prince's practical pronouncements on civil order.

Shakespeare wrote a seven-line part for a demoralized apothecary into 5.1 in order to dramatize Romeo's decision to die. Given the way that Shakespeare and his company worked, the role would most likely be given to an actor who had already played at least one other part by this time, since it would be wasteful to leave an actor capable of playing the Apothecary idle through the first four acts. The audience would doubtless recognize the actor and be aware of any notable previous role or roles within the play. Quite a few actors would be eligible to take the Apothecary's part, their own earlier roles being no longer in play. Which is the best dramatic choice, in the circumstances? The overall design of the play shows a taste for symmetry and irony. Surely it would occur to Shakespeare to make this apothecary of last resort, the purveyor of poison to end Romeo's life, reminiscent of the druggist–friar with whom this whole episode began. It would make splendid dramatic sense for Shakespeare to give his audience the jolt of making the apothecary visibly parallel to the friar, the man who has tried to save Romeo's volatile and precarious life, and thus reminiscent of our first introduction to him as he reflected on medicine and poison, and the self-destructive potentials of human willfulness.[7*]

If you are unpersuaded that this was in fact Shakespeare's design, I will not make any further attempt to sway you; this is a possible and an appropriate bit of dramaturgical byplay, but there is no direct evidence to require it. But if you share my sense that this is at least very likely, you are in tune with an important principle of Shakespearean dramaturgy—namely, that a play that require some actors to play more than one part not only imposes dramaturgical restraints on the playwright, but opens new dramaturgical opportunities as well. Shakespeare sometimes exploits the positive dramatic potentials of such a situation, and reading Shakespeare on his own terms may require an alertness to his ability to make a virtue of necessity.

In order to understand how he worked with necessity, we have, for instance, to realize that he sometimes had to drop characters in order to release their actors for other roles and occasionally felt that he had to go rather overtly on record as having done so, rather than just forgetting them.

It is not always clear in these cases just how he made judgments about whether to explain or let it go. I have tried to account for the case of Lady

Montague, and it seems to me that the shift between the Q1 and Q2/F texts' treatment of Benvolio is a step in the right direction. But why does he bother to explain the absence of the King of France in the Quarto version of *King Lear* when he lets the Fool slip away permanently at the end of 3.6 without either an explanation or a satisfying exit line? (The Folio text drops the apology for France's absence, but does nothing to account for the vanishing of the Fool.) Why is Egeus allowed to disappear at the end of act 4, overruled and unreconciled and apparently unhappy, in the Quarto of *A Midsummer Night's Dream*? (The Folio reinstates him in act 5, but creates a new problem for the role of Philostrate in doing so.) Why, given the importance of Adam in the first two acts of *As You Like It*, is he so unceremoniously abandoned just after his salvation has become the chief focus of attention at the end of act 2? So far, I have found no satisfactory answers—but I would like to emphasize the importance of asking these questions if we are to understand more adequately how Shakespeare wrote his plays.[8]

More subtly, Shakespeare could take advantage of the conspicuously definitive or inconspicuously sly loss of a character by initiating or amplifying another role taken by the same actor. Mercutio's death in *Romeo and Juliet* 3.1 is a conspicuous example. For while it is brought about by a deep dramaturgical logic that allows it both to conclude a major movement of the play and to initiate another, and is thus dramatically sufficient on its own, it also leaves Shakespeare free to redeploy an obviously talented actor. Benvolio's total disappearance at the end of the same scene is an inconspicuous equivalent without dramatic closure, and for that reason we may plausibly infer that is likely to be motivated by the needs of another role to be taken (or resumed) by the same actor, in that it seems gratuitous and retrospectively odd—surely he would otherwise be a better choice than Balthazar to bear the bad news to Romeo in Mantua in 5.1, and to accompany him to Juliet's grave.

Because Shakespeare could count on his audience's recognition of familiar actors inhabiting multiple roles, he could therefore also count on the audience's realization that certain combinations of characters in the same scene were dramatically impossible: overt excuses for an absence, as in the case of Lady Montague, were sometimes desirable for dramatic tact but not (as in the case of Benvolio, despite Q1) for establishing the sheer practical necessity of the omission. To appreciate how Shakespeare worked, we have to stay alert to how he dealt with the audience's awareness that a given role is being played by the same actor who had already played another elsewhere in the play.

Montague's announcement of his wife's demise may strike the reader as a careless throwaway, a facile rationalization for her dramatic absence. That is exactly what it is. Shakespeare could afford to be relatively facile in this case, because actor recognition probably allowed his audience to understand that

Lady Montague had already been dramaturgically disposed of. Shakespeare needed only to take care of explaining to Capulet and the Prince; almost any excuse will do, and better a poignant and dramatically relevant one than sending her off to visit an aunt in Cremona. The actors of Benvolio and the Nurse were also plainly visible to the audience in their alternative parts, but as their absence did not disturb an established symmetry and no one on stage need be bothered, no further explanation was needed. In a sense, this is dramaturgy at the level of diplomacy and damage control, covering up (plus relying on the audience to cover up) some obvious but unavoidable omissions.

But although damage control operations were part of Shakespearean dramaturgy, he built in some more dramatically clever collusions with his cooperative audience. When, earlier in the same scene, Romeo unmuffles his slain (but heretofore unrecognized) assailant, he exclaims "Mercutio's kinsman, noble County Paris!" Paris and Mercutio have never been linked before. Why add the further information now?

The most plausible grounding reason, as you may well have guessed, is that Paris and Mercutio were roles borne by the same actor. If so, we as audience have seen this all along, and have been denied the direct dramatic linkage only so that Shakespeare can here, at a decisive point in Romeo's life, make the connection between the friend who he thought had died for him and the innocent bridegroom of Juliet whom he has just ironically killed through a terrible misunderstanding. Shakespeare has Romeo deliver the genealogical news at the moment of its greatest dramatic impact, forcing us to see the parallel pointlessness of two of the three deaths in which Romeo has been involved—the third being Tybalt, who figured importantly in Paris's mistaken logic about why Romeo was trying to enter the Capulet tomb, and with whom Shakespeare has Romeo make his peace before he dies at Juliet's lips. Much more is recapitulated in the last scene of this play than is openly spoken about; much of it is accomplished through the way Shakespeare took advantage of the practical necessity of doubling roles.

There is one further minor problem that may be resolved by an appeal to doubling. Although the organization of *Romeo and Juliet* is generally strong on symmetry, and the Chorus's opening sonnet in act 1[9+] is echoed by another as prologue to act 2, the Chorus disappears permanently after that. "Chorus" as a technical dramatic term does not mean an ensemble; this function was normally executed by a single actor. In *Romeo and Juliet*, the Chorus speaks typically (though in other plays Shakespeare sometimes handles the Chorus differently) from the perspective of a wise overview. That perspective is the particular specialty of one character within *Romeo and Juliet*. I guess that the actor who played the Chorus may well have worn monastic robes, and disappeared from the play when he had entered it as Friar Laurence in 2.3, thereafter being ineligible to step outside it again.

The dramaturgical strategy of doubling has the disadvantage of putting constraints on who can appear with whom, and occasionally requiring an apologetic explanation for conspicuous absences. It has the virtue of making it possible to amplify the cast of characters without enlarging the company of actors and deepening the dramatic significance of a moment. The advantages outweigh the disadvantages even thus far, especially given that Shakespeare's audiences were probably patiently aware of what could not be done; but Shakespeare had still more to offer. He could organize his doubling in a way that adds to the sheer fun, or creates an arresting surprise in the action.

Much of the time, of course, Shakespeare simply redeployed actors without making an issue of it, and his audience understood the rules of practical necessity well enough not to assume that they were *expected* to notice, or that a given doubling was dramatically significant. It was simply a practical given, until Shakespeare defined it as something more, either through the lines or through parallels and coincidences too obvious to miss. He often did just that.

I alleged in an earlier chapter that Titania's fairy servants in *A Midsummer Night's Dream*, though imaginatively construed as tiny, were actually presented by the same actors who played the Athenian mechanicals.[10+] I cannot prove that this was so, but it is at least more than likely—not just because it would be a happy dramatic effect, but because a consideration of the customary number of actors and the distribution of the play's roles make it practically plausible. The effect is of course ludicrous, and therefore entirely appropriate both in its completing the transformation of the Clowns (which is how they are collectively characterized in the opening stage direction of 3.1) and to the general portrayal of everything else in the pixilated woods.

And while we are dealing with *A Midsummer Night's Dream*, which at least one careful scholar has argued must have required fifteen actors rather than the thirteen I have proposed,[11] let us pause briefly to consider a curious anomaly. Shakespeare usually keeps his major positive roles as free from moral taint as modern candidates for high political office are supposed to be. Yet in 2.1, where we first meet Titania and Oberon, the squabbling between them includes the dramatically gratuitous accusations (which are more evaded than denied) that they have had somewhat compromising dalliances with Theseus and Hippolyta.

Why taint the moral characters of four principal roles, when nothing ever comes of this except the fairy monarchs' blessing on the wedding of their putative paramours? The answer is surely that Shakespeare is having fun with our recognition that both couples are presented by the same pair of actors.

And that in turn explains why there is a sounding of horns between the exit of Titania and Oberon at the end of 4.1 and the entrance of Theseus and Hippolyta in 4.2: it sets the atmosphere for the hunt that never quite takes place,[12+] but more importantly, it covers the time needed for two actors to throw off their fairy robes so that they might enter again as the Duke and impending Duchess. Thirteen actors can do it after all.[13+]

Shakespeare sometimes plays with the brute fact of doubling as a sort of tease to the audience, usually coupled with some useful preparation. In *Richard II*, we can see in retrospect, when examining the construction of the play (but not at the time, so no omission is evident to the audience) that it would have been appropriate for York to appear in the large first scene: he will be a character of crucial importance to the guidance of the play, and ideally would be introduced at its inception. If not then, he might be expected in 1.3, a scene equally large and concerned with the heart of the matter that York will pursue well into act 5. Why is he absent?

The explanation seems to me to be implicit in 1.2, where John of Gaunt bares his conscientious soul to the Duchess of Gloucester, and she to him. Gaunt's speeches cut to the quick of a political philosophy that haunts much of the play, the invulnerability of Richard's person and crown; the Duchess' speeches are mainly more personal, lamenting the death of her husband at Richard's instigation and calling for retributive justice. At the end of the scene, perceiving that Gaunt is morally resolute against acting against the king, however guilty he may be, she turns her attention finally to the Duke of York, Gaunt's brother and her brother-in-law. She asks Gaunt to commend her to York; and then, stumblingly, asks Gaunt to have York visit her; and finally cancels the invitation on the grounds that she is too desolate to offer hospitality.

Why this special emphasis on York, whom we have not met, if it is to end with her backing off? A reasonable answer can be given on dramaturgical grounds without getting into the question of doubling. This is the way York is introduced and highlighted, this is how Shakespeare establishes that he is to be trusted as a sympathetic figure, this is the initial gate through which a sense of his character and a hint of his eventual importance pass into the play, and it is a touching way to underline the Duchess' desolation.

But Shakespeare often loads multiple functions into a dramaturgical maneuver. Here, I think, he is setting up the physical introduction to York, which takes place in 2.1. At the beginning of that scene, we have John of Gaunt in conversation with a previously unseen character, who is not identified. We run through some 150 lines of dialogue, *and* the entrance of Richard and his entourage, without any identification for this second party. It is only after Gaunt's death that the unknown interlocutor names himself as York.

This is superficially odd, in that Shakespeare usually keeps us informed about whom we are dealing with. But if we take into account the dramaturgy of doubling, I think we can see how he is handling the matter. We have not seen York before, but we have seen the actor who played him. That actor had given a cameo appearance as the Duchess of Gloucester, which made it too awkward for him to be in 1.1 or 1.3 as York: the necessary costume changes, much more complicated than the donning of a friar's habit or the doffing of fairy robes, would take more time than the swift scene changes allowed. Instead, Shakespeare has the actor focus on York at the end of the Duchess' scene, and leaves it to our imagination to guess that his next appearance, in masculine garb, means that he is now taking the role of York—and teases us by withholding the confirmation of all this until 2.1 is well advanced.

Falstaff forgets—implausibly, but with wonderfully characteristic elaboration—the name of one of the crucial figures in *Henry IV, Part 1*. In 2.4, he fumbles toward it: "he of Wales, that gave Amamon the Bastinado, and made Lucifer cuckold, and swore the Devil his true liege-man upon the cross of a Welsh-hook; what a plague call you him?" Poins replies "O, Glendower." Why did Shakespeare handle the identification of Glendower this way?

For the answer, consider the ending of the scene. The original texts have Prince Hal concluding it with Peto. Samuel Johnson thought Poins a better candidate than Peto, and editors since then have occasionally emended the text to substitute Poins, who has, after all, been Hal's sidekick since 1.2. But although this emendation seems to make sense at first glance, it is only because emending editors (and approving readers) have not gone far enough into Shakespeare's strategy.

The scene is intricately designed. Midway through Falstaff's subsequent performance in the role of King Henry, the Hostess, Mistress Quickly, is overcome with laughter, and Falstaff, not breaking from his assumed role nor the one he has projected on the Hostess, says "For God's sake, Lords, convey my trustful [usually emended, for good reason, to "tristfull," i.e., teary] Queen, / For tears do stop the flood-gates of her eyes." Mistress Quickly then has one more line, and does not speak again until after the stage direction "Enter the Hostess."

No exit has been registered for her in the stage directions, but it is amply provided for in the lines. Shakespeare has deftly arranged that she be ushered out of the scene when Falstaff so orders. With her go the pseudo-lordly ushers, one of whom is Poins. That gives him plenty of time to change costumes, don a beard, whatever: but Peto takes Poins' usual place at the end of the scene because Shakespeare has taken Poins offstage, and he has taken Poins offstage because he is to appear at the beginning of the next scene as Glendower. When, earlier, he supplies the name that Falstaff has conveniently forgotten, it

is doubtless with a mimicking of Glendower's accent and physical movement—a tiny rehearsal of what we will see in the next scene when the same
actor again introduces us, in a more literal way, to Glendower himself.

Two more examples will suggest the range of Shakespeare's exploitation of the dramaturgy of doubling. The first is well known, though much
controverted; the second is (as far as I can tell) generally unnoticed but
true, and brilliant.

In *King Lear* 1.4, Lear calls for his Fool. In fact, he does so four times.
For the moment, we focus on the conversation that ensues after the third attempt. Impatient Lear remarks that he hasn't seen the Fool in two days. (At
this point, *we* haven't yet seen him at all, despite the potential contributions
he might have made in the opening scene: Goneril introduces him to our attention in her conversation with Oswald in 1.3, speaking of him as if he were
a regular fixture despite his absence so far in the play.) His knight answers
that "Since my young Lady's going into France, Sir, the Fool hath much
pined away," and Lear brushes off this diplomatic remark as something that
has troubled him.

Why does Shakespeare thus link the Fool with Cordelia, when nothing
whatsoever is ever said again to imply a special affection of the Fool for
Lear's banished daughter? Or indeed for *anyone*—we would be hard put to
find evidence in the text that (apart from this one moment) the Fool is even
capable of genuinely personal affections. The answer must by now be obvious. The Fool was absent from 1.1 because Cordelia needed to be present,
and when he vanishes unceremoniously from the play at, or near, the end of
3.6 it is because Cordelia is to be prominent in the last two acts.

In the meantime, Shakespeare has established a curious linkage between
the Fool and Cordelia. He does it by having the same actor play both roles,
but before we know that, he has already given us the Knight's lines, creating
an odd connection between them that will be reaffirmed by the use of the
same actor but will never be alluded to again—except at the very end. This
may be part of a design to reinforce a general parallel—Cordelia is both critical and solicitous of Lear, as the Fool is in his own way—but it is certainly a
preparation for one of the play's most devastating lines.

At the beginning of Lear's last speech, in the final scene of the play, he
says "And my poor Fool is hanged." Commentators have scrambled to
prove that a beloved daughter might be affectionately referred to as "my
poor fool," and thus have missed Shakespeare's point entirely. Relying on
our knowledge of their being supported by the same actor, we can see that
Shakespeare has given Lear a line that is redolent of an understandable mistaken identity, but is a mistaken identity nonetheless. When Lear goes into
his final speech, he has lost track of whose limp body he has carried onto

the stage. As Albany has already remarked, "He knows not what he says." His terrible odyssey, bracketed by the losing and the refinding of Cordelia, and haunted by the Fool's solicitousness and biting satire in the meantime, has come to rest in a madness that can no longer distinguish which role is which. Shakespeare has exploited the advantages of doubling to create a shattering line that loses its power when translated into modern casting habits and modern editorial annotations.

The second example is in a more soothing key. In *As You Like It* 3.1, Shakespeare has the wicked Duke Frederick send Oliver to bring in his brother Orlando, dead or alive. Oliver protests that he can hardly be accused of collusion with the self-exiled Orlando: to his earlier soliloquy confession (1.1) that he has absolutely no reason to dislike Orlando, apart from sheer envy, he now adds that "I never loved my brother in my life." But that does not get him off the Duke's hook. Orlando is to be hunted down, and Oliver will lose all he has if he fails to bring him in.

Oliver is forgotten in the course of the intense development of the love plots through the rest of act 3 and the early part of act 4, but when we get to 4.3, the stage direction reintroduces him: "Enter Oliver."

This does not yet resolve anything dramatically. Shakespeare's design is much deeper than that. Remember that the play is designed for performance, not for readers, and that in the playhouse all we can know is that the *actor* who played Oliver has now come into the presence of Rosalind and Celia. Which *character* has entered?

We simply do not know. We are used enough to the practice of doubling that we know that the use of of the same actor may be incidental. (For all we know, this could be the third brother, Jaques de Boys, who is mentioned in 1.1 and never again until he suddenly appears in the last scene to announce the conversion of Duke Frederick.) The identity of the evidently new character who enters in 4.3 can be disclosed to Shakespeare's audience only when, and however, Shakespeare chooses to give him a name. So far, he is Oliver's actor playing a very different role.

We are then gradually weaned away from the possibility that this really is Oliver in a changed costume. He speaks with a gracious kindness that has never been associated with Oliver; and he tells a tale that speaks of Oliver in the third person as one who was found by Orlando as "a wretched ragged man, o'er-grown with hair"—which is decidedly not the condition of the speaker—and as one who knows that Oliver had rightly been called "unnatural." By the time we are a little more than halfway through the scene, we still have no idea who this is, but we can (virtually *must*) be confident that it isn't Oliver, even though the actor is the same. The tale continues with an account of how Orlando rescued his wicked and unnatural brother from the threat of a snake and the hunger of a lion, and concludes with the identification we have been waiting for: "in which hurtling / From miserable slumber I awaked."

Suddenly, Shakespeare has reversed the strategically misleading dramaturgical tactics by which he has decoyed us away from the truth. This unidentified character, who has spoken so kindly of Orlando and in such harsh judgment of Oliver, this thoughtful right-thinking gentleman who could be almost anyone whom we haven't met before but surely can't possibly be Oliver, abruptly turns out to be Oliver, recovered and reformed. Through an extraordinary dramaturgical strategy, Shakespeare has totally persuaded us of the authenticity of Oliver's moral transformation even before we learn that it has taken place.

Shakespeare's practice of doubling has been well known for a long time; but his dramaturgy of doubling is still an underdeveloped territory. Let me glance at a couple of problems that may illustrate the possibilities of further exploration.

As I mentioned earlier, Benvolio's disappearance at the end of *Romeo and Juliet* 3.1 is entirely unremarked and unexplained (and remains so for the remainder of the play, except in the aberrant Q1 version). That in itself is not necessarily a red flag: when the Fool definitively leaves *King Lear* at the end (or perhaps, though doubtfully, in the midst[14+]) of 3.6, we are given no indication that he will never reappear. Still, the potential usefulness of Benvolio, especially in act 5, may well raise the suspicion that there is more going on than Shakespeare's decision to use Balthasar as Romeo's man (a role he has not taken before, as far as we can tell from the text) to carry the sad message to Mantua and accompany Romeo to Verona and the Capulets' monument. As the final scene involves thirteen speaking parts, I naturally suspect that Benvolio's actor is in there somewhere—but where? My best present guess, however provisional and reluctant, is that he is wearing Friar Laurence's robes, Romeo's parallel and higher counsellor having absorbed the apprentice who had seen him through Rosaline but was not prepared to deal with Juliet.[15*]

This would give that actor possibly three roles, if the apothecary of 5.1 is also included. But that is not necessarily the record for this play. Earlier in 5.1, Romeo's opening soliloquy is arrested by the arrival of another character. The stage direction reads "Enter Romeo's man," and his speech headings are simply "Man" until he exits (Q2 reads "Exit Man"). But Romeo's first line to him reads "News from Verona; how now, Balthasar?"

Q1's direction seems to confirm that this is what Shakespeare had in mind: "Enter Balthasar his man, booted" (i.e., having been traveling). His subsequent speeches are headed *Balt* and he retires with the direction "Exit Balthasar." Q1 continues this identification in 5.3, for it is "Balthasar" who enters with Romeo, speaks to him as *Balt* before retiring aside, and after being haled in as "Romeo's Man" has one final speech as *Balth*.

That final speech as Balthasar is echoed in Q2, and in the first setting of F.[16+] But at the beginning of the scene, both in the character's first entrance and in the headings of his two speeches, it is *Peter*.

This apparently implies that the role of Balthasar, Romeo's man, was played by the same actor who played Peter, the Nurse's servant whose last previous appearance was as he joked with the musicians at the end of 4.4, his speech headings there all reading *Peter* in Q2 and *Pet* in F—and his entry saying "Peter" in F, but "Will Kemp" in Q2.

I will not try to unravel the whole thing here, but I suggest that if you were to undertake the untangling of the role evidently designed as Will Kemp playing Peter, and follow it through where the name Peter leads and where the saucy and clownish servingman manner reappears as "Servingman" or "Servant," you are likely to come to the conclusion that Will Kemp once played Peter, Romeo's man Balthasar, Capulet's unnamed illiterate servant in 1.2, and quite possibly either Samson or Gregory, the bawdy servant jokers from the Capulet household who speak the play's first lines.

The final scene of *As You Like It* is so well prearranged by Rosalind that there is relatively little room for surprise. Substantial portions of the scene are in fact given over to Rosalind (as Ganymede) rehearsing with other characters the promises and conditions that have been set up for the resolution of the main relationships, and Rosalind (as Rosalind, now freed of her doubling as Ganymede) presiding over their completion. This may heighten the suspense for the assembled characters, but the audience has been in on the major secret since the last part of act 1 and has no grounds for doubting that it will all work out or for wondering how. Shakespeare brings about two surprises all the same, both of them gratuitous and rather outrageous.

The first is the introduction of Hymen as master of ceremonies for the assorted weddings. Nothing in the play has offered a precedent for the sudden intervention of a Roman deity, whether or not *ex machina*. Once it has happened, there is a certain appropriateness that falls into place. The figure of Hymen had begun to appear in masques and entertainments for weddings as a classier act than the more traditional Cupid (Hymen might accordingly be recognizable even without naming himself, which he does repeatedly), and Shakespeare's text neither requires nor disallows taking him here as either the Roman god of marriage or a courtly masquer playing the role. In either case, he constitutes a clever solution to the problem of proper marriage rites that arises through the encounter of Touchstone and Audrey with Sir Oliver Martext in 3.3, is further glanced at in the mock wedding of Orlando with Rosalind/Ganymede (as Rosalind) in 4.1, and is echoed once more at the beginning

of 5.4 in the arrangement with the Duke to give Rosalind (if she can be produced) to Orlando in marriage.

If Hymen himself unites the couples, the disputed rules are completely circumvented by a resolution at the mythical level—and if this is a conventional Hymen from wedding or betrothal entertainments, nothing
definitive has happened, no harm is done, and no claim to made about
proper form. Shakespeare never presents a completed wedding ceremony
in any other play, always either interrupting it (as in *Much Ado about
Nothing* 4.1) or sending it offstage (as in *Romeo and Juliet* at the end of
2.6). In *As You Like It*, he plays around considerably with what constitutes
a valid marriage form, and creates a wonderfully ambiguous test case in
the mock marriage of 4.1.[17*] But be all of that as it may, who plays the part
of Hymen, whether he is taken as a real deity or as a member of the celebration, got up for the occasion?

Amiens is one of those who is mentioned as entering at the beginning of
the scene, but that does not necessarily mean that he stays throughout. No
lines are assigned to him during the entire scene. If Shakespeare changed his
mind after writing the opening direction and kept Amiens back, or had Rosalind seize him to escort her and Celia offstage when they exit, the play's
chief singer would be readily available to enter to perform Hymen's songs
and office when he escorts Rosalind and Celia back into the action. I think
that Shakespeare's design was planned and executed along these lines.

The other surprise is the entrance of Jaques de Boys, who was mentioned
in the play's first speech and utterly forgotten thereafter. Shakespeare makes
no attempt to explain how he happens to arrive in the depth of the forest just
in time for his brothers' weddings, bearing the remarkable news of Duke
Frederick's abrupt conversion, which is the simple solution to the exiles that
have been steadily accumulating from the play's beginning. Suddenly everyone is able to go home again, and the happy ending is complete.

That is surprise enough. But given Shakespeare's doubling tricks, there
is almost certainly another. Brother Jaques has never been seen before, and
the audience must wonder who he is until he identifies himself in his second
line. The reader, on the other hand, can see the stage direction "Enter Second
Brother"—but then is left to wonder who he *was*: i.e., since Shakespeare is
unlikely to have left this actor, who is evidently capable of playing a very
front-and-center role at an extremely climactic moment, unemployed for the
whole play up to this point. I suggest that the design is fairly close to the surface, though leaving no definitive clue. Who of the known but absent characters would be the most dramatic presence for the uttering of the portentous
opening line of Jaques' speech: "Let me have audience for a word or two"?
That consideration, taken together with a tendency for Shakespeare to have a

given role make reference to its doubled alternative, makes the best candidate the actor who previously presented Duke Frederick himself. If so, the resolution is doubly complete.

The dramaturgy of doubling provided Shakespeare with obstacles that were more daunting than the bareness of his stage, and difficulties in strategizing that were less easily manageable than a conventionalized acting style. Both have left us with problems of understanding arising from our unfamiliarity with his dramaturgical liberties, the absence of detailed stage directions, and our lack of access to his specific instructions to the players.

We have trouble because he did not. He was not concerned about us, and knew that he could count on his audience to grasp his spatial and temporal manipulations, and could count on his actors to express themselves gesturally in a manner that he could play with.

There was nothing he could do about the limited number of actors in his company. Or, to put it more precisely, there was nothing he could do about the *fact* of this limitation. This chapter has attempted to show that there was a great deal that he could do beyond adjusting to that fact. Having inherited the need for doubling, he managed to turn it into new kinds of imaginative inventiveness. Though he occasionally shrugged to it acceptingly, he just as often transformed it into a means to double significances, the creation of new forms of dramatically concretized metaphor, and the extension of the truths experienceable through the illusions of the stage. I suggest that in this dimension of his dramaturgy, perhaps more than in any other, he shows himself to be a master of his medium, deftly accommodating to the limits that were imposed, hiding the seams of his dramatic garments when that was the right thing to do, exposing them playfully when that worked better, and exploiting new opportunities to make a virtue of necessity.

Many of my speculations in this chapter are moot. I hope that they may be cumulatively persuasive even if less so one by one, and I hope still more that their unprovability does not obscure the main point. And that is that reading Shakespeare's texts in a way that includes an alertness to the dramaturgical possibilities of doubling will bring us closer to his compositional habits of mind, and always opens an opportunity for them to disclose aspects of his design that must otherwise remain hidden. In this department, as in the others already glanced at, I believe that close attention will show that Shakespeare was a masterful practitioner of a dramaturgy that deserves to be learned, and that Shakespeare's Shakespeare is immeasurably richer, more accomplished, and more satisfying than most of the alternatives that have been presented by editors, directors, critics, and commentators over more than three centuries of attempts to make him look good.

7

A GOOD PLOT, GOOD FRIENDS, AND FULL OF EXPECTATION

Shakespeare's plotting of plays and management of sources

What did Shakespeare think he was doing when he wrote a play? There is not the least evidence that he thought he was probing the ultimate secrets of the cosmos, or even of human life. There is no indication that he ever thought he was writing large poems in a superficially dramatic mode. He does not appear to have set out to produce studies in human psychology, or to teach moral lessons, or to subvert the dominant ideologies of his time; nor are his plays coded messages about the occult, or sly allusive critiques of contemporary politics, or allegories of Christian theology, though all of these have been alleged. So what did he think he was doing?

The few oblique, and fewer direct, references to plays that are embedded within those he wrote suggest that Shakespeare thought of his dramaturgical constructs in a variety of ways, which I will deal with in turn; but the most important governing notion appears to be that a play was primarily a dramaturgically enacted story.

"Story," to Shakespeare and his audiences, had various levels of meaning, most of which are still alive. The term shows up within Shakespeare's plays to refer to an episode, a career, even a personal life. Lady Capulet, promoting Paris' suit for Juliet's hand in 1.3, embroiders her praise of Paris by likening his personal qualities to a story: "Read o're the volume of young Paris' face . . . That book in many's eyes doth share the glory, That in gold clasps locks in the golden story." Hamlet, as he is dying, charges Horatio with the task of clearing his name from the wounded reputation that the recent puzzling and confused events will otherwise give him. He does not ask Horatio simply to vindicate him, or to explain what Claudius had really done, or to set forth the heart of his mystery, but merely "to tell my story." Hippolyta, at the beginning of the last act of *Midsummer Night's Dream*, remarks of the Athenian lovers that "all the story of the night told over, / And all their minds transfigur'd so together, / More witnesseth than fancy's images, / And grows to something of great constancy."

These examples all fall short of embracing the entire content of a play, but they share the interesting assumption that "story" does not mean fiction. Late sixteenth- and early seventeenth-century English culture does not appear to have been particularly fussy about rationally rigorous distinctions between sound fact and good fiction, and accordingly blurred the distinction we now regularly make between "story" and "history." Either fact or fiction could be called "history" or "story" interchangeably, and either could be creatively edited and embellished whenever it was retold, especially in the service of a moral truth that seemed more important than mere factuality. Sir Thomas Blundeville's little treatise on the writing of history, published in 1574,[1] advises the would-be historian to suppress the vices and misdeeds of otherwise admirable figures (and the accomplishments and virtues of historical villains) so as to make the result more socially edifying—the same sort of advice that was regularly offered to poets. For the play that ends with the verdict that "never was a story of more woe / Than this of Juliet and her Romeo," Shakespeare's principal source was a translated poem entitled *The Tragicall Historye of Romeus and Juliet*, whose translator offered a preface emphasizing what he claims (with amusing harshness, compared with both his own translation and Shakespeare's later adaptation) to be the moral lessons of the tale.

"Tale" is in fact used with similar ambiguity. In the last scene of *King Lear*, Edgar finally identifies himself, and responds to Albany's inquiry by saying "List a breefe tale," whereupon he swiftly recounts the barest essentials of what we have seen him doing over the previous three acts, adding a quick account of Gloucester's demise to round off (for us as well as for Albany) that previously undisclosed part of the plot. "Tale" is here the factual account of his adventures, the publicly unobserved history of his recent life: the story of Gloucester's tragic life and death since Albany lost track of him.

One more significant datum may be useful. At the end of the Induction to *The Taming of the Shrew*, Sly—the disoriented beggar who is set up as a Lord suffering from amnesia—is told that his players will entertain him with "a pleasant Comedie . . . a play." Sly, starting to enjoy his new role as a Lord, replies "Marrie I will let them play, it is not a Comontie, a Christmas gambold, or a tumbling tricke?" He seems to mean something like "a farce, a skit, or a bit of acrobatics," i.e., forms of entertainment familiar at fairs and common enough in the festivities of wealthy houses but falling short of what we would call a *play*.[2*] The answer is "No my good Lord, it is more pleasing stuffe. . . .It is a kinde of history." It turns out to be, of course, *The Taming of the Shrew*, which is "a kind of history" in that it is a dramatic entertainment that goes beyond skit, farce, or tumbling display by being structured as a story. The representation of this "kind of history" is evidently what differentiates what we would call a play from alternative forms of other public entertainment.

The early editions' titles mingle the variant terms: the Quartos' *The Tragedy of King Richard the Second* becomes *The Life and Death of King Richard the Second* in the Folio text (where it is listed among the "Histories" in the table of contents); the Q *The True Chronicle History of the Life and Death of King Lear* is in the Folio *The Tragedie of King Lear*; the Q1 *The History of Henrie the Fourth; With the battell at Shrewsburie, between the King and Lord Henry Percy, surnamed Henrie Hotspur of the North* appears in F as *The First Part of Henry the Fourth, with the Life and Death of Henry Sirnamed Hotspurre*; F's *The Tragedie of Hamlet, Prince of Denmarke* had been Q's *The Tragicall Historie of Hamlet Prince of Denmarke*;[3] and the last of the Folio's comedies is *The Winter's Tale*. The Epilogue to *Henry IV, Part 2* in the Folio advertises the subsequent *Henry V* with "our humble Author will continue the Story . . .," and act 5 of *Henry V* itself begins and ends with similar references to "the Story."

Three dimensions worth noticing arise from this sketch of considerations, even if we may not assume that Shakespeare was responsible for all the variants in the titles. One is that in general usage, it appears that history and story and tale were roughly equivalent, and that "tragedy" and "life and death" were equivalent subdivisions of the more comprehensive category of history/story/tale, with "comedy" as an alternative subdivision. The second is that what we think of as the Play was normally conceived as the history/story/tale that was dramaturgically delivered. The third is that the locus of the play's significance, whether or not it dealt with matters of historical fact, apparently lay in the trajectory of the story itself, as it appealed to a level of satisfaction, or truth, or appropriateness, that lay beyond the reach of chronicles' purported factuality or the authority of antecedent fictions. The play's the thing insofar as it makes the story come to life.

The story that is brought to life by a play may be, somewhat indifferently, fact or fiction or a combination of the two. Restoration dramatists had a bias toward nonfiction as the foundation of serious dramatic plots, and a preference for historical accuracy in plays drawn from historical material. Shakespeare's generation was not so conservative, but evidently liked what we now frequently call "true stories," and valued them for their historicity. Sensational news events were written up in ballad form and hawked successfully in the streets of London; Bottom is firmly in a popular mode when he contemplates having Peter Quince write a ballad of his amazing "dream" at the end of 4.1. But a ballad is significantly different from what was later insisted upon as objective reporting or strict fidelity to sources, and a title like *The True Chronicle Historie of King Leir and His Three Daughters* (or Shakespeare's decidedly different remake, billed as *The True Chronicle History of the Life and Death of King Lear*) was appealing to an audience with an established tolerance for inventiveness within historical recounting, like modern "docudrama." Whatever kind of truth is in question in these titles, it is apparently not a devoted faithfulness to the chronicles, or even an assurance that the chronicles themselves were reliable in representing the central figure as historically real. Shakespeare manipulated chronicle material much as he did overt fictions, and historical accuracy was apparently of trivial importance by comparison with effective story.[4!]

Hamlet, a play unusually rich with reflections about plays, offers a case study that illuminates two sides of the question of the kind of truth that may be found in a story.

The first appears when Hamlet initiates his plan to test Claudius for a sense of guilt. He asks, as the players are leaving 2.2, "can you play the murther of *Gonzago*?" We tend to read this (and modern editors tend to print it) as if it were "can you play *The Murder of Gonzago*?"—but that is not what it says.[5+] Hamlet asks whether they can enact an incident, not a text. When Claudius asks about it in the course of the performance in 3.2, Hamlet's reply seems to indicate that he supposes it to be based on true history: "This Play is the Image of a murder done in *Vienna*," subsequently adding that "the Story is extant and writ in choyce Italian." The play is the image of what once happened in Vienna, as recorded in an eloquent story. The play is expected to replicate the happening effectively.

"Effectively" takes us to the other side of the matter. Hamlet's plan of entrapment is based on his observation in 2.2 that through an equally eloquent dramaturgy—"the very cunning of the scene"—guilty people, in real life, have been struck to the soul enough to confess their misdeeds. The truth of the image is measurable not simply by its fidelity to its founding story, or to the grounding historical event that it recreates, but also by its effect. In *Henry VI, Part 3* (1.4), York says of his son's death "And if thou tell'st the heavy story right, / Upon my soul, the hearers will shed tears." Hamlet's instructions to the players at the beginning of 3.2 amount to a generalization of the same principle with respect to "the purpose of playing, whose end both at the first and now, was and is, to hold as 'twere the mirror up to nature: to show virtue her feature, scorn her own image, and the very age and body of the time his form and pressure." The "nature" in question is evidently located in the audience's instinct for recognizing palpable, and *pulpitatable*, truth when it is imaged more clearly than the world normally affords, and the dramatic mirror accordingly shows us who and what we are.

The play that Hamlet calls *The Mousetrap* is the enacted story-image of a murder done in Vienna, and simultaneously the image of the internal story of King Hamlet's murderer. The truth of this "history" lies at the intersection between the sources of the story and the evocation of the audience's self-recognition through it.[6*] The mirroring effectiveness of *The Mousetrap* of course is proved not only by Claudius' loss of his composure and bolting from the scene, but also by the calmer uneasiness of Gertrude's "The lady protests too much, methinks," which conceals the degree of self-awareness behind it but clearly reveals that she has glimpsed her own feature in the play. Peter Quince's *Pyramus and Thisby* bungles both sides of the matter, and successfully misses both the intrinsic poignancy of the story and the sympathetic responsiveness of the audience[7*]; Shakespeare's *A Midsummer Night's Dream*, like the stories of the Athenian lovers, manages to be illusion and truth at once by presenting a story that is two steps beyond Theseus' rationalism and one step beyond Hippolyta's sense of evidence. The play's the thing.

Shakespeare employs a cluster of similar literary and dramatic metaphors to refer to subdivisions of the overall story, or to displays of its characters in action.

In *As You Like It* 2.7, Orlando's urgent quest for food to sustain the fainting Adam brings him into confrontation with the Duke and his party, where (once the Duke's kind manner has won him over from threats to gentle pleading) he asks them to search their personal histories for memories of better days and church bells and good men's hospitality and weeping tears of pity. The Duke quietly, and with much understatement, acknowledges that these things are all familiar to their previous experience, and that Orlando is accordingly welcome to share what they now have, just as he has shared the happier world they too once had. Orlando goes to fetch Adam; and the Duke, still making the best of his new station at the bottom of Fortune's wheel, remarks sympathetically to his critical philosopher, Jaques, that "Thou see'st, we are not all alone unhappy: / This wide and universal Theater / Presents more woeful Pageants than the Scene / Wherein we play in."

Jaques' memorable reply, beginning "All the world's a stage, / And all the men and women, merely players," sifts through seven ages—he first calls them "Acts"—of a human life. His agreement with the Duke that the world is a stage, a theater, should not mislead us into thinking that he agrees about anything else. The Duke never suggested that we are "merely" players. His statement raises the notion of the theater to a metaphor that embraces all of human life; Jaques' reply cynically reduces human life to a trivialized caricature, shrinking it to the size of an aimlessly constructed play with a series of unrelated parts played by actors of indifferent skill—just as Macbeth's burnt-out despair leads him, in 5.5, to portray life itself as "a poor Player, / That struts and frets his hour upon the Stage / And then is heard no more," and, alternatively, as a similar deformation of a story: "a Tale / Told by an Idiot, full of sound and fury / Signifying nothing."

When Jaques ends with a bleak sketch of the final act and the final role, "Second childishness and mere oblivion, / Sans teeth, sans eyes, sans taste, sans everything," concluding the poor human drama in meaninglessness, it is Orlando's cue to enter carrying the helpless but noble old Adam, and Jaques' view is decisively and wordlessly rendered inadequate. The Duke's view, vindicated in the same stroke, takes over again with his courteous and respectful welcome to the ancient servant. The story that is the play, or the play that is the story, has deftly refuted Jaques' charge of life's pointlessness. Macbeth's own story, and the larger story in which he plays a part, show us that meaninglessness is not something that belongs to life itself, but a function of Macbeth's having murdered his own meaning as surely as he had murdered sleep, turning his own story into one that no longer makes sense from the inside; Jaques' outside view is definitively refuted by the way the Duke's personal story embraces that of Adam.

The Duke's earlier statement shows him willing to see himself, and others, as being in a way actors in the universal play, but it is a dignified play that is to be grasped with sympathy, rather than a sort of pointless farce to sneer at, as Jaques would have it. The "scene" in which he and his companions are playing is at once the spatial location of impoverished exile in the forest and the story that is coordinated with that location, i.e., their life as exiles and outlaws.

A scene is a little story, or a large one, dramatically presented, just as a story can be either the whole play or some subdivision of it. Richard II, after learning in 3.2 that his Welsh forces have dispersed, hears a second dose of bad news from Scroop, and replies "Too well, too well thou tell'st a Tale so ill." After yet another piece of bad news, Richard has his own tales to tell, and cries out "For God's sake, let us sit upon the ground, / And tell sad stories of the death of Kings."[8+] A bit later in the same speech he shifts from the narrative to the dramatic mode, musing that Death allows a king "a breath, a little Scene, / To Monarchize, be feared, and kill with looks" before dispatching him. Scroop subsequently characterizes his final demoralizing report as "a heavier Tale to say."

Story, tale, scene, act, play are all roughly interchangeable as terms for a narrative or dramatic representation or one of its subdivisions, or for the real-life equivalents. Shakespeare tends to use the smaller-sounding terms (tale, scene) when referring to a smaller constituent part of a larger story, or when looking at the full story from a perspective that diminishes its importance. Terms like "act" and "scene" within Shakespeare's plays appear to mean the natural larger and smaller phases of a dramatic story's development, rather than the formal divisions of the text into acts and scenes: these divisions, though useful for locational reference, are rather artificial, sometimes quite inappropriate and misleading, and almost certainly not part of Shakespeare's design.[9*]

There are other terms that Shakespeare used to refer to what he wrote. One of them is *pageant*. In the general usage of the time, a "pageant" is more often a display than an enactment. In the most literal sense, it could be a *tableau vivant*, a spectacle that is represented with live actors (but without action), a human still life depicting an important historical moment or a moral emblem or some other subject that could be handled approximately as well by a skilled painter or sculptor. Such pageants—the ancestors of the "floats" of modern parades—were displayed in London Lord Mayor's shows of the sixteenth century, and continued to be referred to as "pageants" after they began to incorporate a tiny amount of action and a few spoken lines, as in the intriguing example presented in 1590.[10*] Shakespeare's use of the term normally suggests a significant visual display that may have some dialogue and action to support its meaning, but might be almost as independent of such support as a dumb show.

The Duke's choice of this term, as he reflects philosophically on Orlando's and his own circumstances and attendant stories, is apt, and although he makes it interchangeable with "scene" ("more woeful Pageants than the Scene / Wherein we play in") the addition of "pageant" seems to characterize the *type* of scene appropriately. Hardly anything with any practical consequences for his own story takes place through what we see of the Duke's life in the forest. He does not plan how to regain his dukedom, or try to find out what has become of his daughter, or even attempt to organize his followers. His life is on hold, displayed in his very unducal forest uniform of Kendal green and in his philosophical resignation to what it stands for in contrast to what he once had. It is more of a static pageant than a substantive developmental part of his story, and this sense of mere display may have influenced Shakespeare's choice of language in referring to it. The little cameo account of Orlando tending the faded Adam, as a reprise of the brief scene of its recent enaction, functions more as a pageantic display of neediness and devotion than as an action that makes a difference in the overall scheme of things (we never see Adam again after this scene). The language given the Duke by Shakespeare may reflect this sense of a representation that has much to do with what the play shows but little to do with what it *pursues*.

Similarly, at the end of 3.4 Corin invites Rosalind–Ganymede and Celia–Aliena to observe Silvius' wooing of Phebe: "If you will see a pageant truly played / Between the pale complexion of true Love / And the red glow of scorn, and proud disdain, / Go hence a little, and I shall conduct you." He does not say "Silvius and Phebe." He abstracts them to Love and Disdain, thus objectifying them as a conventionalized representation of a stylized Petrarchan situation: the languishing lover pursuing his aloof and rebuffing beloved, a combination that had begotten many an Elizabethan sonnet. It might as well be presented as a token pageant, as neither party could be likely to find anything new to say; but Shakespeare has Rosalind change the terms in the scene's final line: "I'll prove a busy actor in their play." It is her intervention that changes the episode from a mere stalemated pageant to a *play*, a plot happening that releases their arrested development into a winding path to their eventual marriage. Puck similarly summons Oberon in *A Midsummer Night's Dream* early in 3.2 to observe the behavior of the deranged Athenian lovers (whose action in this scene, while wonderfully entertaining as a display of love-madness, does nothing whatever to advance the plot): "Shall we their fond Pageant see? / Lord, what fools these mortals be!"

The play remains the thing. The pageants that go into its displays of its situations, and the scenes that advance its complications and resolutions, are peculiarly dramaturgical components by which it is a play rather than merely a story, but it is the story at the heart of it all that carries the chief burden. A genuine play is not a pageant or a scene or a show, but a kind of history. And therefore the story line must be made clear.

Like many plays of the sixteenth century, the traveling troupe's version of the murder of Gonzago begins with an elaborate dumb show, in which the actors silently mime the outlines of the plot (Ophelia correctly refers to it as a "shew" that "imports the Argument of the Play"). The dumb show[11] was a once-popular dramaturgical device that fell out of fashion before Shakespeare began writing plays, though it did not disappear entirely: its appearance in the play at Elsinore is one of the ways in which Shakespeare establishes this play as being deliberately in an old-fashioned style. (Hamlet complains to the players, at the start of 3.2, about "inexplicable dumbshows," and his complaint is subtly echoed by Ophelia's puzzlement at the dumb show that opens *The Mousetrap*, as she wishes that someone would explain what it means.) This *Mousetrap* is not like Agatha Christie's, depending for much of its dramatic effect on hidden information and wily misdirection. All the major details are disclosed in the opening dumb show, just as (in a much sketchier fashion) the Prologue to *Romeo and Juliet* tells us the essence of the story before its representation begins, and as the Argument was sometimes prefixed to published plays. Shakespearean dramaturgy is full of surprises, but they rarely (and almost never during the early half of his career) are such as need to be hidden from the audience in the main plot line. The importance of the story did not become unfashionable, and remained at the center of Shakespearean dramaturgy even when the dumb show hobbyhorse was forgot. If the story was more or less familiar, that was apparently a dramaturgical advantage.

When Shakespeare and his contemporaries talk about "the story," they—like Hamlet and Peter Quince—frequently mean not the plot of the play but rather the sourcebook that originated the narrative on which the play is built. And that in turn reminds us of a fundamental fact about Shakespeare's stories: Shakespeare rarely invented them.

The modern insistence on literary originality had not yet come to be, in Shakespeare's time. There was little legal encouragement for it, because there was nothing quite resembling modern laws of copyright; and there was far less cultural encouragement for originality, because readers and audiences generally preferred competence, and competence was more easily achieved by following established and approved ways and models than by striking out on one's own. No one expected radical originality in literary or dramatic works. Faithful imitation was as normative in literature as it is now in learning tai chi, golf, the arias of Mozart's Queen of the Night, and the techniques of basic journalistic reporting. Successful imitation of excellent models (especially classical or modern continental models) was a praiseworthy accomplishment, not a pitiable dependency or a reprehensible poaching.

Shakespeare imitated others' stories, lifting them both wholesale and retail to form the plots of his plays. Out of all his nearly forty plays, there are fewer than five for which we have not located sources that account for virtually all of the plots' main elements—and it is likely that some of those were derived from sources now lost.

This of course does not mean either that Shakespeare disvalued plot as a dimension of his dramaturgy, or that plot was one area in which he showed no real creativity. Quite the contrary: the evidence already presented indicates that he thought of plot as the central dramaturgical consideration, and the ways in which he adjusted his sources as he appropriated them demonstrate remarkable plotting creativity and (even better) show us something about his values as a plotter of plays, an inventive manager of stories.

The relentless search for Shakespeare's sources has resulted in the identification of a surprisingly large number of texts that he evidently consulted in the building of his plays. In some individual plays, we can track the certain or probable traces of over a half-dozen separate sources.[12] Some of the candidates that have been proposed as sources are questionable: they offer parallels that might be mere coincidences, or details that might well have been derived from other identifiable (not to mention lost) texts. But when we insist on hard evidence—a specific small historical event that Shakespeare could not imaginably have invented independently of a particular chronicle that uniquely reports it, or unusual names that occur in one previous version of the story but in no other, or a complex story line that is known from only one pre-Shakespearean work and is replicated in detail in Shakespeare's plot— we are forced to the conclusion that Shakespeare frequently researched his story in three or four history books when one might have been enough, brought together two or three very different kinds of sources to form a richer plot than can be found in any of them taken alone, and felt free to make major changes in the source materials in order to come up with a better story.

There are many terms in literary criticism that are so central, important, and frequently used that critics mistakenly assume that they are talking about the same thing when they use them. Some procedural definitions are accordingly in order at this point.

By *story*, I mean the chronological report of the connected events by which a coherent happening begins, develops, and ends. The happening may be an episode in English history, or how a young couple meet and somehow make their way to marriage, or the narrative version of how a given person came to be what she is or of what took place in an important two-hour or ten-minute contentious encounter. The story may be rendered in five crisp sentences, or may take hundreds of pages to tell, but it is still the same story if the essential outline is preserved. When Peter Quince says that "Pyramus and Thisby (says the story) did talk through the chink of a wall," it is unnecessary to track down a particular version of that once-famous story: this detail is a regular part of its various retellings, including one that is five sentences long.[13]

A *plot* is a story as arranged by the teller of this version of it, and a *dramatic plot* is the story as enacted. The story as such is the chronological order of indispensably relevant events, beginning in the mode of "once upon a time" like its efficient exemplar in the Prologue to *Romeo and Juliet*: once upon a time, in Verona, there were two households that had an ancient quarrel, and . . . The plot, by contrast, may secure a more vivid and arresting beginning by following Horace's advice, plunging *in medias res* and picking up the earlier part of the story later through what the characters tell us about it. The *plot* of *Richard II* begins with bitter mutual accusations between Bolingbroke and Mowbray; but the *story* really begins with the death of Thomas of Woodstock, Earl of Gloucester, apparently by Richard's order, in that this is what makes sense of the Bolingbroke–Mowbray confrontation and underlies much of what follows: it is not dramatized within the play, but its presence is significantly felt. The plot of *Henry IV, Part 1* begins with King Henry's momentary relief that the civil wars are over, and his hopeful intention to turn the leftover energy to a common effort in a crusade to Palestine; but the story starts earlier, as the play discloses by reaching back to events depicted in *Richard II*, the return of Henry to England as Lord Bolingbroke seeking to be Duke of Lancaster (and perhaps something more) in order to fill out the *res* in whose *media* the plot begins.

In dealing with plot, I am dealing only with the substantive events presented by the play together with the earlier substantive events it remembers and calls to our attention as part of the story. Entertaining speeches or bright (or even moody) passages of dialogue do not belong to the plot as such unless they bring about some happening that changes the shape of events. Mercutio's dazzling account of Queen Mab in *Romeo and Juliet* 1.4 does not properly belong to the plot; the plot as such is put on hold while he carries on with his inventive display, which could theoretically have been inserted as appropriately into *A Midsummer Night's Dream*. Neither do *pageants* belong to the plot if the spectacle they present has no effect on anything but the appetite for entertainment (the final performance of Peter Quince's *Pyramus and Thisby* contributes only marginally to the advancement of the action, and the brief pageantic display accompanying "Which is he that killed the deer," which takes up *As You Like It* 4.3, contributes not at all), nor do *scenes*, if they do not make any difference in the flow of action (like all of the above, *As You Like It* 5.3, featuring two pageboys singing "It Was a Lover and His Lass," makes a contribution to the play, but does not enhance or adjust the plot). The task of plotting may include setting up the conditions for a pageant, a scene, a musical entertainment, a debate on the nature of satire, or a discourse on the formal evasions used by courtiers to evade the charge of "giving the lie." But although these latter may form a more or less important part of the play's overall accomplishment, they nevertheless are not part of the plot as such unless they belong to the process by which the story is moved along.

The plot is the story as rearranged, and generally *managed*, by the playwright in his serial presentation of the enactment that is the play. It is his dramatic fashion of delivering the story. The way I have chosen to use the term requires that I may not say (as many, who use the term differently, do) that *King Lear* features two intersecting plots, one gathered around Lear's family and another gathered around Gloucester's. In the usage I adopt (in the hope of greater clarity), I am required to say that *King Lear* has one plot only, and that it embraces two distinguishable but intersecting major stories that make up one more inclusive story. (If you prefer another critical language, please bear with me: I think this one pays off.)

Most of Shakespeare's plays are focused on one primary story and derive from one principal source. The titles of the tragedies and the histories generally indicate the focal story, and direct us to Shakespeare's point of departure in telling it. *Romeo and Juliet* depends on *The Tragicall Historye of Romeus and Juliet*, Arthur Brooke's rendition in English verse of Bandello's Italian story, and both *Richard II* and *Henry IV, Part 1* are mainly derived, almost predictably, from the massive and comprehensive *Chronicles of England* by Raphael Holinshed. Beneath the undisclosive titles of Shakespeare's comedies are usually central stories (although substories of secondary interest frequently eddy around the main stream) which are normally indebted to a specific source: *As You Like It* leans extensively on Thomas Lodge's *Rosalynde*, a romance-novella in which a great deal of sophisticated plotting had already been invested before Shakespeare made it his "story," including the Celia–Oliver and the Phebe–Silvius diversions as well as the fortunes of the title character.

All the same, Shakespeare's plotting took on further complexities that were not necessarily in the job description of writing individual plays. He added the adventures of Touchstone and Audrey, and a Jaques who interacts with almost everyone, to the already well-developed plot bequeathed him by Lodge's *Rosalynde*—not to mention various substantial changes in Lodge's scheme. *Romeo and Juliet* remains preoccupied with the title characters in Shakespeare's version, but although Brooke's *Romeus and Juliet* provided Shakespeare with a lengthy, ample, and adequate sourcebook, he nevertheless considerably amplified some of the characters, invented new and significant plot functions for them, and changed the arrangement of the happenings significantly. In *King Lear*, on the other hand, Shakespeare hardly devotes exclusive attention to the central character: his addition of the substantial story of Gloucester and his sons was scarcely required, and changes the nature and focus of the plot considerably all by itself—not to mention other changes made within the Lear story. *Richard II* is nearly as much the story of Henry Bolingbroke as that of the title figure, and Shakespeare turned to Hall's chronicle as well as Holinshed's to build his plot, and probably also to Samuel Daniel's *Civile Wars* and the anonymous play *Thomas of Woodstock*. *Henry IV, Part 1* is only in part about King Henry himself, and Shakespeare went well beyond what the chronicles could provide as he altered and amplified their stories to accommodate the antics of Falstaff and the tavern scenes and to encompass the life and death of Hotspur. In general, he did not approach the task of plotting as if he wished to get it over with as quickly and efficiently as possible.

Historical material may appear at first to require more plot shaping and to allow less tolerance for invention than fictional stories, but the difference is in fact not great. On the one hand, the chronicles were written much more in the fashion of stories than of records of fact, sometimes with overall thematic preposessions and influential intent; and poets and dramatists had already shaped some portions of the history into individual and memorable plots. On the other hand, while Shakespeare probably did not have the option of having Richard hang Bolingbroke for treason and remain king until old age, neither would he likely get by with having Romeo and Juliet raise a family in Mantua. Certain givens in both well-known history and well-known fiction were rather unassailable (the effect of Quince's play of *Pyramus and Thisby* absolutely depends upon this), but readers and audiences appear to have had a high tolerance for invention within familiar stories (whether or not they were labeled "true"), and Shakespeare could tamper with the less central historical facts.

He invented Gaunt's illness, his sending for Richard, Richard's visit, and Richard's formed intent to confiscate Gaunt's property, all of which are fit coherently together to make 2.1 one of the most important scenes in this revised story. He changed the historical York (who broke his staff of office and joined the Bolingbroke faction early on) to the highly principled and statesmanlike dramatic character who reproves Bolingbroke for breaking the King's decree of exile, monitors his movements personally, and functions as a reliable point of reference to guide us through Richard's abdication and the accession of the new King Henry IV. Shakespeare could also compress and rearrange a set of discrete events, that took some three weeks according to the chronicles, into the single scene of act 4, with powerful and intense dramatic result.[14*]

Shakespeare could, and did, pick up hints about adjusting and plotting these stories by reading two or three (perhaps even four) different accounts, and could make up minor story management episodes even if the main lines were harder to tinker with. But he was sometimes remarkably bold in his management of the received stories. The pairing of Hal and Hotspur in *Henry IV, Part 1* is utterly essential to the way in which Shakespeare orchestrates and focuses the contention between the royal cause and the substantial rebellion that challenges it. It is important to Shakespeare's design that the two are of about the same age. That is not what he found in his history books: far from being Hal's contemporary and youthful rival, the historical Hotspur was older than Hal's royal father, Henry IV. The interests of dramaturgy transcended the rights of history, or of any other story, when Shakespeare designed his plays.

A Midsummer Night's Dream is one of the few plays for which no substantial extant source material is known, so it is impossible to be sure whether it was all Shakespeare's invention or was built on a lost source or sources. Either way, it is notable that the plot is far more complex than it need be, and very decidedly dramatic rather than merely fictional. Two pairs of Athenian lovers seen through their comedic difficulties, quarreling royal fairies resolving their problems via amusing byplay, and the organization and performance of a hilariously bungled play, all coming to a happy convergence at the ducal wedding feast? Surely this did not all come to Shakespeare ready-mixed in a single lost text: it is specifically dramaturgical plotting with a strong flavor of Shakespearean expansiveness. And that (the wheel having come full circle) brings us back to *King Lear*.

More than fifty different versions of the King Lear story preceded Shakespeare's play. He consulted at least four[15] of them in the course of forming his plot, but the result was not a mere conflation of selected precedents: he did things with the story that had never been done before.

The most obvious novelty was his fusion of the Lear story with an analogous tale that he found in Sir Philip Sidney's *The Countess of Pembroke's Arcadia*. Sidney's *Arcadia* was extremely well known, and appears to enjoy the distinction of being the first work of English literature to be translated into a European language. The story of Gloucester and his two sons as presented in *King Lear* would doubtless have been recognized by various members of Shakespeare's audience as a borrowing from the *Arcadia*—the tale of the Prince of Paphlagonia (told by Sidney in II, 10), who made the mistake of trusting his wicked son while he abused and rebuffed the devotedly faithful son, and paid for his error by being ruined at the hands of the former to a state of blind helplessness from which only the loyalty of the disowned latter could rescue him.

Does this addition enhance the play? It is routinely observed that it supportively parallels the story of Lear and his daughters, but of course it is equally easy to argue that the play is weakened by combining two similar stories in one plot: one may see too much coincidence, and thus too great a strain on credibility. It is highly unlikely, however, that either Shakespeare or his audiences would have made such a judgment. The love story of Orlando and Rosalind in *As You Like It* is not rendered less credible by the inclusion of Silvius and Phebe; quite the contrary, Shakespeare's plotting seems to imply that such a parallel makes a romantic event more statistically probable, or at least enhances its plausibility and thus its credibility and appropriateness.

Accordingly, he spends little effort on getting us to accept the subsequent liaison of Celia–Aliena with the reformed Oliver. After Orlando and Rosalind have fallen for one another so swiftly in 1.2, and Phebe has tumbled abruptly for Ganymede in 3.5 (while Silvius has been proclaiming and demonstrating since 2.4 the power of his love for Phebe over him—not to mention that the Touchstone–Audrey alliance has been thrown in meanwhile), Shakespeare evidently supposes that another case of love at first sight will be all the easier to establish, especially when it rounds things out so symmetrically. All he has to do is to imply such a thing silently through a little stage business when

Oliver so gracefully and attractively presents himself to the two girls in 4.3, and then reinforce it via Orlando's wonderment at the news: "Is't possible, that on so little acquaintance you should like her? that, but seeing, you should love her? And loving woo? and wooing, she should grant?" and Oliver's reply, "Neither call the giddiness of it in question; the poverty of her, the small acquaintance, my sudden wooing, nor [her] sudden consenting: but say with me, I love *Aliena*; say with her, that she loves me" (5.2)—capping it off with Rosalind's witness, a few lines later, that "there was never anything so sudden . . . for your brother, and my sister, no sooner met, but they look'd; no sooner look'd, but they lov'd; no sooner lov'd but they sigh'd . . . they are in the very wrath of love, and they will together." Step back three (arbitrarily labeled) acts, and this alliance seems out of the question; but after romantic matching has become the principal preoccupation of forest society, the courtship of Oliver and Celia can be easily and convincingly short-circuited into place.

I guess that, for the original audiences of *King Lear*, credibility was increased rather than diminished by having two similar stories combined in a single plot, especially when their beginnings are enhanced by Gloucester's general lament in 1.2 (as he exits after hearing Edmund tell of Edgar's putative treachery) that things are falling apart all over, and that Lear's irrational repudiation of Cordelia and Kent is of a piece with Edgar's apparent unnaturalness. There is, however, one further factor, important in the evaluation of Shakespeare's plotting, that bears on the question of dramatic plausibility as well as on Shakespeare's use of his sources.

Shakespeare makes radical alterations in his presentation of how the connections of his source materials are worked out. I will return to this in the next chapter, but for the moment I want to emphasize that his alterations of character are a significant factor in the cases just discussed. Lodge's Rosalynde is a coquette, only gradually won over to the risk of serious romance, and his Orlando is a stylized suitor; Shakespeare makes them both winsomely spontaneous, reserving what Lodge had invested in her for the conventional Petrarchian Phebe and rendering Orlando tongue-tied rather than poetic at their first encounter: that makes a difference in the credibility of abrupt love at the parallel level of Celia and Oliver. Likewise, his grounding of Lear's troubles with his daughters in Lear's own irascibility and preoccupation with his dignity makes the parallel with Gloucester less artificial than mere abstract similarity would leave it: their different practical entries into their troubles, fortified with the difference between the flatly malicious Edmund and the patience-tried Goneril, creates a new dimension in what might otherwise be flat analogues. Character is itself an important side of the dramaturgy of plotting.

The importation of the Gloucester story contributes more to effective plotting than just this reinforcing parallel. On the level of practical story management, it offers a convenient way of bridging between discrete phases of both stories. The shift between the state of affairs at the end of 1.1 and the new state represented in 1.3-4 requires enough imagined time to permit Lear's knights (and to an extent, Lear himself) to try their hostess Goneril's patience to somewhere near its limit. Shakespeare knew that an intervening scene, involving a different place and a different story, would dislocate our sense of time (though not necessarily our sense of continuum) enough to permit Lear's story to be resumed at a later stage of development without our experiencing a continuity gap of the sort that he evidently wanted to avoid: he need only inform us that things have gone very much as Goneril had anticipated at the end of 1.1. A similar bridge is provided for the Gloucester story by the concentration on Lear in 1.3-5: we then pick up again with Gloucester, Edmund, and Edgar, at a more advanced stage of their story, feeling that we have arrived directly from Lear, just in time for the next major development in Edmund's scheme.

By this technique of separating stages of one story by inserting scenes drawn from another, Shakespeare was able to distribute the action of *Richard II* and *Henry IV, Part 1* over various parts of Great Britain and over several months of his sources' chronology, without missing a beat. On a smaller scale, he could also cover the gaps between developmental stages of the love stories of Orlando and Rosalind or Romeo and Juliet (unless he wanted to make a dramatic point out of a gap, as he does in *As You Like It* 3.4 and *Romeo and Juliet* 2.5). In doing so, he could make further dramatic points by inserting particularly apposite scenes.

Between the first two forest love scenes starring Orlando and the still-disguised Rosalind (3.2 and 3.4), Shakespeare places the first scene of the "romance" of Touchstone and Audrey, which consequently comes off as something of a playful parody. After we leave Juliet at the end of 3.3, anticipating Romeo's arrival for their wedding night, Capulet finishes planning with Paris in 3.4; Paris and the Capulets leave the stage near dawn (with Lady Capulet on her way to prepare Juliet in accordance with her husband's instructions), and Romeo promptly appears with Juliet at the upper window to greet the dawn, having evidently consummated their marriage offstage while her father and suitor arranged another wedding for her. What we see just before the Montague–Capulet troubles break out for the second time, with fatal results, in 3.1, is the sole children of the two houses accompanying Friar Laurence offstage to be joined in marriage. Romeo's refusal to be riled by Tybalt in the next scene is intolerable to Mercutio but not to the audience: we know exactly where he's just coming from even though we did not witness the wedding itself.[16+]

Such intermixing of scenes in *King Lear* makes it relatively easy to move Lear from the court to Goneril's household to Regan's to Gloucester's to Dover, and even to send Cordelia into exile and bring her back for her invasion of Britain with the French army, without ever rousing a sense of discontinuity or even of overcompression. Whether he could have accomplished this without engaging and interweaving a second story so that he can move between them to disguise the shifts in time and space and sustain our sense of temporal and spatial integration, is questionable. But as it is, he makes the continuity happen in the audience's dramatic experience. It is not absurd to suppose that the reason for Shakespeare's importation of a second story into that of King Lear—the first time in over fifty recountings that anyone had attempted such a thing—was motivated at least as much by the advantages to continuity as by the virtues of parallelism.

Unlike true parallels, which never meet, Shakespeare makes his multiple stories interpenetrate, well beyond the needs of convenient plotting. Gloucester is the linch pin that joins the two *King Lear* stories, but Shakespeare provides other trivial bits to make them seem to belong together: he has Regan mention to Gloucester that Edgar is Lear's godson, and allege that he was "companion with the riotous knights / That tended upon my father" (2.1). Gloucester seems to accept that Lear is Edgar's godfather, and professes not to know whether he mixed with Lear's knights, but neither point makes any dent in the rest of the play, which does not even provide for any form of recognition between Lear and Edgar to support this artificial connection. These are not genuine story elements but, like Edmund's gratuitous introduction to Kent in the first scene, merely localized linkages, just enough to establish a connection that Regan can exploit to the slight disadvantage of both Lear and Edgar, and Shakespeare can exploit as an untested but effective connecting of the two stories, as a sort of reminder that all the principals are interconnected and may the more plausibly affect or even show up in each other's stories.

Less superficially, Shakespeare takes advantage of the characterizations of Goneril and Edmund to bring them together in a liaison that serves both their ambitions and the plot. When Regan, who is presented as less bold and self-serving than Goneril, is widowed and thus free to court Edmund's attention, the two stories are joined in a set of dynamics that Shakespeare manages to arrange, through other clever plotting conjunctions, in such a way as to make the bad faction self-destruct. Goneril murders Regan because of her jealous possessiveness of Edmund, jeopardized by Regan's obvious intent to take advantage of her widowhood (and Edmund's ambition) to advance him as Goneril is not yet free to do; Goneril dies by her own hand upon the discovery that her husband Albany has found out what she is up to—which in turn derives from Oswald's attempt to capitalize on the bounty placed on

Gloucester's head on account of his aid to Lear, which gets Oswald killed and puts Edgar in possession of Goneril's letter to Edmund, which in turn sponsors not only Albany's awareness of Goneril's treachery but also the final showdown between Edmund and Edgar.

Shakespeare's plotting through all of this is as intricate and complex as the last sentence, and more readily intelligible. And it is all his own: his sources offered no suggestions about how to combine two stories that had never before been brought together. However liberal his dramaturgy allowed him to be about time and space, he tended to take few such liberties with the plot connections of his own versions of his story or stories. He did not usually ask his audience to pretend that somehow this or that state of affairs has come about. He made it happen, either before their very eyes or in well-advertised offstage segments of development.

The most stunning example of Shakespeare's independence of his source stories, and the most striking example of his originality in plotting, is also to be found in *King Lear*.

Those post-Shakespeareans who knew the Lear story only from Shakespeare were evidently disturbed about the cruel injustice of his ending, and may have been unaware that this was Shakespeare's deliberate revision of a gentler tale that he had inherited. Nahum Tate's 1681 revision of the play catered to the more decorous taste of his age: Lear survives along with Cordelia, who is romantically linked with Edgar. For more than a century, Shakespeare's *King Lear* did not appear on English stages: Tate's cosmeticized version was substituted. Samuel Johnson testified that Shakespeare's ending had so bothered him that he could not bring himself to reread it until he eventually produced an edition of Shakespeare. We moderns, used to brutality and carnage in our entertainment diet, may wonder patronizingly at the squeamishness of the eighteenth century in this regard, but even we need only a little reflection to realize that Shakespeare's *King Lear* ends with a great deal of gratuitous devastation. It is not fair. Far from delivering poetic justice, it is neither just nor poetic. No one should sneer at either Tate or Johnson for wanting a more satisfactory conclusion.

I do not know whether either Tate or Johnson knew any other versions of the Lear story (though I guess that they had both read at least Spenser's brief retelling), but Shakespeare's audience did. They had not read all of the fifty-plus versions that preceded Shakespeare, but the general story was evidently well known, to judge from its frequency of appearance and the glancing allusion to it in 1590 by Thomas Fenne, who evidently assumes that his readers will know the general outline of the Lear story as "but a tragicall history of Leyr, sometime King of this land, which is so sufficiently set down and made manifest in their English Chronicles" (though not yet, as far as we know, in any play).[17] *The True Chronicle Historie of King Leir*, authorship unknown, was produced by the Queens Men and Sussex's Men in 1594[18] and was published in 1602. Shakespeare's audience knew what to expect.

But they were wrong. The cleverest among them may already have caught on to Shakespeare's tendency to deliver dramatic surprises, on an increasingly large scale, but even they could not have anticipated what Shakespeare was going to do with this well-known story.

All of the versions of the Lear story before Shakespeare end with Lear being restored to his throne. When he dies peacefully, years later, Cordelia succeeds him. Shakespeare teases us with hints of that approaching ending as Cordelia is gradually revealed as coming with the posse, in the form of the French army, to rescue her father. Lear recovers his sanity and station under her ministrations. The local forces are in considerable disarray on account of the Goneril–Edmund–Regan triangle and the indecisiveness of Albany. At the beginning of 5.2, Lear and Cordelia parade across the stage with their troops. *All* the dramatic signals are green for the traditional victory of the Lear–Cordelia side. When we hear the battle noises in the middle of 5.2, climaxed by the trumpet call for retreat, we *know* that Lear's side has won, because it has always been so.

And that is exactly where Shakespeare meant to place us, so that Edgar's simple report, "King Lear hath lost, he and his daughter tane," can be as devastating as possible.

The modern reader expects this, because Shakespeare's version of the story is now the only one that is widely known. But put yourself in a seat at the Globe on opening day, and try to imagine the shock waves sent out from Edgar's announcement. This cannot be; this will not do; this is outrageous! And so it deliberately was. The coherent buildup toward the traditional ending has been abruptly shattered, and our distress is part of Shakespeare's design. And this is only stage one of a great reversal: schooled by this numbing surprise, we are now to be confronted with the unprecedented, unjust, unacceptable, brutal, and nearly unimaginable murder of Cordelia, and Lear's unanticipatable relapse into the craziness in which he dies. Shakespeare has set us up to expect a repeat of the traditional story so that he might wreck this expectation spectacularly.

His plotting relied on borrowed sources, but he was by no means confined to what they told him. Like most accomplished story tellers, he cribbed from what was available but always had his own adjustments to make, always passed on a story interestingly different from the versions he knew. Not all audiences thought his version simply better; but it is difficult to deny that they are dramatically more ambitious and more effective, once one learns to receive them according to Shakespearean dramaturgical principles.

What values guided Shakespeare's adjustments of his stories and his structuring of their plots?

Some are already apparent from the examples I have given. Shakespeare likes to establish *personal interconnections among the various roles*, and he takes trouble to see to it that *events are brought into close relationship with one another*, creating and sustaining a momentum as well as creating a sense of enhanced coherence.

He also tends to build his stories on *the personal projects of the major characters*, informing us amply about what they want and how they will (and will not) pursue it as they collide with the cross-purposes of other roles. He sees to it that our sympathies are attracted by certain characters and repelled by others (in this process, the *moral definitions* are important), so that we get involved and become partisans of specific ways of working the story out. In order to emphasize the character-based purposefulness on which the stories are built, I would like to attend to a couple of apparent exceptions, though most of my discussion of character will be reserved for the next chapter.

Fate is routinely contrasted with free will, mainly for rhetorical purposes: but fate is never the deciding factor in Shakespeare's plays. Gloucester, in 1.2, laments that disruptions in the stars are causing weird behavior on earth, including Lear's puzzling actions in 1.1, and now Edgar's unaccountable plot against his father. At his exit, Edmund scoffs at this evasion of responsibility. "I should have been that I am, had the maidenliest star in the firmament twinkled on my bastardizing." The cause of happenings in the human world is human action, which in turn derives from human character as it deals with situations that are often unpredictable, and often surprising. Fate has nothing to say about it. *Will* is in control, as Friar Laurence had mused in the garden but then failed to convince Romeo. What Gloucester blames on the stars should rather be credited to Lear's imperious anger and Edmund's malevolent cunning, as Shakespeare has Edmund himself remind us.

We do not like Edmund (though we may be impressed by his craftiness and resolution), but we cannot deny that he is right about the rules of the game. As the play moves on, various speeches attempt to account for evil in the world—stars, demons, malevolent gods, the deterioration of the cosmos from old age, organic disorders. All of these were either commonplaces or popular suspicions. They all ring false. All real harm can be traced to willfulness, sometimes operating through misunderstanding and sometimes directly malicious, but there is no effective room for fate in the equation by which the action is organized.

There is a good deal of talk about fate, stars, and inexorable providence. In *King Lear* there is talk about astrological conjunctions that make people who they are, adultery that begets unnatural progeny, and gods who kill us for their sport. In "That Old Black Magic," the addressee is said to be "the mate that Fate had me created for." It all amounts roughly to the same thing. The projection of outside forces that cause our situations and govern our behavior is the work of an imagination that "gives to airy nothing a local habitation and a name," in the words of Theseus at the start of the last scene of *A Midsummer Night's Dream*.

Shakespeare made Edmund "rough and lecherous," just as he made Kent heroically loyal. Apart from dramaturgical convenience, there is no other explanation for either of these, just as there is no explanation for why Albany finds out Edmund's treachery just in time to save Britain, while Edmund has a change of heart just a bit too late to save Cordelia. It is a truth of life as well as of drama that the comic and the tragic may differ only by a small margin of timing. Unless we appeal to Shakespeare's power to determine just what happens, and how, and what is more appropriate in the design of a given play, there is no use asking why. Let the characters speculate as they will, some things just happen. Shakespeare accordingly often makes things just happen. The drama lies not in their happening, as if human lives are grist for the mill of inexplicable machinery either run amok or managed by inscrutable higher powers, but in the ways in which characters respond to what the routinely chance happenings of the world present to them.

Romeo and Juliet may seem to sing a different tune. The Prologue speaks of the "fatal loins" of the Capulets and Montagues, and calls the lovers "starcrossed." At the end of 1.4, Romeo is apprehensive about "Some consequence yet hanging in the stars" that will lead to his death, but bravely faces it, and "he that hath the steerage of my course" is invited to take charge. When, in 3.1, he realizes that Tybalt is dead, he exclaims "O I am Fortune's fool!" When, in 5.1, he learns of Juliet's death and burial, his first response is "Then I defie you Stars." At the end of his final speech (5.3), Romeo still talks of "the yoke of inauspicious stars," and calls once more upon the one who steers his course—now a "bitter conduct," an "unsavory guide," and a "desperate Pilot," crashing Romeo's bark on the rocks. Even Friar Laurence gets into the act, telling the newly wakened Juliet that "A greater power than we can contradict / Hath thwarted our intents," while the Prince has an even more doubtful theological opinion, telling Capulet and Montague that "Heaven finds means to kill your joys with Love."

The most searching theory of how it works in *Romeo and Juliet* lies not in the decorative references to Fate, but in the musings of Friar Laurence when we first meet him in 2.3, philosophizing on a flower that can be medicinal or poisonous, depending on how it is used. Romeo has apparently just entered in the background,[19+] unseen by the Friar, but obliquely glossed by his moralizing application of the lesson to the human world:

> Two such opposed Kings encamp them still
> In man as well as Herbs, grace and rude will:
> And where the worser is predominant,
> Full soon the Canker death eats up that Plant.

It is probably unnecessary to catalogue the instances in which Friar Laurence subsequently chides Romeo for his haste, his bullheadedness, his lack of restraint, his self-destructive impetuousness. But Shakespeare sees to it that, whatever may have happened spontaneously and by chance between Romeo and Juliet, and whatever the impediments may be to their happy resolution, the story and the plot unfold according to what they do about it. Laurence's cooperation is weakly motivated, considering his misgivings, but is indispensable to the plot and is thus dramaturgically decreed. But the driving force, as often resisted as abetted by the Friar, is the lovers' headstrong urgency, which comes from within rather than from without.

At the key turning point in 3.1, Shakespeare goes beyond the call of duty—and beyond his source—to show Romeo quite capable of realizing that he has no quarrel with Tybalt and that the latter's insults and accusations have no claim on him. After Mercutio's death, he changes his stance: he suddenly takes Tybalt's challenge seriously, adopts Mercutio's obviously false interpretation of what has happened, blames Juliet's beauty for having made him temporarily effeminate, and expresses his new resolve and project in words heavy with ironic self-evaluation: "Away to heauen respective lenity: / And fier-eyed fury, be my conduct now."[20+] He winds up an unfortunate fool, but not the fool of Fortune. Shakespeare makes him unmistakably responsible for what he has done, having proved that he knew better only moments before.

And so it remains for the rest of the play. The driving momentum, the secrecy and misunderstandings that lead to the hastening of Juliet's marriage to Paris, the precariousness of communications between Friar Laurence and Romeo,[21+] all contribute to the formation of desperate situations. But it is Romeo who buys poison and rides to his suicide at Juliet's tomb, and it is Juliet who decides not to go with the Friar but rather to stay with Romeo in death. This is not fated. It is brought about by the deliberate actions of those involved. We can see that their responses are just what we might have expected from them, but we are by no means asked to suppose that they had no choice. "He who hath the steerage of my course" is Romeo himself.

A Midsummer Night's Dream provides a test case of a different kind, in some ways more loaded in favor of outside forces. Oberon and Puck drug

Titania, Lysander, and Demetrius, and we see all three enter into bizarre behavior as a result. But just what difference does it make?

Lysander is temporarily plunged into a callous break with Hermia and a temporary infatuation with Helena. Demetrius is redirected back to Helena, his first love, and stays there. Titania has a crazy fling. And Bottom is, for a while, made to be literally what he has always been metaphorically.

In fact, all of this magical and pharmaceutical playfulness has to do with the interpenetration of the literal and the metaphorical. The Demetrius we meet in 1.1 is unlikable and fickle, having deserted Helena and insinuated himself between Hermia and her true love Lysander. This is exactly what happens to Lysander in the forest, under the influence of Cupid's flower. When Puck's application of Dian's bud has restored him to his proper love for Hermia, he wakes to discover that Demetrius has recovered his more natural self, and belongs to Helena once more; his own inexplicable crush on Helena, if he remembers it, has appropriately vanished.

"But Demetrius is still drugged!" my students regularly tell me, like Athenian mechanicals. Yes, Oberon daubed him about one hundred lines into 3.2, but the point is that he has been *restored* rather than merely arbitrarily transformed, as Demetrius elaborately informs us in the dignified voice newly bestowed upon him as he wakes in 4.1. The bungled homeopathic magic has come out right, and has brought him home. That is what counts, not how he got there.

Young men are notoriously fickle, the play reminds us, and neither magic drugs nor administering fairies *need* to be imagined in order to find temporary defections and permanent recoveries credible, just as we don't really have to postulate Puck in order to come to terms with the occasionally fruitless attempts to churn butter, failed batches of beer, clumsily spilled ale, or funny pratfalls mentioned early in 2.1. Young women, on the other hand, are jealous, and the undrugged comportment of Helena and Hermia is no less crazy than what goes on with Demetrius and Lysander under the flower's influence. Nothing goes on that requires an explanation from outside control, as Theseus aptly observes in 5.1 (having already observed in 1.1 that Demetrius' fickle desertion of Helena for Hermia was something that he had wanted to speak with him about).

Demetrius' recovery, which no more *requires* flower-power than his original defection did, solves the problem, and all four lovers wind up contentedly rounding off their dearest hopes, free at last to choose marriage with the right partner. The choices are older than the plot, having been in place at the ultimate beginning of the story, before Demetrius appears at the beginning of the plot. The lovers finally have what they want, and they have it because they have, despite temporary confusions, realized and decided that this is where they truly belong. Much of the fun is a result of the fairies' interference, but what actually happens is no more extraordinary than Phebe's abrupt infatuation with Rosalind as Ganymede. The backbone of the plot, and of the story it manages, lies ultimately in the deliberate choices of the principals, just as Phebe resolves her own story by choosing to marry Silvius rather than merely abiding by her earlier agreement to do so by default.

Rather than abstracting further generalizations about Shakespeare's plotting values from the evidence, I would like to explore the overall question by turning to *As You Like It*, because of its peculiar advantages.

This is a play that has essentially one source only, Thomas Lodge's *Rosalynde*, so we can watch Shakespeare's changes without having to deal with the eclectic borrowing he used in other plays; and the source in this case was a highly competent literary fiction, so that the story had had already been thoughtfully plotted by Lodge. Shakespeare's alterations are accordingly much easier to isolate and evaluate.

When Shakespeare's story is compared with Lodge's, it becomes readily clear that Shakespeare's inclination to establish personal relationships among his roles, already evident from the previous examples, is firmly operative in the ways he adjusts Lodge's established plot. Interconnections of kinship, friendship, acquaintance, and respect for reputation abound in Shakespeare's plays, and in *As You Like It* there is almost a systematic linking of major parts drawn from all these techniques of making connections. Lodge's two kings, the banished Gerismond and the usurping Torismond, are not related; Shakespeare's two dukes are brothers, thus compounding the wickedness of the usurper as well as echoing the Oliver–Orlando story. That of course means that Rosalind is not only the best friend of the usurper's daughter, but her cousin as well, and Shakespeare emphasizes this kinship repeatedly. Lodge has Torismond banish both girls; Shakespeare has Frederick banish only Rosalind, so Celia's decision to abandon the court and accompany her friend and cousin into exile all the more strongly affirms the bond of love between them. In Lodge's story, Torismond embraces the Orlando character upon learning who his father is; Shakespeare has Frederick react in the opposite way, souring on Orlando upon learning that he is the son of a man whom everyone but Frederick had loved.

You will have noticed that in addition to supplying a variety of closer personal connections, Shakespeare's revision of Lodge also creates clearer moral distinctions. Frederick disliked the universally beloved Sir Rowland de Bois, rather than (with Lodge) compromising his unpleasantness by being fond of that honored man. Lodge has Torismond punish Oliver's equivalent for abusing his brother: far from allowing Frederick take Orlando's side, Shakespeare his him send Oliver to bring Orlando in, alive or dead.

Even qualified moral taints are removed from Orlando when he moves into Shakespeare's play. In the wrestling scene, Lodge reports that the champion wrestler (who is not directly connected with the usurper, whereas Shakespeare makes him "the Duke's wrestler") has killed an old man's two sons in the ring, and in the final event the Orlando character kills him in turn. Shakespeare has Charles leave three sons in critical condition, but not dead, and settles for Charles being left thoroughly defeated and unable to speak. (It is also worth noting that Shakespeare sets Charles free from the sheer brutality in which Lodge had left him, endowing him with the moral concern with which he approaches Oliver in 1.1 and sparing him the deaths of the old man's sons. Even Frederick, though deprived of the mitigating grace of admiring Sir Rowland and disapproving of Oliver, is not allowed to do any permanent harm.)

Given Shakespeare's interest in binding events close together, we might well expect that a transition from the source story to the Shakespearean play would involve a closer rationalization of connections. In fact, nearly the opposite is true. Shakespeare dismantles much of Lodge's plot logic.

Lodge's wrestling matches are presented as part of a strategy by the usurping Torismond to distract his subjects from political questions and keep them from thinking of the banished Gerismond; Shakespeare gives no explanation for them. Torismond's banishment of Rosalinde is a calculated and motivated move, whereas Frederick's banishment of Rosalind is presented abruptly, with a scattered set of rationalizations and excuses that keep us from knowing whether he even *has* a motive, and is encapsulated in "Thou art thy Father's daughter: there's enough." Lodge gives us a period of flirting between the lead characters, while Shakespeare settles emphatically for love at first sight. Lodge's equivalent of Oliver undergoes a well-meditated conversion while he is in prison for abusing his brother, and his journey to the forest when released and exiled is to find his brother and beg his forgiveness. Shakespeare's Oliver goes to Arden with malice in his heart, on an ugly mission prescribed by Duke Frederick: his conversion is abrupt and offstage, and turns mainly on his rescue from a hungry lion through Orlando's gratuitous and heroic action in the name of natural brotherly love.[22*] The conversion of Duke Frederick (who is thus spared by Shakespeare from the death in battle bestowed upon Torismond by Lodge) is almost outrageously arbitrary, prepared only by the previous exaggeration of his tyranny and the flimsiness of his earlier motivations and by the spate of happy endings prodigally bestowed upon the residents of Arden. Dramaturgical license apparently makes it as easy to reform a shallow tyrant as to get him killed, and such a change is more in keeping with this play's tone, despite its audacious abruptness.

This curious derationalization is not confined to comedies. *The Chronicle History of King Leir*, played and published just a few years before Shakespeare tried his hand at the same story, spends a substantial part of the first two scenes establishing a rationale for the command performance in which Leir's daughters display their love for him. The problem is that Cordelia refuses to marry, and so Leir, with thoroughly benevolent intention, rigs a show in which Cordelia will acknowledge that she is ready to do anything he asks, whereupon Leir can match her with his favorite candidate. Shakespeare neither exploits this rational preparation nor alludes to it. He simply gives us the event, starkly and abruptly, with no explanation to make it seem reasonable.

Similarly, Shakespeare has the blinded Gloucester request that he be led to Dover so that he may end his miserable life by jumping off the cliff—not so that he may thank and encourage Cordelia, who he knows has landed there, or perhaps take his leave of Lear, who has been taken there by Gloucester's order, but just to jump, as if there aren't easier ways to do oneself in than a leap from the White Cliffs after a long hike. Goneril and Regan, in the meantime, move from their disposition at the end of 2.4, where Lear is to them a troublesome and self-willed old coot who doesn't know his place and can damn well soak in the storm if that's what he chooses, to the sudden revelation by the trustworthy Gloucester in 3.4 that "His daughters seek his death." We have not seen either Goneril or Regan in the interim, and no explanation is forthcoming for their unaccountable new murderous intent. It is a new axiom for the play, evidently adopted because useful and justified by being along the same trajectory as their other deteriorating attitudes toward Lear since the beginning, but at any rate not requiring—or at least not given—an explanation.

It is hard to avoid the conclusion that one of the principles of Shakespearean plotting was simply to stay flexibly in charge of the action, with limited accountability. Far from being logic-driven, his plays often dissolve the logic of his sources, and place the action within what may be called *a matrix of general appropriateness*, within which he can make connections and cause happenings merely by dramaturgical decree, without having to contrive a persuasive explanation or a detailed rationale. Shakespeare's audience is kept informed about the characters and their projects, and given clear moral guidance about how to take sides. Token motivation, like token spatial definition, apparently served as well as rationalized coherence in the task of bringing this about. Shakespeare could evidently get by with cutting corners if he made things turn out As They Liked It; it appears that he could also abbreviate the plot connections toward tragic disappointments, once he has established (or evoked our foreknowledge of) a pattern of mishap and thwarted intents. He made his audience see where the play was going, and his audience was apparently expected to be cooperative with his ways of taking it there. His plotting, like his other dramaturgical modes, counted on a measure of audience participatory imagination.

THERE IS OF COURSE more to be said. More will be said in later stages, some of which will inevitably qualify what I have proposed in this one. But this is enough for the moment: quite enough, I hope, to establish at least five main points:

1. that plotting the play (that is, telling the story in the eloquent and flexible language of Shakespearean dramaturgy) was one of the highest values—perhaps *the* highest value—underlying the composition of Shakespeare's plays;

2. that Shakespeare leaned heavily on the work of others in setting the main outlines of his plots, but combined, selected, modified, added, subtracted, and sometimes entirely redefined his sources, making the stories very much his own;

3. that Shakespeare's plotting strategies included the establishment of interconnections among persons and events (even to an unrealistically exaggerated extent), close linkages of events, and non-naturalistic manipulations of space and time such as to create a sense of relentless connected progression in the action together with a sense of the interrelatedness of its principal elements;

4. that Shakespeare characteristically generated his dramatic stories especially through the projects explicitly undertaken and pursued by the significant characters in his plays (including the turns of story that come about through cross-purposes and collisions between projects) and clearly—sometimes exaggeratedly—engaged audience sympathies to create a sense of emotionally plausible outcome; and

5. that Shakespeare deliberately diminished the role of rational logic in his storytelling, substituting for it a general sense of appropriateness though which he could move the story by efficient shortcuts in order to arrive at an accomplishment and a conclusion that would seem satisfactorily apt.

But what, then, is this guiding principle of satisfying aptness, if Shakespeare's plotting tactics are enlisted in its service? This too will require later qualification, but for the moment I think that the capstone of the plotting lay in Shakespeare's establishment of characters' projects and their claims on audience sympathies, together with the creation of apparently appropriate (though partially surprising) impediments to the happy ending to which the audience's partiality has been summoned, and the organization of an eventual but non-inevitable resolution either through the somewhat improbable (and thus relieving) success of the projects we have backed or through their non-inevitable but unavoided (and thus poignant) defeat by plausible causes.

Or, to put it another way, Shakespeare organizes the action so that we are soon attracted to some characters and alienated from others, we are quickly made aware of what they want, and firmly brought to take sides with the obviously more appealing plans and persons against the counterplans and persons (and inconvenient circumstances) that impede the resolution we prefer. The forces we experience as negative are usually identifiably so from early in the story, even if Shakespeare gives us surprises in how they come (either temporarily or decisively) to dominate the action; but the means by which they are overcome are usually even more surprising and occasionally almost whimsical. That makes it important for Shakespeare to keep up the illusion of a densely connected system of happenings while in fact using illogical dramaturgical liberties to manipulate the happening in the designed direction, with the flavor of fresh, though sometimes sorrowful, surprise.

Shakespeare's plotting of plays is, in its ingenuity, its license, and its unfamiliar styles of purposefulness, is closely akin to his other modes of dramaturgy. It makes ample use of his techniques for manipulating time and space, and accommodates to the restraints and opportunities presented by the restrictions of his cast. As my discussion of the matter has skimpily observed, it is also importantly coordinated with his dramaturgy of character—and it is to that subject that we now turn.

8

STUFFED, AS THEY SAY, WITH HONORABLE PARTS
Shakespeare's dramaturgy of character

When Hamlet is told that the players are on their way to Elsinore, he responds in a fashion that bears on the question of how Shakespeare dealt with the creation and management of characters. Notice how Hamlet refers to the players in 2.2. While Peter Quince called his players by their proper names as they assembled for the first rehearsal in 1.2, and then slipped into calling them by their specific roles as they began to walk through the play in 3.1, Hamlet does neither. He refers to them in terms of *types of roles*. "He that plays the King shall be welcome; his Majesty shall have tribute of me. The adventurous Knight shall use his foil and target; the Lover shall not sigh *gratis*, the humourous man shall end his part in peace, the Clown shall make those laugh whose lungs are tickled o'th'sere; and the Lady shall say her mind freely, or the blank verse shall halt for't. What players are they?" Hamlet cannot call the players by name, because he doesn't yet know which company is in question. But he can recite a catalogue of role types that are likely to appear in their performances, whoever the players may be.

Interestingly, Hamlet continues in this vein even after he is more adequately informed. Rosencrantz answers his question with "Even those you were wont to take delight in, the tragedians of the City," and Hamlet confirms his familiarity with them by greeting them as "good friends" about one hundred lines later in the same scene. But his specific greeting to a boy actor is again in terms of the lad's usual female roles, with only an oblique allusion to his own budding manhood: "What, my young lady and mistress! By'r lady, your ladyship is nearer to heaven than when I saw you last, by the altitude of a chopine. Pray God your voice, like a piece of uncurrent gold, be not cracked within the ring."

Shakespeare provided his plays with ample instances of kings, clowns, and outspoken ladies, but he did not usually write as if he were ordering his characters from a catalogue of established role types. He caused Hamlet to think in such terms, but he did not design Hamlet as one of them, any more than he designed Hamlet's soliloquies in imitation of the player's long narrative set speech which Hamlet admires. There is an inevitable type dimension in the majority of the figures who inhabit Shakespeare's plays, and I will attend to some of the more extreme instances shortly; but for the most part, he only *based* the design of personnel on the conventional societal and fictional types from which they were drawn—kings and princes and dukes, servants and attendant lords and ladies-in-waiting, soldiers and friars and romantic girls (and their smitten suitors), shepherds who might be seen at a rural market and shepherds who might be seen only in affected pastoral poems. It is what he did beyond those typologies that is most notable, and one of the symptoms of his interest in taking them beyond mere types is his tendency to give them names of their own.

Most of the time, the plays' speeches are headed, and their entry directions are provided, with personalized names rather than generic ones: Laertes, Hippolyta, Northumberland, Glendower, of course, but also minor figures like the servant Peter in *Romeo and Juliet*, the shepherd William in *As You Like It*, and the ephemeral Curan who passes by over about a dozen lines in 2.1 of *King Lear*. All three of these latter are named in the dialogue, but in other cases a specific name is gratuitously provided in headings although never heard by the audience. *Romeo and Juliet* 1.5 merely numbers both the servants and the elder Capulets as they speak (the one referred to as Potpan speaks simply as "2." and even the master of the house is momentarily reduced to "1. Capu."), but the first entry in 1.1 names one servant *Sampson* and heads his speeches accordingly even though his name is never spoken and he himself disappears after this scene; and the ruler who speaks and is addressed (and referred to) exclusively as "Prince" throughout the play first enters as *Prince Eskales*.

Personal names that might easily and conveniently, like the last example, be replaced by titles sometimes cling tenaciously nevertheless. In *Richard II*, the title figure enters and speaks as "King Richard" at the beginning of 1.1 and remains "King" throughout the scene, subsequently entering as "King" in 1.3 and the two scenes that follow—but otherwise his speeches and stage directions are always simply "Richard" throughout; and Bolingbroke goes by that name almost exclusively throughout the play's directions and headings (never "King Henry" or "King"[1+]). On the other hand, the relevant title sometimes takes over, as it does with Prince Eskales. Oswald is addressed by name three times in *King Lear* 1.4, but is otherwise unnamed: all his stage directions and speech headings are "Steward." In *Henry IV, Part 1* the role now usually referred to as "Hal" first enters the play in 1.2 as "Henry, Prince of Wales," and on three later occasions (3.2, 4.1, 5.5) enters as "Prince of Wales," but otherwise appears in stage directions and speech headings exclusively as "Prince."

If the directions and headings are mainly accurate reproductions of what Shakespeare wrote (and I think it difficult to imagine otherwise), they may be taken to suggest that Shakespeare tended to think of his *dramatis personae* more in terms of the play's specific story than in accordance with Hamlet's role types; and that while he often identified a minor dramatic functionary as "Servant" or "Messenger" or random "Lord," he leaned toward concretizing even these with gratuitous names. Even titles and offices are, after all, effectually surrogate names: the usurping Duke Frederick is named only twice in the text of *As You Like It*,[2+] and his older brother is never named at all; but the consistent use of *Duke* for the former and *Duke Senior* for the latter in all the stage directions and speech headings is the supporting equivalent of names in Shakespeare's systematic and personalized distinction of the two of them. Occupations too may be convenient identifiers that do not reduce roles to mere abstract types. The two carriers who open 2.1 in *Henry IV, Part 1* enter namelessly as such, and are only "1. Car." and "2. Car." in the speech headings throughout their brief appearance, while the offstage ostler is addressed simply as "Ostler" three times by "1. Car."; but the ostler is also apparently called "Tom," his predecessor is identified nostalgically as "Robin the Ostler," and the anonymous 2. Car. calls his fellow "neighbour *Mugges*" as they exit. The gratuitous personalization is far more conspicuous than the routine occupational labels. Shakespeare tended to personalize his characters even when it was functionally quite unnecessary to do so.

One further difference between Shakespeare and Hamlet is an occasional exception that qualifies the rule just sketched. Sometimes Shakespeare evidently thought in terms of neither the role name nor the role office, but rather of the actor he had in mind for the part. The Second and Third Quartos of *Romeo and Juliet* read "Enter Will Kemp" in 4.5, emended in F to a more story-correct "Enter Peter."[3+]

All the same, there are striking instances in which Shakespeare does seem to have shared Hamlet's sense of role types. "And let those that play your Clowns," Hamlet instructs the players at the beginning of 3.2, "speak no more than is set down for them."

The generic term "clowns" is one of the cases in point. In the most striking scene played by Bottom the Weaver in *A Midsummer Night's Dream*, his adventures with Titania in 4.1, his entrance is signaled by "Enter Queen of Fairies, and Clown," and his speeches are given neither as those of *Bottom* (as they are consistently in 1.2) nor as those of *Pyramus* (as they are occasionally in 3.1), but as spoken by *Clown*, in every case, including his final speech (even though it follows the stage direction "Bottom wakes.") Shakespeare is quite aware that this is Bottom the Weaver, who plays Pyramus, and that it is simultaneously Will Kemp, the most accomplished comic actor in his company; but he is evidently thinking of this part, as it reaches its full flower in 4.1, especially in terms of the generic type to which it belonged: the Clown.

Indeed, the whole cast of the Pyramus and Thisby play are registered as *Clownes* as they enter at the start of 3.1, and again as they exit some 110 lines later, though they are at least as differentiated from one another as the Three Stooges. Personalization is a special case of type rather than an alternative to it.

As You Like It's Touchstone is clearly unlike all of the above, except in his basic function as a provider of comedy. Still, from his first appearance (signaled by the direction *Enter Clown*) to his last, his speech headings are never other than *Clown* or its abbreviations. He is a clown with a difference: a courtier who capitalizes on his ability to parody courtliness, and obviously a clever comedian where Bottom is a dolt. Although he is called a Fool more than a dozen times, he is clearly not anybody's fool: in 2.7, Jaques praises his deft wit and envies his license, speaking of the advantages of taking on the same role and uniform to further his own satirical projects.

The introduction of this "clown" in 1.2 as a "natural" fool (i.e., as a mere simpleton) turns out to be a misnomer. He, unlike Bottom, is decidedly clever. Unlike the amusingly unromantic Bottom with the doting Titania, he even has an adopted life of his own in his relationship with Audrey, though it is crude and lecherous in keeping with one of the traditional properties of stage clowns. But he does not clearly have a name. The unique stage direction beginning 2.4 attends to differing levels of representation: "*Enter Rosaline for Ganimed, Celia for Aliena, and Clowne*, alias *Touchstone.*" Rosalind addresses him by that alias shortly afterward, and Corin does so twice in 3.2, but the parallelism in the stage direction suggests that Shakespeare may have thought of him as *playing* Touchstone, as the girls played Ganymede and Aliena: he may never have had a real name in Shakespeare's mind.

Lear's Fool has no name. He is referred to by other characters, and by Shakespeare himself in speech headings and stage directions, only as Fool. A corollary of this namelessness is that he has no personalizing traits: he has no reflective and revealing asides such as we get from Edgar in the midst of his Mad Tom disguise (Edgar is sturdily personalized, and is never called Tom in speech headings or stage directions), no private plans or aspirations, and no more dramatically evident grounds for his attachment to Lear than might be attributed to a cocker spaniel. He teases or whimpers as the dramatic needs of the moment may dictate, and is scolded or patronized accordingly. If he sometimes sounds insightful, he is scarcely credited for it as a thinker,[4+] and his alternations between amusing Lear and galling him show no more personal concern than one may expect from a detached heckler. His only recorded personalized trait is his pining for Cordelia, which we hear about for a moment but never see—and this too is not different from the response of an abandoned dog, and is without implications for the play apart from its mediating cue for a role-doubling. He is a case of virtually pure dramaturgical function, a type kept as a type, left in a state of partial abstractness for maximum efficient deployment as a useful voice.

Fools and clowns were traditionally exempt from participating in the main action in the drama of Shakespeare's time. They scamper about being silly and crude (sometimes ineffectually lecherous) and thus making the audience laugh, or being clever and satirical and thus making the audience reconsider; but they normally have no effect on the plot, even if they hover close to it.

The type spectrum that may be labeled Clown/Fool is dramaturgically endowed with unique and privileged properties for creating interesting side effects without making a serious difference in what happens. Shakespeare thus labeled and employed them. What we think of as the gravediggers in *Hamlet* are brought into 5.1 with "Enter two Clownes," and their subsequent speech-headings are "Clown" (or its abbreviation) and "Other." After "Other" is sent away, we have three bursts of irreverent song, one headed (in the midst of a speech labeled *Clo.*) simply "*Sings*" and the other two "*Clowne sings.*" The text never presents either of them otherwise than generically, despite the memorable vividness with which the lead clown is represented. In our seven-play canon, four of the plays have explicit clowns (or fools), another (*Romeo and Juliet*) withholds the label but provides at least one (and perhaps another) role that is clearly clownish, and one (*Richard II*) dramatically withholds clownishness where we are probably expected to expect it.[5+] That leaves *Henry IV, Part 1*, where clownishness is amply provided by Falstaff (and supplemented by Francis). None of our plays really interrupts the hypothesis that Shakespeare was habitually thinking of clowns as such.

An alternative role type with a totally different set of properties (and not on Hamlet's list, being less commonly employed) was the *bastard*. Shakespeare made substantial use of this type occasionally, the most notable instance being *King Lear*'s Edmund.

Like other dramatic bastards, Edmund fits the type both literally and metaphorically. The opening scene of *King Lear* offers us an Edmund whose father makes a point of his illegitimacy, but who responds with three brief speeches that are polite and are headed with his name; but in 1.2, where he shows his hand as villain, Shakespeare shows that his bastardy is not incidental.

The opening direction is *Enter Bastard*, and his speech headings are all *Bast.* until the last twenty lines, when on the cue of Edgar's "Some villain hath done me wrong!" his manner adjusts to the new situation with fake brotherly solicitousness, and his speech headings are *Edm.* In his next appearance, 2.1, he enters as *Bastard* and his speech headings remain *Bast.* for the rest of the scene. In 3.3 and 3.5, he enters as *Edmund*, but always speaks as *Bast.*; so also in 5.1 and 5.3. In 4.7, where his treachery makes him the Lord of Gloucester, he does not speak—but his brief appearance is ushered in as *Bastard*.

Neither the stage directions nor the speech headings were meant for the guidance of readers or members of Shakespeare's audience. They were the necessary appurtenances of a text that was submitted to the company of actors to be copied into individual parts for the actors to learn. They were not available to the audiences who attended the performances, and the play-book was deliberately withheld from publication. Their presence in the subsequently published texts is therefore not part of the dramatic happening, and is something of a historical accident—but they are nevertheless probably authentic clues to the dramatic *design* in the mind of the author who penned them.

I assume that the difference between "Enter Edmund" and "Enter Bastard," and the same shift in speech headings, is not intended as a shorthand instruction to the actor about how to comport himself at this moment but rather a casual reproduction of how Shakespeare was thinking as he laid out the play, and therefore a privileged glimpse of how he was thinking out his play. It *may* have been a directorial instruction rather than a news leak: Don John, the bastard villain of *Much Ado about Nothing*, is thus regularly labeled in the parentheticals of the play and is thus a bastard to readers from the start (and comports himself accordingly), but he is never identified as such, or other than the rebel brother of Don Pedro, until 4.1. Shakespeare had ample opportunity to communicate his design in detail during rehearsals, but may have deliberately notified his actors in advance. In either case, he apparently perceived the character he had named Edmund primarily in terms of a type-role of the Bastard, a type that was understood conventionally as a social reject and thus by reflex an antisocial disturber of the peace or, pushed further, a diabolical extreme of the same type, like Edmund himself.

Shakespeare was free to endow bastards or clowns with individual traits as well as the general characteristics of the type matrix, and he did so. Touchstone is unlike Bottom and both are unlike Lear's Fool, though they are all fool/clowns. As fool/clowns they conventionally make little difference in the main action; by contrast, bastards are always busy at the heart of the main action. That is to be expected: there is little point in deliberately postulating a bastard who is otherwise just as moral as everyone else, unless to correct prejudices about the irregularly born that made "bastard" a defamatory epithet and deprived literal bastards of legal rights.[6+] Clownhood is not a status that affects the plot, but bastardy is: bastards must interact effectually with those whom they subvert.

Bastards need not be individualized to the same degree as their victims (just as clown/fools need not have names in order to be effective), or indeed much at all. *Much Ado*'s Don John is made up of little more than sour melancholy and spiteful mischief, a sort of anticlown. Edmund has ambitious schemes, panache, reflective intelligence, even (at the end) a pitiable wistfulness. But it seems evident that in both these cases, as with the clowns, Shakespeare was taking his point of departure from the type rather than from the individuating differentiations that he created for them as Edmund and John (or Bottom and pseudo-Touchstone), rather than as Bastard and Clown (or Fool), whatever their speech headings may be. That is to say, bastards and clown/fools, like servants and messengers, have a dramaturgical job to do. They may be decorated with their own personal styles and agendas as it may suit the playwright's whim, but their principal dramaturgical importance is determined by what they can do for the play. Their types provide their driving force; their personalizations give them a useful versatility and intrigue.

Shakespeare's treatment of clowns and bastards is an especially overt example of how he regularly designed his *dramatis personae* in general. He saw to it that the important figures in the enterprise be apprehended in both typical and personal terms: we know in general what to expect; we trust this one, we like that one, we hope that these two get together eventually, and in the meantime we perceive the sourness of those who mean to interfere with what we want sweetened. He regularly gives us names and faces and specific memorable traits that hide, while supporting, his practical engineering.

His character design, that is to say, had two quite different agendas. He had to make a story work, and staffed it with roles that were recognizably suited to bring it about (thus the types of young lovers, tyrannical or benevolent rulers, loyal lords, dutiful servants, nasty villains, and bumbling subordinates, all in various slight shadings, as the backbone of the design, with a seasoning of clowns to entertain and well-placed interveners to cut dramaturgical corners where needed). He also wanted his audiences to be engaged, and sometimes arrested unexpectedly, and therefore endowed his principals with personalities that made them charming or intriguing, and gave many of his trivial agents a gratuitous vividness that made their departures mildly regrettable even after their business was done.

In terms of sheer dramaturgy, his first priority must have been to make the story work effectively. The technically anonymous chessmen through which the game is played must be given motives for their moves, and our interest in the game itself must be spiced by dramaturgical strategies that get us to care about what is happening. Any given agent in the story is a member of the happening, and must be delivered to us appropriately.

Appropriateness, in this case, may be dealt with in either of two directions. Reading Shakespeare's text, we are captivated by Juliet's sudden shattering of her previous poised courtliness as she asks Romeo, in the dark, if he really loves her; we wince as Richard falls to pieces on the walls of Flint Castle. If we go further in this direction, we notice that Shakespeare has made this happen: he causes us to like this one so much, distrust that one entirely, long for this to happen or that not to take place, care about the discouragements and satisfactions of fictional figures designed to be seen enacted by professional players for a price on a random afternoon. Shifting to the other direction, we think through Shakespeare's dramaturgical strategy, and wonder what he is up to, why he is teasing our experience in this particular way, what he has in mind in creating our loyalties and expectations and hopes and anxieties as he does, and how it all relates to the delights and poignant disappointments to which he so diplomatically brings us.

We meet characters full-face. Shakespeare rarely slides them unobtrusively into the picture, withholding their full force until later: his usual style is abrupt and strong, the way we hit Orlando in the opening lines of *As You Like It* and Sampson and Gregory at the opening of *Romeo and Juliet*, and the way we get a firm taste of Benvolio and Tybalt a few lines later and of Rosalind at the start of the following scene.

Shakespeare usually contrives to have a given role make a personal impression on us before we know what its dramatic function is. The ending of *As You Like It* is an outrageously conspicuous but in fact typical example. Shakespeare has ordained that the closure should be more generously complete than the forest of Arden can offer, and therefore needs to tell us that everything has been quietly resolved so that everyone may go home, having lost nothing despite having given everything up. Any messenger would theoretically do for the delivery of the wildly extraordinary message about the tyrant's conversion and retirement. It is entirely typical of Shakespeare to bring in, without any explanation whatsoever, the middle brother of Sir Rowland's family, and have him open his resolving news by identifying himself as such.

What I am on the way to suggesting is that when it comes to the presentation of characters, Shakespeare thought in a duplicitous way that he made no great attempt to hide. On the one hand, he had to manage the story, direct the experience, make the play happen to his audience as *feelingly* as he wished; and on the other hand, the conditions of making his audience have that experience included disguising from them, not entirely but at least most of the time, that such manipulation was taking place.

I do not know how conscious Shakespeare was of this double game, but there can be no question that it was an essential part of his trade. His audacity at the end of *As You Like It* suggests that he was well aware of how he was managing us, and quite willing to draw our attention to the artifice. The messenger role is accordingly explicitly invested with the maximum available decorative credentials: however out of the blue, the newsbearer happens to be the brother of our two happiest protagonists. Nothing in his speech, or in the scene's reactions, suggests a family reunion. Had he identified himself as a monk or a casual observer or a disappointed courtier, there would be no need to adjust the speech Shakespeare gave him apart from the arbitrary opening self-identification. This is a privileged glimpse of Shakespeare's dramaturgy of character, and it says that a needed or desired dramatic happening may be characterized, like a scarecrow or a Halloween trick-or-treat costume, in whatever way the dramaturge might suppose to be the most generally effective.

Effectiveness in a member of the *dramatis personae* did not require any serious degree of personalization. The resolving 2. Bro. of *As You Like It* discloses nothing of the preoccupation with Aristotle that had been bestowed on his equivalent in the Lodge source text, nor any other distinguishable personal trait. He does not express the play's customary reverence for old Sir Rowland or even show that he notices that his two brothers are in the scene he addresses. He differs from an anonymous messenger only in Shakespeare's arbitrary label, which he announces with no evident awareness of its potential social implications. He therefore provides a good occasion for making some distinctions in Shakespeare's dramaturgy of character.

Shakespeare seems usually to have organized the personnel of his plays in three descending steps.

As his plots were mainly borrowed from already accomplished narratives, he adopted them as already stocked with *roles*. A *role* is a part, a personage in the story, a figure who makes something happen or is subject to a happening or at least witnesses a happening. Theoretically, a given role can be dramatically concretized in any number of ways: it may be restricted to a few words of a messenger (as in the servant's response to Romeo's 1.5 inquiry about who that lady is) or elaborated into a small dramatic performance by an analogous messenger (as in the servant's response to Capulet's charge in 1.2). There are no rules for the personalization of roles; there is only dramaturgical strategy and whim.

Shakespeare's usual way of presenting a given role was in terms of a *type*, i.e., a dramatically familiar set piece that had certain preordained conventional properties that could easily be evoked by indications of social position, costuming, or behavior—cf. television sitcom dads, obnoxious neighbors, dumb blonds, ministers, manipulative kids, nurses, and rock-star wannabees. Many of Shakespeare's minor roles are simple occupational types, provided with typical functions and occasionally endowed with names. Attendants, messengers, gentlemen, officers, citizens, servants, even Lear's precious knights peek briefly into their plays, do what their types are automatically authorized to do, and disappear unceremoniously. Many of Shakespeare's more substantial roles do little more than enact a type: Duke Frederick in *As You Like It* is a tyrant and virtually nothing else; Lear's Fool is simply that. Even the major parts are types: but they are also characters.

I prefer to reserve the term *character* for the roles (whether or not they are also types) to which Shakespeare adds a more personal level of differentiation—a special way of speaking, projects and reactions that give the role a personal and moral dimension, and especially grounding characteristics that are gratuitous to the role and the type but give us a sense of personalized presence. Shakespeare may have thought of Edmund and Bottom especially in terms of the bastard and clown types to which they were conformed, but he wrote parts for them that concretized them into *characters* who project the illusion of individuated life.

Somewhat surprisingly, the same formula obtains for major operatives in a play as for casual intermediaries. Being important does not require being personalized. The decisive Prince of *Romeo and Juliet* manifests no individual life beyond an implicit wish to govern fairly, and Tybalt conducts himself like a machine driven by feud and protocol. Duke Frederick in *As You Like It* is a simple sour tyrant, unlike his counterpart in Shakespeare's source, but gets the play's needs done; his exiled brother, the nameless Duke Senior, is entirely ineffectual, despite being the theoretical pivot of the major resolution, and Shakespeare gets by with it all because he has made us more interested in subsidiary happenings that do not require the intervention of either duke. In terms of characterization, Frederick needs only to be "humorous"; his brother needs to be only a philosophical liberal whose policy may be quietly assumed as the appropriate happenings proceed under Rosalind's direction, her daughtership to him being inexplicably reserved to the final scene and then presented in a manner as token as his presence in the action has been. In *Hamlet*, King Claudius is left almost equally uninteresting despite his centrality to the plot: we have the arresting attempt to repent in 3.3, but that turns out (if we keep track of the whole happening) to be a localized moment, dramatically jarring but without implications for the rest of the story. Shakespeare manipulates his characters to make the play work, neglecting them or engaging them as the story provides or requires. He shows no loyalty to their inner life unless it serves the purposes of drama.

Hereafter, I will use the terms role, type, and character in this differenti-ated way—which is admittedly artificial and awkward, but may get us closer to the principles of Shakespearean dramaturgy.

This chapter began with a reference to Hamlet's response to the news that the players were coming. There is another dimension in that happening which has a deeper relevance to Shakespeare's dramaturgy of character. It is that Hamlet cheers up at the news.

He does so just after having disclosed to Rosencrantz and Guildenstern a state of gloom so powerfully sketched that it has become one of the most fre-quently quoted passages of the play, and so deeply pervasive that Rosen-crantz expresses doubt that Hamlet will welcome the impending dramatic entertainment, which of course results in emphasizing his spontaneous de-light. We have seen variations on Hamlet's gloomy mood from his first ap-pearance onward, and have been informed of several reasons for it. His depression is not news to us, whatever it may be to his newly imported and prying old friends, even if we may not have understood why he seems so deeply and thoroughly stuck in it. But his sudden good cheer *is* news: how can he light up so quickly from such darkness on the basis of this announce-ment? How is Shakespeare managing his key character in creating this strange and abrupt transformation?

The simple answer, which is close to being adequate, is that his being in charge of the play meant that he was free to define and redefine roles as he chose, even if they are also characters. He was not obliged to supply a con-vincing motivation or explanation. Adjustments in character might be as abrupt as changes in space and time. Hamlet responds with delight simply because it serves Shakespeare's purposes to have it so: he need not anchor the change in a rationalized transformation of Hamlet's state of mind. This was not Shakespeare's carelessness but simply his taking charge, dramaturgically akin to the rerationalization of his sources in writing parts of *As You Like It* and *King Lear*. Characters were his creation, and at his disposal.

A character, in this sense, need not be an important role. Capulet's ser-vants who initiate *Romeo and Juliet* 1.5 have the task of defining a new space and clearing the floor for the dance, and could have been left as a small band of functional stage hands, trivial roles restricted to trivial types; but Shake-speare gives them some cameo below-stairs dialogue as they grumble about the lazy Potpan and set up a later tryst with Susan Grindstone and Nell. This is hardly necessary for the play's workings: Nell, Susan, and Potpan are never heard from, or about, after this momentary burst of chatter. But it does assist the transition from the brooding conclusion of 1.4 to the party atmosphere of 1.5, it does provide a pleasantly distracting cover for the practical business of setting up the stage, and it gives us a glimpse of the larger world in which the key story is embedded. This is not *merely* a cover for practical rearrangements: the parallel and more amplified opening of 2.1 in *Henry IV, Part 1* gives us cameos of the bypassing carriers that are personally richer than anything we get in the portrayal of Mortimer, the pretender to the throne.[7+]

Role, type, and character are not adequate analytical categories, in that they do not isolate the elements of Shakespeare's major design of the action, or hierarchize his structuring of the story. That is because he was often whimsical in his distribution of characterization. He allows the engagingly characterized Touchstone to dominate the opening of the climactic final scene of *As You Like It*, and then suddenly substitutes the characterless Hymen to preside over the next phase. His dramaturgy of character was utterly indecorous by neoclassical standards, and refreshingly delightful to those who, unlike Philip Sidney and his heirs, do not object to the mingling of kings and clowns. Character is an unpredictable variable in Shakespearean dramaturgy, and that was apparently a liberty that he enjoyed, and made deliberately enjoyable.

To endow a role with character is not to remove it from the primary dramaturgical value of *functionality*. A personalization that is gratuitous to the extent that the role could function well enough as a routine type alone may nevertheless be a strategic piece of dramaturgy. The illiteracy of Capulet's servant, which he bemoans amusingly in *Romeo and Juliet* 1.2, is not technically required of the role (the role, in fact, at least as Capulet has projected it, virtually excludes illiteracy as an option), nor necessarily a property of the type (though common enough in household servants), but it is nevertheless dramatically and dramaturgically appropriate: it is an occasion of minor fun, and an indispensable functional device for arranging that Benvolio and Romeo find out about the feast and its therapeutic possibilities.

That Shakespeare had a leaning toward such specific differentiation even in minor functional roles is indicated also by the first scene of the same play, where he bestows the name Sampson on the braggart who later shows his true cowardly colors when the chips are down: since the name is never spoken, Shakespeare's audience was never let in on the tiny private joke he had in mind and probably just forgot to build into the spoken lines. Prince Eskales is thus named in the stage direction that brings him into the scene some ninety lines later, but the audience never hears the name, and thereafter, for the rest of the play, he is simply the Prince—a type who speaks and behaves as a type, privately individuated with a name in Shakespeare's mind and written text, but not really endowed with personalized character.

The Nurse is always the Nurse, her role being paramount in creating her eligibility for her important place in the play's action. Her type was not as clearly conventionalized as that of the Prince, though it was probably recognizable as something like "the Older Household Servant Confidante."

Shakespeare could probably have left her at such a type level without compromising his management of the play, but he goes on to make her one of the most vivid *characters* in *Romeo and Juliet*, endowing her with specific traits that personalize her memorably.

But a close analysis will reveal that this is less gratuitous than the characterization of Capulet's servants: virtually every one of her individualizing and personalizing traits has a dramatic function somewhere in the play. Her heedless garrulousness, established in her first scene, gives us good drama later in the play, as in 2.6, where Juliet pleads with her to get to the only point that matters, and in 3.2, where her rambling lamentation occasions a wonderful responsive performance through Juliet's having to guess at the meaning of the Nurse's distracted and fragmentary remarks. Her earthiness in her first long speech (1.2) reappears later to make Juliet blushingly display her innocence by contrast. Above all, her initial demonstration of her endearingly heartfelt devotion to Juliet (whom Shakespeare characterizes her from the start, though without further mention, as having clearly adopted in place of her own lost daughter Susan) earns her our confidence as the one who must reliably foster the forbidden liaison that the sheltered Juliet cannot pursue without sturdy help. Further analysis of the traits that Shakespeare has invested in her will show that they are virtually all functionally purposeful for the working-out of the play: these samples are only part of her dramaturgical makeup, but enough to establish the point.[8*]

What characterizes a character is usually not just for fun, nor for gratuitous personality studies, but for the sake of the play's needs. Whether the traits were invented by Shakespeare to anticipate the needs, or the subsequent uses of them inspired by their having already been invented, is indeterminable; but their dramaturgically convenient interconnection can hardly be denied. But there is an uncanny and utterly convenient relationship between functional traits and memorable personalization, and the critics who generally preferred Jonson to Shakespeare in the two generations after their deaths made an exception in the case of Shakespeare's characters: they, according to the critics, were the one thing that Shakespeare did better.[9]

One of Shakespeare's richest accomplishments in the dramaturgy of parallel types is his creation of Sir John Falstaff in *Henry IV, Part 1* (a character who resembles the Falstaff of *Henry IV, Part 2* and and the Falstaff of *The Merry Wives of Windsor*, but should not be confused with them).

Our first impressions of Falstaff are likely to be a sense of an irrepressibly fun-loving rogue with a quick mind and a supple and evasive tongue, whose nocturnal bunglings as a highway robber seem more naughty than wicked. As the play moves on, we gradually awaken, catching up with Hal's established perception at the end of 1.2 (which will probably have shocked us initially as being coldly manipulative, and perhaps inadequately appreciative of a jolly good fellow) to see him increasingly as an irresponsible bad influence, a knight without honor or serious morality, and a person quite unworthy of the trust of the future king.

Shakespeare's audiences are likely to have had a different sense of the unfolding of Falstaff.

The more educated would see in him the lineaments of the empty braggart soldier whom they had met in school through Plautus' *Miles Gloriosus*; the less educated would see the same thing as filtered through English dramatic imitations of that same type, e.g., in *Rafe Roister Doister*. In either case, Falstaff would have been more rapidly self-disqualifying for them than for us, because they were more familiar with the ultimate, as well as the proximate, properties of a character made in that type image. And that Falstaff was made in that image was already well hinted before Shakespeare made it hilariously obvious in 2.4, through Falstaff's lengthy account of the battle he didn't fight, with his outrageous and rapidly growing exaggerations of the opposition, his totally fraudulent boastfulness about his own valiant stand against them, and his sudden deflation when the truthful witnesses come forward.

But still more telling would have been the audience's recognition of a familiar pattern in the general relationship of the immoral elder to the important and impressionable youth. This was a standard structure in the morality plays that had substantially faded from dramatic repertoires but were still apparently much alive in memory, to judge from Shakespeare's allusions to them. The Young Man (named Manhood in *Mundus et Infans*, Man in *Nature*, Humanity in *Four Elements*, and the title role in *Lusty Juventus*) falls under the influence of the type role generically known—and often referred to in the lists of *dramatis personae*—as "The Vice" (Folly, Pride, Sensuous Appetite, and Hipocrisy are this type's specific names in the respective plays).[10] The Vice is usually an older figure, normally rude in manners and bawdy in speech, who attempts to lead the Young Man astray from the path he was meant to follow. Eventually, the Young Man comes to his senses and rejects the Vice, who is then occasionally carried away by a demon,[11] defeated and disgraced, and flailing with the dagger of lath (a toy dagger that was worn in real life by children and fools) that was apparently one of the Vice's standard attributes.[12]

The banter of 1.2, where Falstaff attempts (unsuccessfully) to tempt Hal into participating in a robbery, while carrying on richly with bluster and hypocrisy, would have been enough to evoke this familiar structure. That Shakespeare had it explicitly in mind, and wanted his audience to see it, is demonstrated in 2.4. There, Falstaff enters to Hal and spouts "A king's son? If I do not beat thee out of thy kingdom with a dagger of lath . . ." and the point is indelibly secured. It is yet more thoroughly made when, later in the scene,

Falstaff rehearses Hal for his pending interview with King Henry by playing the part of the Prince, while Hal plays the role of his royal father. Hal (as Henry) chides Falstaff (as Hal) for keeping bad company: "There is a devil haunts thee, in the likeness of a fat old man . . . that reverend Vice, that grey Iniquity, that Father Ruffian, that Vanity in years . . ." No one could mistake the meaning. Shakespeare here has Hal identify with his father's anxiety about his apparent wildness, and assimilates Falstaff explicitly to the type he has been conformed to and has already identified himself with: "That villain-ous abominable misleader of Youth, *Falstaff*, that old white-bearded Satan." At least some members of Shakespeare's audience are likely to have remem-bered that when Manhood succumbs to Folly in *Mundus et Infans*, they go to Eastcheap to dine and drink wine at a tavern.

Hal's comportment in 1.2 and through the subsequent robbery episode, especially when glossed by his soliloquized intent to shape up as a good prince after a little more playtime, had already, by the time of the mock inter-view, established that he was not really vulnerable to Falstaff's malign influ-ence, despite superficial appearances. Now he reaffirms more pointedly the principles of his soliloquy at the end of 1.2, showing that he knows the moral theory as well as the political. Falstaff's wonderfully ingratiating self-promotion (through the role of Hal, which he is still playing) comes next, but no one but he can be surprised when, in answer to his grand conclusion, "Banish plump Jack, and banish all the world," Hal answers—as Henry, but also as himself—"I do; I will."

Falstaff as braggart soldier is recognizable, harmless, and entertaining. In his very different, but compatibly parallel, type as the Vice, he is recog-nizable, harmful, and at least superficially threatening. By the end of act 2, the informed audience can feel confident that the hints of 1.2 are now con-firmed and fulfilled, and it is virtually Game Over for Falstaff as Vice. Hal is safe. If Falstaff survives in his parallel type of braggart soldier (which is precisely what he does), his type as Vice has been irretrievably emasculat-ed. Emptied of his capacity to harm, he is reduced to a resonant buffoon, sometimes amusing, often annoying, never dangerous. The Vice has been effectually banished; Shakespeare and Hal can afford to put up with the Braggart Soldier for a while longer, for which Shakespeare must have known that we would be grateful.

That Falstaff is a knight, rather than an ordinary ruffian like Gadshill, is one of the notable complicating features of the character that Shakespeare built on the frame of a Braggart Soldier and a corrupting Vice. It is also typi-cal of Shakespeare's handling of character. Shakespeare generally delineated his roles with an eye to a decorum about social status, which was apparently expected by his audience.

Rulers tend to speak rather grandly, even when they are delivering routine pronouncements or being astonishingly stupid, and are apparently intended to move and gesture befittingly. From *Hamlet* onward, Shakespeare experimented increasingly with the deliberate breakdown of these norms as a way of dramatizing personal disintegration—cf. the language and behavior of Hamlet's exit with "Hide fox, and all after" (4.2) and Lear's analogous exit with "Come, and you get it, / You shall get it by running. Sa, fa, fa, fa." (4.6)[13+]—but the dramatic effectiveness of such unbecoming departures obviously depended on the same decorous expectations.

Servants and workmen, at the other social extreme, tend to speak in a colloquially vulgar way, in prose rather than verse and usually with some malaproprian bumbling of language,[14+] and probably carried themselves accordingly (Touchstone's "bear your body more seeming, Audrey" (5.4) is doubtless an understated reproach for the posture Shakespeare had directed her actor to assume as a visible statement of who she is and isn't). His plain folks usually accept the places that life has given them, and those who aspire to something greater (Bottom's moment in the sun, Pierce Exton's dream of advancement through murdering Richard II, Osric's deferential flattery to Hamlet, Oswald's ambitious glee at the prospect of killing Gloucester—interestingly counterpointed by his contempt for Edgar in his momentary self-disguise as a peasant) are regularly parodied or disgraced. They also tend to be preoccupied with the trivialities of their own situations, and to provide little more than homely local color (they almost never do anything that has a significant effect on the action, at least not deliberately).

Despite a growing fashion of others' plays about middle-class life, Shakespeare offers few characters who occupy the social ground between the well-established (kings, peers, ranking clergy, leading families) and the members of the supportive infrastructure (servants, soldiers, laborers, shepherds). Searching our restricted canon, I find no representative of the regular merchant class apart from the unsuccessful and compromised Apothecary of *Romeo and Juliet* and the ambiguous hostess of the Boar's Head in *Henry IV, Part 1*. No one has a situation of potential legitimate upward mobility. The Apothecary is barely scraping by and the hostess has all she can do trying to get Falstaff to pay his debts; neither shows even the wistful dreaminess that the other mechanicals have about Bottom's chance of a windfall pension (which even they do not dream about for themselves, nor does Bottom). Only someone as vulgar as the Nurse thinks of the money that will be in Juliet's dowry (1.5), and Capulet's delight at Paris's suit never results in anyone's saying that she is on the brink of becoming a countess.

Most of the major roles have standing, with no attention to vulgar questions like earning money; others have humble trades or stable servitudes in the employ of those with standing. Nobody beyond the Apothecary and Mistress Quickly runs a business or makes a financial deal or is otherwise engaged in what kept the city of London flourishing. There are of course exceptions to be found in the rest of Shakespeare's plays, but they remain few. He specializes in two very distinct strata of society, and keeps them in their places. Their dramatic relationships are mainly by contrast rather than by interaction. When they interact, social climbing is in question only for the rapacious wicked. Audrey never registers that she is marrying into the court, and while Oliver supposes his newfound Aliena to be a genuine shepherdess he contemplates only his willing self-demotion to her level; Polonius warns Ophelia that Hamlet's status dooms her romance. Social place is part of the essential definition of a role, and only the unsavory people raise any question about it.

Shakespeare does *not*, however, bestow attractiveness and personal interest only on the privileged, or even only on the important movers of the story. Thus Capulet's servants in 1.5 are inserted, with their complaints about lazy Potpan and their plans for the below-stairs party, partly to give us instant emotional distance from brooding Romeo so that we can receive his next intensities with renewed attention, and partly to widen the play's scope for a moment in order to reestablish perspective (more "partlys" could be easily generated). Similarly, the Ostler and the Carriers who open the second act of *Henry IV, Part 1* offer an indirect buffering into what follows them, while giving us a momentary glimpse of the ordinary low-life world: they have no more part in the subsequent action than Capulet's servants, and are never heard from again, but they have in the meantime given us a delightful cameo of the stables.[15]

But this is a norm of Shakespearean dramaturgy, not an absolute rule. The lower classes are not always so colorful and self-preoccupied. When, in *Richard II* 3.4, the attempt of the Queen's ladies to distract her from her moodiness is interrupted by the entrance of the gardeners, she decides to eavesdrop, opining that they will "talk of state: for everyone doth so / Against a change." Shakespeare has set up three competing expectations. The usual one would be that the gardeners will turn out to be a comic interlude, but as he means to surprise (and perhaps momentarily disappoint) us about that, he offers two alternatives. One is that they will talk about gardening, as Capulet's servants talk of their situations and the ostler and carriers are typically concerned with theirs. The alternative expectation (that they will talk politics) has just been voiced by the Queen, but she is intensely preoccupied with her own situation and may well be thought to project it unrealistically upon the ordinary workers.

Shakespeare uses this dual anticipation to surprise us yet again: the gardeners begin talking about gardening, all right, but in an elegant versified manner that is utterly unlike what we hear in the stables or in the hasty preparation of Capulet's ballroom; and the gardening talk, which uses eloquent political metaphors to describe weeding and pruning, soon turns to a political conversation using gardening metaphors. Both expectations were right, and both wrong. The gardeners have been restylized from the laborers we probably anticipated, upscaled to where they can be accepted as at least token gardeners while being more convincing as anonymous and astute political commentators who make better general sense than any of the other voices of the play, as they buffer us gently from the ambivalent self-defeated Richard of 3.3 to the abdicating Richard of 4.1. Like typical working-class types, they have no effect on the action and are never heard from again; but Shakespeare has allowed them more elegant and relevant voices than his usual practice might have dictated, and I guess that anyone who attempts to imagine them speaking like Capulet's servants or the stablemen of *Henry IV, Part 1* will probably agree that their sustaining of the high tone of the previous scene was prudent dramaturgy on Shakespeare's part.

In *King Lear* 3.7 we are treated to a different surprise. As Cornwall works his vengeful and brutal will on Gloucester's eyes, a nameless servant steps forward to challenge him, boldly but uneloquently, precisely on the basis of his servantly duty to serve Cornwall well. Regan's surprise—"A peasant stand up thus?!"—will be shared by Shakespeare's audience, who have rarely seen low-life types enter so abruptly and decisively into the action. The servant is killed; Cornwall directs that he be thrown on the dunghill, but then acknowledges his own mortal wound from the servant's dutiful sword. In this play of extremes, an anonymous underling has changed the course of British history and is tossed out to rot. In the Quarto version (but not the Folio), other servants, who will never make a difference or be seen again, discuss the desperate condition of a Britain in which the likes of Regan—who has dispatched the upstart, apparently with a sword taken from another and less valiant servant, and probably by stabbing him in the back—can do what she is doing. The servants' roles have here reverted to the helpless and ineffectual buzz (no talk of revolt, only of moral confusion and the need to serve the blinded Gloucester) that usually define their place and types. In the meantime Shakespeare has roused one of their number to a heroic stance that he takes care to make credible within the type (including his deferential moral apology before his attack) while taking it beyond normal expectation, with serious results. Shakespeare's dramaturgical practice was not only to accept traditional norms and expectations, but to subvert them strategically from time to time for good dramatic effect.

On the whole, Shakespeare is fairly careful to keep roles in their social places. Ladies-in-waiting are allowed to be sassy, but must remain respectful.

Earls must defer to Dukes, so much so that in *King Lear* 2.4 Gloucester is caught in a dilemma of allegiance and appeasement between the powerful and moody Duke of Cornwall (who has effectually commandeered Gloucester's residence because it is at the moment more convenient than his own) and the powerless though nominally royal Lear to whom he is still loyal. Orlando, kept by his brother Oliver in a place that is beneath his birthright social station *and* in violation of the terms of their father's will, has a stronger and more persuasive complaint than Edmund's nearly unimpeachable critique of the unfairness and irrationality of discrimination against bastards—but he still acknowledges not only that "the courtesy of nations allows you my better, in that you are the first born" but also that "I confess your coming before me is nearer to his reverence."

But the social stratification is bisected by another dimension. No matter where a role may stand in the social order, Shakespeare regularly sees to it that roles that can make a difference (which usually does not include ordinary servants or clowns/fools, no matter how close to the action they may be) are sorted out *according to their claims on our sympathies.*

Both Shakespeare and Ben Jonson used the classical observation that life is like a play. The most striking difference between their uses of this *topos* is that Jonson, typically, placed himself and us as spectators, watching the world's drama, while Shakespeare (just as typically) saw us all as actors. Jonson kept his audience relatively distanced from the roles that carried out his plays, objectively detached and therefore readier to appreciate moral logic; Shakespeare involved his audience's sympathies, and not only allowed but virtually required that they take sides sympathetically as the roles pursued their competing projects, the evoked sympathy being a shortcut to moral truth. Jonson's dramaturgy tended to be like what we might expect from Jaques as he discloses himself in *As You Like It* 2.7, what Sir Philip Sidney called the comedy of scorn: Show the face of folly for what it is, and thus motivate the viewers to despise and avoid it. Shakespeare's dramaturgy was more like what Duke Senior might have practiced—what Sidney called the comedy of delight: show what deserves to call upon elemental human sympathy, and bring the audience to rejoice in the happy outcome of those whom they have learned to care for.[16]

It is demonstrable, as I remarked previously, that in this scene Shakespeare is making topical allusions to contemporary controversies about satire. I would not be the least surprised if he was also simultaneously glancing at two alternative philosophies of dramaturgy (and had Jonson partly in mind as being of the Jaques school). Hamlet's advice to the players in 3.2 provides an appropriate gloss on *As You Like It* 2.7: "The purpose of playing, whose end both at the first and now, was and is, to hold, as 'twer, the mirror up to Nature; to shew Virtue her owne feature, Scorne her owne image, and the very age and body of the time his form and pressure." There can be little doubt about the values disclosed in Hamlet's mirror. Scorn is not being awakened to dutiful vigilance, as it was in Jonsonian comedy, but rather shown what it really looks like, which is not flattering.

Shakespeare's portrayal of Jaques and the exiled Duke comes as near as he ever got to juxtaposing purified images of Virtue and Scorn as dramatic ways of showing alternatives in human nature, and it is at least equally clear where he stood in these instances and in his general practice as a playwright mirroring nature. Scorn, however justified, is inferior to sympathetic understanding. Virtue sympathizes.

Genuinely bad roles are usually defined with unmistakable clarity. *As You Like It*'s Duke Frederick is exaggeratedly perverse, disliking Orlando because everyone loved his noble father (who evidently disapproved of Frederick, as we do: here Shakespeare departs importantly and effectively from his source) and exiling his daughter Celia's best friend because she is the daughter of the rightful Duke and is attractive enough to upstage Celia. Oliver hates Orlando, but confesses that this is entirely irrational, as everyone else who knows him loves him. Edmund declares himself a dedicated villain in his soliloquy that opens the second scene of *King Lear* and never varies from that commitment until the play is almost over. Shakespeare sees to it that we know who the real enemies are, and alienates our sympathies from them no matter how smoothly they may seduce others: it is one of the notable habits of Shakespearean dramaturgy to keep the audience better informed than the roles, and we are not fooled by the genuinely bad even if onstage roles often are.

Genuinely bad roles never become sympathetic until their power is gone, but it is notable that Shakespeare often arranges a touch of sympathy at that point. Cornwall's whimper as he makes his last exit (*King Lear* 3.7) suddenly humanizes him into winning a touch of sympathy for the first time; Edmund's wistful "Yet Edmund was beloved" as he lies dying and muses that two women have died on his account (together with the curiously awkward "Some good I mean to do / Despite of mine own nature") raises his standing a notch or two. Laertes partially redeems himself from his perfidious attempt to murder Hamlet by dying with forgiveness and apology. Even Claudius, whose wickedness is somewhat softened by the honest soul-searching of his abortive prayer, might attact a touch of sympathy with his final plea for help. One may suspect that Shakespeare had decided that an unqualified attitude of Good Riddance at the death of villains makes for less successful tragedy than a hint of human kinship at their end.

Rather bad roles are treated similarly, especially when Shakespeare has built in a mediating excuse that may be called upon. Richard II is mainly unsympathetic for three acts of the play, but has been kept vaguely eligible to enter a plea of Guilty with an Explanation. Once he is a powerless prisoner, Shakespeare treats him gently and gives him speeches that may superficially seem self-pitying but on closer inspection are dignified self-criticisms with virtually no special pleading at all. Falstaff, after progressively disqualifying himself from our sympathy, lies apparently dead in *Henry IV, Part 1* 5.4, evidently slain by Douglas as a sideshow to the long-awaited combat between Hal and Hotspur, and is given a gentle and appropriately restrained eulogy by Hal. It is only after Hal's exit that we discover that Falstaff was merely playing 'possum and, having been effectually and affectionately concluded for this play, has survived to entice us to its sequel.

Sympathetic roles (or relatively neutral roles) that go bad rarely recover our sympathies except in this token way. Roles that make a bad impression have to be made sympathetic or stay where they are. I see no genuinely morally ambiguous roles in our small canon of seven plays. Demetrius comes close in *A Midsummer Night's Dream*, but even in his nastiest moments his threats against Helena sound hollow through their exaggeration, and we have been warned that he is not really himself. Richard II comes still closer, but is systematically protected by the thematic suggestion that he is a good man unfortunately surrounded by poisonous advisors, a suggestion that is reinforced by his never appearing without them in the first two acts and doubtless further enforced by advisory stage business in 1.3 and perhaps in 2.1.

The closest we get to moral ambiguity in our seven-play canon is probably Jaques in *As You Like It*, who is characterized by Duke Senior as having been immoral (2.7, this being the Duke's explanation of Jaques' savage satirical bent, and a hint—pointless to the action of the play—of why he remains so aloof from the local society's wholesome mood). But however critical Jaques may be in the course of the play, there is never a suggestion that we are in danger of his harming or corrupting anyone, and the ambiguity of his role and type and character is therefore of a different order from those few roles who carry bad previous records into other Shakespearean plays.

Moral crossover—which in Shakespearean dramaturgy is usually the redemption of immoral roles rather than the corruption of moral ones like Laertes—is the usual way in which Shakespeare deals with what a later dramaturgy might prefer to handle through an initial ambiguity. Oliver is an abominably unnatural villain in the early part of *As You Like It*, yet winds up engaged to Celia. I have already discussed the clever way in which we get persuaded that he has totally changed even before we know that the change has taken place, and wish now merely to glance at some of the other dramaturgical strategies by which Shakespeare makes this plausible as well as simply accomplished.

The early emphasis on the brothers' natural inheritance from Sir Rowland establishes that Oliver is temporarily derailed, much as Demetrius is at the beginning of *A Midsummer Night's Dream* (though with far more serious moral consequences). Demetrius can be redeemed by undergoing a bit of a penitential ordeal as a silly quarreling lover, coupled with a medicine that brings him to his senses (those who are puzzled that the same dosage that deranges Lysander can heal Demetrius are thinking too much like Athenian mechanicals). Oliver has been more obviously on the far side of the moral line, and must accordingly be subjected to a deeper penance (loss of his lands, exile in the forest, degeneration into a wretched ragged man o'ergrown with hair), a threat to his life (a serpent and a lion), the heroic example of kindness and nature on the part of his brother in rescuing him at great risk, and the general redemptive atmosphere of the pastoral/forest "greenwood" scene as distinguished from the wicked court, capped off by his willingness to surrender his worldly goods to Orlando while he remains with the shepherdess Aliena. (Thomas Heywood remarked that pastoral drama contrasts the craft of the city with the innocency of the sheep cote, and *As You Like It* fits the formula, though it finally purges the court and takes the courtiers sensibly home.) That, coupled with the stunning introduction of the reformed Oliver before we recognize that it is he, is enough to reverse the artificial and ungrounded villainy of his earlier days. Do not look for psychological continuity, even though its shadow is there. This is dramaturgy, not case study.

Goneril and Regan are good examples of roles who move in the opposite direction. Despite the strong modern impulse to read their later state backward into their first scene, and psychologize them into villains from the start, both of them begin as basically good. Not notably good, let alone heroically, but basically. They cooperate with their father's odd (but hardly crazy) testimonial dinner project, and they give their command performance toasts as toasts are given on such occasions, declaring eloquently how much they love him. If there is any insincerity in what they say, it is the insincerity of the ceremonial occasion, in which it is appropriate to use exaggerated rhetoric, which is hardly the same as crafty lying. (The same rules obtained in the dedication of books in Shakespeare's time, and anyone whose naturalistic bent makes it impossible to imagine that Shakespeare intended Goneril and Regan to be recognized as behaving appropriately in their protestations of love is invited to have another look at Shakespeare's fulsome words in the dedication of *Venus and Adonis*.)

There is a lot of confusing yes and no in the dramaturgical design of this first scene. Are Goneril and Regan vying for land grants? Yes, to the extent that we focus on Lear's announcement that he will give away his kingdom in proportion to his daughters' love. No, to the extent that the scene opens with

Gloucester and Kent *already* knowing what the division is. No also insofar as Goneril and Regan have already received their shares when Cordelia gets her turn to speak. Is Lear going to say *"Very* sweet: let me lop off a county or two from your sisters' lands," or "A bit disappointing: Goneril gets two more counties from the remainder and Regan one"? Of course this is absurd. The deal is both done and not done at the same time; the daughters are competing and not competing; the situation is both a normal retirement ceremony and an outrageous demand for self-serving insincerities; and Cordelia is both coura- geously honest not to get into the game and a sullen brat to insist at first on saying nothing whatever. At the end of the scene, her sisters scold her for scanting her obedience, and the charge is apt. Goneril and Regan end the scene with practical—and utterly unvillainous, however ungenerous—plan- ning about how to deal with this unpredictable and irascible old man.

It is only by gradual subsequent stages that Goneril and Regan shift from being wary to being weary, from reluctant permissiveness to insistent discipline. Their hearts harden by slow, then faster, increments. Once they have hardened enough to produce the ending of act 2, Shakespeare speeds up the process and quite abruptly turns them, without adequate explanation, into Lear's malevolent enemies, the essential bonds having been broken and the essential damage al- ready having been done to an extent that allows Shakespeare to project upon them a leap to the next major stage of moral monstrosity. From there on, they are too far across the moral line to be retrieved other than by extravagant tactics like those used in Oliver's case. And retrieval is not Shakespeare's design for them. They end, as they did decidedly *not* begin, as deserving disappointed and miser- able deaths, in murderous and suicidal despair.

Shakespeare takes them across the dramaturgical chessboard in a series of discrete moves, according to the rules of the dramaturgical game, and takes them to the point of no return. It is orderly but not logical. Their end is not implicit in their beginning. Their beginning only acknowledges, through Cordelia's critique[17!] and Kent's oblique hints and Cordelia's parting remarks to them, that something considerably less generous than their protestations of love could come to be, and that Cordelia would rather commend her father's welfare into more reliable hands. From then on, it is increasingly a matter of morality, in which they inch under pressure to the brink (which is in 2.4), and then (not in 2.4, where they are still rationalizing their behavior at the end, but rather off stage while Lear struggles against the storm and everything else) tumble to where there is no scrambling back. The moral line can take a considerable amount of dramatic work to cross, in either direction; once it is crossed, it is normally assumed to require a great deal of dramaturgical ma- nipulation either to rise or to fall to the other side. There are a few cases of late rehabilitation, almost all of them prepared for by Shakespeare's earlier management.[18+] There are also a few cases of late moral defection, but they are rare and usually very qualified.[19+]

I will stop there, though there is obviously more to be said. I want to spend the rest of this chapter addressing the discomfort that many readers are likely to have with the way I have presented Shakespeare's dramaturgy in the matter of roles, types, and characters. This is an especially sensitive area in modern critical sensibilities, and I want to try to provide a context of thought that might make my treatment seem more plausible, and less unwelcome, than it may at first appear to be.

Modern taste tends to be especially preoccupied with the artistic depiction of character. Painters, photographers, biographers, novelists, actors are all regularly praised for their successes in rendering a sense of deep, rich, highly individuated, and original character (or scolded for failing to do so). I am trying to show that Shakespearean roles were basically unoriginal, presented more as general types than as unique individuals, often endowed with individual traits only insofar as those traits were dramatically functional within the play's needs (though sometimes apparently just for fun), not only uncomplex but usually quite simplified, and with most of what mattered displayed on the surface rather than hinted at in their putative depths. I do not suppose that many readers will instinctively find my approach congenial.

For that reason, I want to confront this disparity more directly, in the hope that I might dispel some of the inevitable misunderstanding and make a decent apologetic case for my claim that the kind of dramaturgy I attribute to Shakespeare aptly represents how he really made his plays—and my further claim that whether or not we find such a dramaturgy instinctively congenial, it not only makes far more sense than any alternative way of reading Shakespeare but even vindicates itself through his plays as being *at least* as fine and accomplished a dramaturgy as any modern alternative.

Originality, as I argued in the last chapter with respect to Shakespeare's plots, was not as high a value in the popular artistic efforts of his time as it is (or pretends to be) in ours. Popular taste, then as now, showed a tendency toward novelty, modishness, fashion-consciousness, new-fangledness—but we know this especially because it was frequently criticized as shallow, a disvaluation of tradition. In literary art in general, there were two main trends that tugged at the dominant traditionalism.

One was classicism, which sought to reform what was wanting in the established traditional by appealing to the more polished and authoritative ancient literary models in Greek and Roman literature, and their more recent imitations in French and Italian. Spenser's grand attempt to gather traditional romance and allegory into epic proportions in *The Faerie Queene* was succeeded by Milton's use of Homeric tactics as the best way of displaying the epic dimensions of the very unclassical story of *Paradise Lost*. They were, in a sense, approaching the same kind of project with significantly different hierarchies of traditional literary allegiances.

The other trend was a more self-consciously "modern" manner that tried to break new ground. The Petrarchan tradition of love poetry, with its carefully stylized situations and attitudes, represented in finely tooled sonnets, no sooner reached its highest point of English poetic accomplishment than it was challenged by the irregular liaisons that Donne rendered in colloquial language, rough verse, and startlingly daring similes and metaphors.

In all of this, Shakespeare's allegiance seems to have been much more grounded in a satisfaction with the received traditional than in either the classicizing or modernizing trends. Of *course* he made considerable use of the fruits of the classical revival, and wrote plays in classical settings that show a deep assimilation of classical values that were no longer prominent in his received tradition. And of *course* he exploited the accomplishments of new experimentation: he kept up with shifting tastes and even invented new techniques, new words, new characters, new major plot twists on his own. But while no generalization can be made on these matters unqualifiedly, I suggest that it is more appropriate and rewarding to read the Shakespearean dramaturgy of roles in terms of a modified traditionalism than as if it were a novelty (or a genius's anticipation of twentieth-century taste) that shows signs of a traditional background.

The beginnings of opera were rooted in an attempt to express character as well as the ancients seemed to have done. The nature of the project precludes any notions of what is now generally meant by "realistic" or "naturalistic" representation: the *dramatis personae* of these early experiments were singing their parts, after all, and the goal was to make the handling of the musical line as expressive as well-tooled gesture might be—i.e., not a matter of fancy singing, or of delightful melodies, but a *dramatic* mode of music, dedicated to bringing out the ways in which the individual roles responded to their situations and defined their dispositions toward their next moves in the drama. It had little to do with making them appear to be interesting individuals.

The value of character in the thousands of representations of the Madonna and Child from the beginnings to Shakespeare's time is relatively trivial. Both roles must be rendered in a way that is appropriate. From the beginning, this was not a domestic scene, but rather a hieratic icon. Hence Mary, in the early stages, is rendered with a posture and expression of solemnity, and Jesus tends to look more like a tiny man than a baby, often holding a significant attribute (most often, a scroll, to which he points with a composure beyond his naturalistic years).

As the image was gradually domesticated over the centuries, with steady attenuation of gold backgrounds and halos and an equally steady increase in the babyizing of the original tiny man (along with the desolemnization of Mary, who becomes progressively more motherly), it quietly carried two lessons for our purposes.

One is that originality in the handling of the roles was not a particularly important value. The same image, over and over, with only minor variations, continued to express what was appropriate. Signs of discontent with the type are hard to find. Reproducing it recognizably, rather than inventing a new way of doing so, seems to have been the dominant aim. When it gradually got to the point of being more or less Mother and Baby, free of the Byzantine formulae of representation and in the hands of painters who knew more than five ways of posing them, the characterization of both remained conservative despite its freedom to break loose. The type had absorbed sufficient meaning that fidelity to it was enough to satisfy the task, so long as the faithful rendition was done well enough.

The other lesson is that even at the height of the image's domestication, when the occasional painter might have felt that something had been lost in the centuries-long process of arriving at Woman with Child, there was no discernible attempt either to stir up new interest by innovations at the domestic level or to regain lost hieratic ground through some form of otherworldly characterization. No painter felt the need to break free enough to have Mary threaten Jesus with a spanking, in order to enliven the traditionally placid scene; I have not yet found a painting that shows her weeping over a sleepy or distracted Jesus as if to show that there was much more going on in her beneath the surface. The surface, as in the case of the physical structure of paintings, or indeed the earth itself, was where the real action was: hidden depths were not to the point, and were not pursued.

There is nothing inferior about a type-based dramaturgy of roles. It is a style with its own integrity. If it tends to exclude a form of audience appetite (and a repertoire of actors' skills) that are of special importance in the modern dramatic world, it compensates by maximizing the importance of another dimension of acting skills and feeding another form of audience appetite.

It is, I suggest, little more than a curious failure in self-knowledge that prevents audiences with a taste for ballet and opera, or even a taste for well-written and well-acted television comedy series, from recognizing that a dramaturgy based on stylized types can deliver great drama in any of its modes, as long as the audience is willing to relax into how it works rather than fighting it off with prepossessions about how a tragic role ought to be designed or how an actor ought to play a serious part. The reading of Shakespeare has been unhappily distorted by the mistaken assumption that a great play must be supplied with roles who are to be seen as iceberg tips, their self-manifestations being mainly symptoms of deep psychological rumblings where the action really takes place. Such a reading appeals to the clever, appeals to a psychotherapeutic culture, appeals to those who have been trained to read works written in just such a way. But it does not read Shakespeare on Shakespeare's terms.

It is not by random chance that Hamlet is the role and character most fascinating to twentieth-century Shakespearean interpretation. He gives the most room for interpretive ingenuity. I will attempt later to give a different accounting of Shakespeare's Hamlet, in keeping with the unpopular principles that I am here advancing. For the moment, I will say merely what those principles are.

Shakespeare drew his roles primarily from a repertoire of established and recognizable types, just as he drew his plots mainly from traditional or popular stories. His expertise was exercised mainly in the finesse with which he deployed their typical attributes, dispositions, mannerisms, and expected behavior within the texture of the play's action, and the deft skill with which he provided them with concretized traits that were appropriate to the type though not necessarily implicit in it, and decidedly helpful to the overall play. In his style of dramaturgy, the nature and meaning and value of his roles are normally displayed on the surface. What you see is what you get. Nothing important is hidden. He personalized many of his characters memorably, but rather as Raphael personalized his Madonnas: exquisitely but on the surface. He intermixed them with others who are presented with hardly any interesting personal qualities at all. If we look into a role for something that does not seem to be processed on the surface of the action, we are usually asking an irrelevant question, or overlooking a fairly plain answer. The focus of attention that is invited is a concentration on the manifest unfolding of the play, as appropriated through an understanding of how he wrote them. Whatever is not there is not part of the experience he designed for us. Whatever is there should be carefully understood. "Carefully," of course, means in accordance with the principles of Shakespearean dramaturgy.

9

A TASTE OF YOUR QUALITY: COME, A PASSIONATE SPEECH

Shakespeare's language,
especially his dramatic verse and prose

For the student of Shakespearean dramaturgy, an extraordinary revelation flashes out from a generally unmemorable exchange in *As You Like It* 4.1. Jaques enters with Rosalind (who is still in her Ganymede disguise) and Celia (probably all at the same door: Jaques' opening line suggests the continuation of a conversation rather than its initiation), and he is apparently in an uncharacteristically sociable mood: "I prethee, pretty youth, let me be better acquainted with thee." After a bit of banter, in which Jaques' somewhat stiff self-promotion is deflated by the supple replies of Rosalind/Ganymede, Orlando enters with "Good day, and happiness, dear Rosalind." Jaques, having obviously failed to ingratiate himself with Ganymede, retires with a lame excuse: "Nay then God buy you, and you talke in blanke verse."

The Duke has long since alerted us to Jaques' perceptiveness, beginning with his own first scene a full two acts ago. Our experience of Jaques has on the whole confirmed the Duke's judgment that, however warped his attitudes may be, Jaques is never to be easily dismissed as a keen-eyed observer of life. But how did he know, from a single line, that Orlando was speaking blank verse?

Shakespeare obviously expected at least part of his audience to know what blank verse was, and (more importantly) to realize that Orlando was speaking it in a scene that had commenced with some thirty lines of prose. That seems to indicate that Shakespeare's actors had a way of delivering verse that was recognizably different from their delivery of prose.

The English language is structured in such a way that you are likely to produce at least one line that is as blank-versy as Orlando's in any given minute that you speak. We are not here dealing with that sort of coincidence. One might argue that Orlando's six words are stylized in a way that the preceding prose is not, but it would be hard to make a case that the line is in itself conspicuously verse-like: heightened prose, such as we would alternatively expect from Orlando in this context, regularly offers at least as much stylization as we can find in his one verse line. In the subsequent prose (for the rest of the scene contains no further blank verse) one can easily isolate ten-syllable sequences that would make decent candidates for better blank verse than Orlando's: from what is probably Rosalind's best speech, we can pick "in all this time there was not any man," "yet he did what he could to die before," "and being taken with the cramp, was drowned," "and worms have eaten them, but not for love." What was the tipoff for the one authentic blank-verse line in the scene?

I see no way of avoiding the conclusion that there must have been a differentiation of acting style between passages of verse and passages of prose— e.g., something like the difference between the manner of speaking and delivery used when explaining something to a dozen friends and acquaintances at an informal gathering, and the manner used in explaining to 150 strangers in a rented hall.

Something of this kind must, I guess, have been in play when Shakespeare's actors moved from prose to verse or *vice versa*. After some two hundred lines of prose banter with Falstaff in 3.3 of *Henry IV, Pt. 1*, Hal greets the sudden summons to war with twelve lines of verse, and everything about the moment suggests that he must change his bearing conspicuously as he turns from tavern-play to the serious business he was born to. (Falstaff's answering couplet is obviously the expected parody thereof.) When the Athenian mechanicals of *A Midsummer Night's Dream* shift from the lumpy prose of their ordinary discourse to the exaggerated poetry of their roles in Peter Quince's play, Shakespeare's skilled actors were likely to have accompanied the change with a shift from notably slouchy movement to equally exaggerated posturing. The country wench Audrey was almost certainly standing, however silently, in a decidedly prosaic way when Touchstone admonished her to "Bear thy body more seeming, Audrey" (*As You Like It* 5.4). When the original Orlando entered into the casually insinuating manner of Jaques and the informally sassy rebuffs of Rosalind/Ganymede, he must have done so with a physically and vocally obvious difference that set up Jaques' recognition that something in the presentation of these six words (the words themselves being rather undistinguished and unarresting as poetry) has changed the tone.

I will generalize bluntly in a way that I consider basically accurate and useful, though I will qualify it later. Shakespeare wrote verse when he wanted a high-style formal presentation by his actors; when he wrote prose, it was because he wanted a more casual manner of delivery. (What I have called "heightened prose" occurs when a speaker has built up to, or near, the condition of verse: I have not yet noticed that Shakespeare ever starts a scene, or a character, in this mode.) This differentiation contained the seeds of a later shift in his manner of writing verse, and in his actors' style of delivery—but that is beyond the scope of this book. For the moment, I say merely that I consider Shakespearean verse to be the normal dramaturgical environment of heightened acting (and a more formal mode of acting to be the medium through which verse was offered), pushing the mood into a higher key where he had access to a very uncolloquial rhetorical extravagance that verse, supported by an uncolloquial manner of presentation, could make seem appropriate in a way that prose (delivered in a different way) apparently could not.

I certainly would not deny that Shakespearean prose can support rhetorical extravagance, and often does. But it is of another sort. Rather than attempting to describe the difference, I suggest that it can at least be detected by imagining the actor accidentally belching in the middle of the speech. Falstaff's kind of extravagance, or the eloquent prose speeches of Hamlet or Jaques, would go relatively unharmed; but try the verbal posturing of Richard II or Romeo, and it is not hard to see that some serious damage would be done. Prose tends to accompany histrionic deflation, and to signal a relatively unbuttoned casualness that may have its own eloquence but is closer to ordinary speech.

Relatively early Shakespearean plays are predominantly in verse. That releases them to extraordinary language performances that no one could dream are direct imitations of regular speech: it is rather like the liberties created by modern musical drama, where anyone can suddenly break into song without the audience feeling puzzled, or required to pretend that it is the "natural" thing to do in the circumstances, while the song itself is free (if not required) to rhyme as well as to stray beyond the ordinary intonations of speech. And, like modern musicals, a verse play apparently raised the audiences's expectations that some such arias of poetic verse would be bestowed from time to time. After the delicious appetizer of *Romeo and Juliet* 1.5, Shakespeare was not only entitled but probably expected to come through with something like Romeo's extravagant rhapsody on Juliet in 2.2. *Richard II*, which is from the start mannered and stylized in verse—and contains no prose at all—can (and does) get virtually operatic in its provision of brilliantly lyrical speeches, and parallel heightened modes of presentation. Extravagances in expression, such as the Duchess of York's grandly structured speech on the vials of blood and the tree of genealogy in 1.2; extravagances in action, such as Richard's sitting on the stage floor in 3.2 and his moralizing in 4.1 upon the transfer of the crown and upon the mirror he is about to shatter; and extravagances of mood, such as Richard's long speeches as he experiences successive stages of abandonment in 3.2, 3.3, and 5.5, are all part of the fabric of a formalized verse-style presentation, and probably could not have been done in prose any better than *Aïda* could make its mark through blank verse without music. But that touches on another question that needs dealing with.

"Richard is a poet," said Mark Van Doren in an unfortunately influential essay on the play, "and his tragedy arises from the fact that he loved poetry more than his kingship, more than power, more than life itself." Van Doren, writing a prose that deliberately approaches the poetic, has seduced many readers into a theory that sounds lovely but does not keep faith with the text. It is of course true, and dramatically striking, that the play contains moments when Richard's poetic extravagances are underlined by collisions with more practical reality, making him seem conspicuously poetic (as well as self-indulgent). In 3.2, as he sits upon the ground to tell sad stories of the death of kings (try doing *that* in prose), Carlisle admonishes him that "Wise men ne'er sit and wail their woes."[1] Even more pointedly, his extravagance with the mirror concludes with his startling act of smashing it on the platform and his bitter lines "Mark, silent King, the moral of this sport,/ How soon my sorrow hath destroyed my face," Bolingbroke confutes his performance laconically with "The shadow of your sorrow hath destroyed / The shadow of your face." Game, and set, for realism; poetry loses, 4-6, on the strength of Bolingbroke's backhand.

But it was not always so, in terms of the distribution of the poetics of the play. Richard's lyricism lingers in the mind, so vividly that my students have often been startled, on rereading the play, to discover that this rather matter-of-fact prosaic[2+] toss-off line is not in the least a consistent feature of Bolingbroke's character, let alone its essence. In 1.3, it is Richard who delivers the curt replies, while Bolingbroke embroiders his response to the sentence of exile: "But who can hold a fire in his hand / By thinking on the frosty Caucasus" etc. Richard is similarly, and even more rudely, abrupt with the dying John of Gaunt, who not only rhapsodizes elaborately on England but gratuitously rings the changes on his own name ("Old Gaunt indeed, and gaunt in being old" and so forth), only to be undercut by Richard's prosaic (literally verse, but verse deliberately approaching the condition of prose) reply, "Can sick men play so nicely with their names?"

Richard is not a poet. Shakespeare is. And as a poetic dramaturge, Shakespeare invests his *Richard II* lyricism not in particular characters as part of their makeup but rather in particular situations that can make good use of it, distributing it (and the putdowns of it) to the characters who occupy the appropriate places in a given scene's dynamics. In *Richard II*, which tends to specialize in pathos, the underdogs are lyrical, elaborating the scene's capacities to evoke sympathy; the ones in power tend to be antilyrical, thus underlining the pathos further as well as qualifying it. But nobody but Shakespeare himself owns the poetry, or the antipoetry, and he doles them out according to what makes the play work better, and by no other rule.

Shakespeare's poetry, supported by his verse style in general, pushes at the limits of expressiveness through the first half of his career. But that does not mean that his prose was a holiday, or some form of de-versified relief: the distribution of highly intense passages in Shakespeare's plays suggests that he was quite aware that we can't keep that pace for long without an interval of something less demanding, but his prosework is deftly crafted to contribute to the movement of the play and not an invitation to yawn and stretch, or grab something from the refrigerator (or crack some nuts, the notorious Elizabethan equivalent).

There has been a considerable amount of work on the place of rhetoric in Elizabethan education and prose practice. This, when attended to (it is not a subject that everyone finds attractive), has had the virtue of reminding us that the writing of prose was then an art, not just a transcription of one's stream of consciousness. The writer of prose was often as attentive to rhythm, music, structure, and well-chosen figures of speech as the writer of verse. Shakespeare's prose, while occasionally a deliberate and striking imitation of just what might have been said on the street or in the stables or among below-stairs servants, is usually tooled to be not ordinary but extraordinary talk, the sort of thing that one might wish that one had said rather than an accurate recollection of what was really uttered. It is shaped, that is to say, in accordance with good rhetorical principles.

"In accordance with" is meant to be significantly different from "by calculation from." The modern study of Elizabethan rhetoric has the virtue of showing that educated people of Shakespeare's time actually thought about how they wrote or said things, but it often has the concomitant vice of suggesting that Elizabethans used their rhetorical training the way unimaginative novice chefs use cookbooks. One rhetorically enthusiastic scholar, summarizing her own exposition, claims that

> An analysis in these terms is essentially of the kind proposed by Ascham and Erasmus, and we can learn from it much about the means of Shakespeare's art. To both writers, one would imagine, the playwright would have been seen not only to have started with a body of received patterns or formulae, but to have written his plays from them, finding always new ways in which to vary them.[3+]

Whatever one may imagine Erasmus and Ascham to have supposed, or however one may imagine their book reviews of the first collection of Shakespeare's plays, there is no reason to think that Shakespeare wrote like this or was heard like this. The seasoned chef has long since internalized what the cookbooks have to offer, and operates out of experience and tactful imagination. Members of Shakespeare's audience probably did not nudge one another to say "Golly, what a nifty zeugma!" or "Did you notice how well the last few anacolutha varied the topoi?"

Having taught a course entitled "Rhetoric and Composition" more often than I needed or deserved, I opine that just as (according to an American proverb) good whiskey doesn't need water and bad whiskey doesn't deserve it, so instruction in rhetoric is not so much like learning to spell as it is like learning to sprint. Some are swifter than others at spelling, but given enough time, patience, motivation, and pedagogical skill, almost everyone can be brought to a high level of proficiency. But in sprinting, if you don't start out swift, you don't end up swift: the clumsy and slow can become less slow and less clumsy, but not by much, while teaching things about pacing, efficiency of movement, and technique may improve the performance by the small margin that makes the difference between first place and fifth, but cannot make a winner out of a slewfoot. The native speakers who have a genuine facility with language are not significantly improved by instruction in rhetoric, and those who lack such facility are as often deformed as improved by it.[4+]

Shakespeare had facility. He would probably have been more readily able than we are to identify the figures of speech he used, according to the received technical classifications, just as a well-trained pianist can name the chords as well as the notes she plays; but at this writing, the last smart piano performance I heard was by an old jazz musician who had never learned to read music and did not seem to be seriously disadvantaged by that oversight. Shakespeare wrote deft prose because he was skilled with language, not because he knew how to classify his maneuvers. A study of his rhetoric is good if it alerts us to the artfulness of his composition, but misleading if it leads us to suppose that each paragraph is a dish derived from rhetorical recipes.

It is probably obvious that I can't write a chapter on this general subject without addressing the issue of Shakespeare's imagery. It is obvious to me, at any rate, since although the baneful influence of Caroline Spurgeon's *Shakespeare's Imagery* seems finally to have faded, it has not altogether disappeared. Her book is a dedicated and searching piece of work, but is marred by her enthusiasm for the importance of her subject (she believed that she was turning the key that opens the heart of the plays' mysteries) and further marred by the heedless way in which her assumptions were pumped into the minds of naive and trusting students by well-meaning but uncritical pedagogues. Crudely stated, the Spurgeon theory is that when a Shakespearean play contains a particularly large number of figures of speech drawn from the same overall field of reference (e.g., a notable number of similes and metaphors derived from gardening, or merchandising, or politics), this indicates something significant about how Shakespeare saw the essential meaning of his story. Thus Spurgeon noticed how frequently the speeches in *Macbeth* are cloaked in language related to clothing, and argued that the fabric of the play is tailored to show that Macbeth is dressed up in a kingly role that proves too big for him, and must fall because it doesn't fit. Similarly, the essence of *King Lear* is to be found in Shakespeare's dogged use of animal imagery, which shows that he is thinking that the basic significance of the action lies in the ravenous and inhumane ambitions of Edmund and the bestial ingratitude of Lear's daughters, demonstrating that Shakespeare thought the source of evil to be the untamed wolfish disposition that lies near the heart of most persons and leads them to prey on others.

If you had fun watching me try to slip animal images by in the last sentence, and clothing images in the one before it, that only shows that you are awake and have a kind sense of humor. If you didn't notice (my students usually don't when I try this sort of thing on them), that doesn't mean you aren't alert: is simply establishes the point that we don't habitually receive this kind of rhetorical trope by categorizing it in some artificial way (routine essays on "animal imagery" normally include some birds, such as kites and pelicans, but ignore Juliet's being called a lamb). Even my blatant and unfinessed bits about clothing and beasts are likely to be grasped according to what they are attempting to mean rather than being referred to a notebook analysis of the verbal vehicles through which the meaning is expressed.

Native speakers tend to receive words as transparent, or at least translucent—they are busy focusing on the meaning rather than on the construction by which it expressed. Something that is overtly poetic may redistribute one's attention to embrace an increased alertness to sounds and figures of speech as such, but this is a specialized and trained way of listening, not an ordinary one, and usually requires a specific mobilization on the part of the hearer. In a culture that regularly uses language that is loaded with rhetorical schemes and tropes, the figures of speech are not particularly conspicuous, just as touches of slang do not call special attention to themselves in casual shoptalk (though they would in a formal lecture). It is the poverty of our own expressiveness that makes Shakespeare's language seem unusually poetic, and diverts our attention to the mechanisms that create that effect. It is understandable that some folks are fascinated by what we call "imagery," but the attempt to foist this on Shakespeare is misguided. He was being effulgently expressive, not dropping a verbal system of gilded crumbs and stones to guide the reader through the play.

I do not mean to dismiss image-counting as nonsense, but merely to put it in place. Shakespeare appears to have written rather spontaneously,[51] with a internalized sense of form and technique. He set down what seemed appropriate, and it is entirely legitimate to try to reconstruct his sense of appropriateness by attending to what he set down, as long as we are aware that the mechanical way in which we must do this does not imply that he was equally mechanical in making it available. It is more like a matter of tone, which almost always takes precedence over what is literally said: he wanted this or that tonality, and therefore used a metaphor or simile that would express it, quite possibly without consciously realizing that he was dipping repeatedly into expressions drawn from beasts or clothing to drive his points home.

He bent grammar and experimented in vocabulary similarly, inventing new words and novel local constructions in a language that was then still almost as malleable in these respects as it was in spelling, following an instinctive feel for what he could make the language do rather than pondering which rules and strategies to follow. Some subliminal results may appropriately gather in the reader's or hearer's mind, as a reverberation of the spirit from which the writing originated, and the rhetorical patterning may be appropriately analyzed to show how that result comes about. But the crude claim that any talk that glances at clothes or creatures will make us think of what gets glanced at and take our focus off the key point can only be called a contrivance that critics should quit cultivating.

And that brings me to another point about Shakespeare's (and others') verse. It is still somewhat fashionable to treat sheer sounds, the phonemes by which words are physically formed, as if they had a power of independent significance and communication. Did you in fact notice that I stuffed the last sentence of the previous paragraph with an absurdly high proportion of "hard" or "harsh" phonemes? If so, were you also aware that the sentence before it was composed of "soft" and "melodious" sounds, like the murmuring of innumerable bees? If not, all is well: advance three spaces and congratulate yourself for keeping your eye on the meaning. If you *did* realize what I was deliberately doing with the music, you may have an unusual talent for keeping track of the flavors of language while not missing a beat in the communication—or you *may* have a semipathological (but curable) condition that distracts you from what is being said in order to attend to minor elements in how it is expressed.

Shakespeare's verse and prose are concerned with meanings. Like all people who love language, Shakespeare expressed his meanings with a habitual instinct for appropriatenesses of various kinds, and the results almost always produce good music, good texture, and good sense—not from contrivance, but from a rich command of the possibilities of apt expressiveness. Naturally, his language regularly reaches out to metaphors and similes that are sometimes the most precise way of locating a meaning, and sometimes expansive stunt-pilotry that stirs our minds to places that explore what is beyond the possibility of precision. Naturally, the formation of his sentences (the "schemes" of traditional rhetoric, as distinguished from the last sentence's concentration on "tropes") gives us balanced and poised organizations of expression where that is the right effect to capture, and disordered breakdowns of control where he wants to show a character's confusion or frenzy. But there is no reason to suppose that he, or any other of his skilled contemporaries, ever made a conscious decision that it was time for an animal image or an oxymoron or a chiasmus. Writers of his time had a more ample repertoire of spontaneous expressive devices than we have. We can catalogue the results, but we should not make the mistake of supposing that he used such a catalogue to order up the right way of putting this or that utterance.

One more topic should follow more obviously than it does. No one can study Shakespeare for very long without being asked to consider rhetoric, imagery, sound-texture, verse. But it is, unfortunately, possible to spend quite a lot of time pursuing the subject without running into explicit attention to proverbs.

On the surface, it may well seem that a Shakespearean text would be a hostile environment for proverbs. This is a playwright who almost never repeats himself, even though his audience might be grateful rather than disappointed for his recycling of a choice line or phrase here and there. But even when, in 3.1 of *Henry IV, Part 2*, he has King Henry quote ex-King Richard's parting words to Northumberland, and there no need to do other than quote verbatim the same speech he wrote for the occasion in *Richard II* 5.1, he writes an entirely new version that is as paraphrastic of the original as you or I might do on the spot. Proverbs, like clichés, are notoriously invariable: the quintessentially uninventive way of addressing a situation. Shakespeare mocks clichés, but he uses proverbs—and uses them in the standard proverbial manner, neither with irony nor with a new twist—extraordinarily often. Because many of them are no longer in circulation, we do not sense their frequency as readily as Shakespeare's contemporaries would have done; but in fact they occur often. Why?

It is an interesting question to speculate on, and I invite you to do that. I will spare you my own speculations, since there is no real evidence to ground them on, but I will not forbear to toss in a couple of thoughts that may be relevant.

One is that there is a generally shared sense that there is a significant difference between clichés, hackneyed phrases, vacuous truisms, and tired old saws on the one hand, and proverbs on the other, even if we may not always agree which is which in specific cases. Those who have a lively sense of language perceive the former as dull, lazy, routine, brittle, and unhelpful, while the latter, when aptly used, are seen as resonant, appropriate, insightful, decisive, and wise, both taking from and giving to the occasion an ordering focus that clarifies understanding and evaluation. Proverbs, for this reason, are the traditional repository of folk wisdom, the basic first brave step in philosophizing. It is hardly accidental that the character in our seven-play canon who comes closest to being the philosopher, Friar Laurence, is the one most richly provided with proverbs.[6+]

The other thought is that while Shakespeare avoids repetition, he is fond of grounding his plays in the familiar—familiar situations, familiar responses to them, familiar character types, familiar values, familiar problems, familiar stories. Proverbs are familiar language formulae at their best. Shakespeare tinkers with routine greetings and salutations, expressions of general contentment and approval, and formulations for taking leave; he finds new ways for characters to say the equivalent of "yes" and "no," "please" and "thank you," "you're right" and "I disagree." The distribution of proverbs into otherwise highly inventive styles of speech has, I think, the effect of letting the language tag home-base intermittently, keeping in touch with its best roots and reassuring us that the governing intelligence behind the play, for all the unfamiliar and extraordinary expressiveness with which it has generally endowed the characters, has not forgotten that enough is as good as a feast.

Even aside from the various ways in which he embroidered and manipulated it, Shakespeare's language is the most immediate and obvious impediment to reading his plays as they were meant to be understood. This is a problem that can be managed, and is in fact less of a problem than it usually seems at first, but it is nevertheless a problem, and must be confronted.

Shakespeare employed an unusually large vocabulary—around 30,000 words. Many of them were not in general circulation—some of them were apparently his own invention[7]—though most of them were probably intelligible to those who had at least small Latin and some grasp of the remnants of Medieval English that were still, like worn coins, being passed around. Almost four centuries later, we have much more trouble with the basic nature of Shakespeare's language than his contemporaries did (though perhaps they had more trouble than we usually suppose).

Our trouble comes mainly in two forms. The more obvious one is that many of the words are opaque to a modern reader, having vanished from currency long ago. In a way, this is the lesser of the two problems, even if it seems the more daunting. When we run into words we know we don't know, the cure is easy: a minute with the great *Oxford English Dictionary*, which guides us to the meaning of a given word at various periods in the history of the language; or with C. T. Onions' *A Shakespearean Glossary*, which uses the principle of the *OED* (Onions was one of its early editors) but skims off the Shakespearean vocabulary and places it in his time; or just a glance at the notes in an annotated edition (though this is slightly riskier, as the editors have not always done their homework) will usually put us on track. The same techniques as we use for unusual words in modern texts will do for Shakespeare, though for Shakespeare we need dictionaries of a more specialized kind.

The less obvious difficulty with Shakespeare's language is that it is sufficiently close to our own that we are constantly tempted to forget that his characters speak a version of English that is consistently different from ours, and that a gap of four centuries makes more difference in familiar items than an ocean's worth of contemporary distance. Everyone interested in the English language has savored modern differences in national usage through examples like "I'm mad about my flat," or "I'll knock you up in the morning." What we know we don't know may require the trouble of looking up, but that is less of a problem than what we think we recognize, unaware of the shift in meaning that has taken place. "The Duke is humorous," says LeBeau to Orlando, in *As You Like It* 1.2. Our instincts are to read something like "jolly, playful, amusing." But LeBeau's meaning—and Shakespeare's—is drawn from the old medical theory of humors, and carries an opposite sense: the Duke is moody, disgruntled, disturbed.

This too is not as large a problem as it may seem, though it is a problem to be wary of. In the case of false cognates, the context will usually tip us off to the realization that the word means something other than we are used to. Just before calling the Duke "humorous," LeBeau has said "Yet such is now the Duke's condition, / That he misconsters all that you haue done" ("misconsters" being close enough to "misconstrues" that we can ride with it, at least on a provisional guess; the dynamics of the statement require some such meaning); and just after, he adds "what he is indeede / More suites you to conceiue, then I to speake of." The extra *e* in *suits* and *speak*, the standard *u* for *v* in *conceive*, won't throw anyone off for more than a moment. The whole package makes it clear that "humorous" is a thumbnail version of the other parts of LeBeau's characterization of the Duke's mood, and cannot possibly mean what we normally intend by the same word—must, in fact, mean nearly the opposite. Close and careful reading, with an alertness to what does not quite fall into place, will often be enough to keep us from being misled about shifted meanings.

Learning to cope with Shakespeare's language requires more than being aware of the shift of meaning in *humorous*, though that shift is important to know.[8] The general condition of the language was also different in Shakespeare's time.

The rate of change had increased considerably over the preceding century. To begin with, there was a substantial burgeoning of vocabulary. We cannot be precise about this, since the surviving texts are obviously only the tip of the iceberg (and we know that many texts have been lost), but it has been estimated that ten thousand new words entered English during the Renaissance period, an increase of over 25 percent from the end of the Medieval era.[9] That is roughly analogous to what has happened to English in the twentieth-century expansive development of scientific and technical vocabulary, together with the specifically late twentieth-century flowering of computer-speak, correction of gender bias, proliferation of acronyms and official euphemisms, adoption of new words invented in other languages, and absorption of coinages from a prominent popular psychotherapeutic culture.

Such sudden growth tended then, as it does now, to erode the sense of a classical standard of formally proper language and style. Just as English has seen, over the past hundred years, the gradual abandonment of oratorical models and grand prose, and the overall breakdown of conventional distinctions between formal and colloquial usage,[10+] so the English of Shakespeare's time was reprocessing the public sense of linguistic decorum, and producing books in styles that aspired to be more lively than "correct," poems that substituted shirtsleeve directness for the earlier stately poise, and plays in which characters use colloquial idioms, casual grammar, and slang.

Along with this came, especially in literary and dramatic writing, a taste for novelty and inventiveness. This produced not only new words made up for the occasion (usually out of Latin roots or as variations on existing words, so as to leave them generally intelligible despite their unfamiliarity) and new importations of "nonliterary" words into literary works, but other forms of inventiveness as well. There arose new verbal strategies for expressing familiar moods, attitudes, emotions, and the like, so as to make them more feelable rather than merely recognizable. New ways developed for achieving the effect of grandeur, sweetness, elegance, and eloquence. New techniques were required for dealing with a changing sense of the relationship between writer and reader, which had begun to include the assumption that the writer's personal state of mind was relevant to the occasion, rather than being an impertinent consideration that should be carefully excluded from the official pronouncement. In some respects, it was a whole new ball game.[11*]

In short, Shakespeare wrote at a time of maximum freedom and reorganization in the arts of language, when language artists were *self-consciously* readjusting what they had inherited and trying to expand the capacities of English. Conventionally, that period is regularly called by linguists the time of the formation of Early Modern English. The label is appropriate, because the movement was so successful. In the midst of it, English became supple and pliable to dramaturgical needs in a way that had never happened before and has not happened since.

A proper reading of Shakespeare should accordingly include not only an appreciation of how well it all came out, but also a sense of the dynamic effects at the time. What may look a bit old-fashioned from the perspective of Later Modern English was at the moment daring, adventuresome, and excitingly inventive, full of unprecedented vitality and governed by a remarkable command of both linguistic tact and linguistic creativity. We will probably never see its like again.

10

THE PURPOSE OF PLAYING . . . AT THE FIRST AND NOW

The aims of Shakespearean dramaturgy

I was told many years ago that an American had presented himself at the British Museum (now the British Library) requesting a copy of the British Constitution. The American Constitution is a relatively brief document that underlies all American federal law, and is in general well known (though not necessarily understood) by all Americans. A moderately well-read American quite naturally supposes that references to the British Constitution, which crop up from time to time in books and articles on British history, point to a parallel document which the Founding Fathers of the United States perhaps imitated. The British Constitution is not a document at all, but rather a complex of customary institutions linked and defined by an accumulation of authoritative legal precedents—more similar to the way a human body is organized than to the birth certificate that bestows upon this body its legal authorization together with its rights and responsibilities.

Shakespeare wrote with an Elizabethan/Jacobean dramaturgical accent that differed significantly from what was usual in the plays of fifty years before, or fifty years after, his career as playwright. The constitution of his dramaturgy was more like the British Constitution—a set of customs, techniques, conventional assumptions, organizational practices, and stylizations that had become more or less coherent, although not systematically rationalized—than the American Constitution, whose dramatic analogue may be found governing late-seventeenth-century plays, whose critics enforced a more unified and rationalized dramaturgy derived primarily from Aristotle's constitutional *Poetics*, as elaborated and interpreted by the commentators of the Renaissance.

In this chapter, I will try to follow through with the hints of the opening chapters of this book, in an attempt to bring together some of the peculiarities of Shakespearean dramaturgy as more concretely elaborated in the intervening chapters, in the hope of securing an overview of what Shakespeare was doing, and by what general rules, and in pursuit of what values. This is, in short, a summary chapter on the Shakespearean accent and on the constitution of Shakespearean dramaturgy. It will generalize in ways that deserve qualification, take shortcuts that leave important considerations out of view, specialize, oversimplify, and leave far too much unsaid. But there is no other way to sketch the basic map, and much of what it fails to say will be provided in a subsequent book.

I start at the abstract level of aesthetics. Art is expected to be satisfying in some notable way. Traditionally, the satisfaction has been thought to arrive characteristically through the experience of some sort of beauty, though some leaned toward other effects such as grandeur, fidelity to truth, brilliant performance, delicacy, power. Some artists have aimed rather at entertainment, effective shock, moral edification, subversion of values, wit, ponderous gravity, amusement. A few artists have cared about understanding the philosophical principles of what they were doing; probably most of them settled for knowing what worked, what felt right, what made sense to try next. I think Shakespeare clearly belongs in the latter category.

The philosophical principles of art, however, remain a legitimate concern of those who try to understand it as thoroughly as possible. Serious reflective art criticism about drama, which is at least as old as Plato and Aristotle, made a firm mark on the English scene with Philip Sidney's *An Apology for Poetrie* and was rapidly refined through the work of continental commentators and theorists whose work was progressively absorbed into the English discussion. It was firmly present in Shakespeare's time, especially through the dramatic and critical accomplishments of Ben Jonson; it became more thoroughly entrenched in the English scene when the theaters reopened after the 1660 Restoration of the throne, after having been dark since 1642, when the movement that led to the civil war and the temporary abolition of the monarchy had closed them down. A new form of drama, built on different dramaturgical principles, supplanted what had previously been written and performed. New theaters were built according to different architectural principles, new plays were written according to a different sense of dramaturgy, and, as we have already discussed, the industry of rewriting the plays of Shakespeare, to conform them to Improved Standards of Dramatic Sophistication, began.

At the heart of the new aesthetics of drama by which critics and commentators and architects and actors and audiences and playwrights were guided lay what became known as the Doctrine of the Unities. I have touched on this subject early in the book, and have little to add to what I said then; but at least a brief recapitulation is in order.

There were three major principles of unity by which a well-written play was to be governed.

The Unity of Place dictated that the general locale in which the play was initially set must not be changed: if we start *Romeo and Juliet* in Verona, the brief episode with Romeo in his Mantua exile (5.1) will seem incoherent, so its content should be absorbed into a later Verona context—say, a conversation with Balthasar as they arrive at the Capulets' tomb. We cannot spread *Henry IV, Part 1* over various parts of Northumbria, Wales, and the Home Counties. Just as 1.3 manages to bring the incipient rebels to the king, to answer his summons, thus permitting them to start their plotting near to where the play began, so it should be contrived for Glendower to meet with them in the same vicinity if possible—and if not, the meeting should be reported rather than staged. Each scene should have a stable location with stable dimensions. The masquers en route to Capulet's feast should exit before the servants come forth to redefine the place as Capulet's mansion; the Flint Castle scene in *Richard II* (3.3) would work better if set within the castle, with Richard receiving informative messengers who will prepare us for his reception of Northumberland's embassy, with an eventual entrance of Bolingbroke to the same room where the scene should begin. For a whole play to unfold within the same room was ideal, and was often accomplished by what French dramatists had perfected as *liaison des scènes*, a dramaturgical practice in which the stage is never cleared but always leaves a character to be entered to for the next episode, thus guaranteeing that the place has not changed. If this should be too constraining, it is permissible to move about somewhat in the same neighborhood, at least during intermissions.

The Unity of Time projected the parallel ideal of an absolute identity between playing time and represented time; but if it is asking too much to squeeze all the plans, complications, counterplans, new developments, and processes of resolution into a two- to three-hour time scheme, it was allowed to pretend that a full twenty-four hour day's work could be shown between the audience's lunch and dinner. If the original story took weeks or months to work itself out, the plot of the play should be designed so as to catch the crucial final period of resolution, filling us in on what had gone before. If the opening of *A Midsummer Night's Dream* projects a further four days before the wedding, this should be changed to "tomorrow night," and the play redrafted accordingly. *King Lear* is on the right track in closing 1.1 with the news that Lear will spend the night (not next week) with Goneril and Albany, but the suggestion that his visit to Regan will be a full month later stretches things out too far. *Hamlet* would need a lot of tightening in this regard.

The Unity of Action requires that there be a concentrated focus on one central happening. Other supportive byways can be accommodated (the Paris–Juliet project fits well), and even more marginal doings are tolerable as long as they relate well to the main business (one should probably cut back the attention given to Falstaff and the wild side of Hal, as the play now seems to spend a disproportionate amount of attention on enjoying this stuff for its own sake; and the Touchstone–Audrey–William–Martext adventure strays too far from the principal story; and just what *is* the main action of *A Midsummer Night's Dream*, anyway? Isn't it really all over by the end of act 4?).

Such principles were already taken quite seriously during Shakespeare's writing career, and I suggest that *The Tempest*, probably the last play over which he took full charge, cannot be adequately understood without bearing them in mind. They are not silly, even though they no longer claim our loyalty. Samuel Johnson is too much appreciated for his commonsense observation that if we can sit in a London theater and pretend that we are watching a scene in ancient Rome, it is not too much of a strain to imagine that the next scene is taking place in Egypt: but try that out in temporal rather than the more familiar spatial terms, and see whether it is as easy to follow a play in which an opening Wednesday scene is followed by one set on the previous Friday, which then yields to another placed a year later. Shakespeare did not invest in the Unities as they were being formulated in his time. It is plain that he appreciated some of the values that they were intended to secure, and he accordingly disguises shifts in time and space and offers superficial unifications of action, but he was entirely unrigorous, and frequently nonrational, about how he did so.

His appreciation was expressed in a different dramaturgy—one that could manipulate time and space to give an overriding impression of continuity and coherence rather than confining the action to literally rationalized temporal and spatial containment. I will not add to what I have said already about Shakespeare's appreciation of the dramatic values of unifying space and time and his manner of honoring those values through a more flexible dramaturgical idiom, a traditional dramatic constitution that was already in the process of being replaced by a a more centralized and explicit set of principles. As for the Unity of Action, there is much more that needs to be said.

We now smile benignly on the Unities of Place and Time as they were propounded for over a century after Shakespeare stopped writing plays—and as they still leave their marks in the division of scenes and the suppression (or addition) of stage directions in popular editions of those very plays. Cinematic techniques have, along with other influences, restored to us a capacity to follow spatial and temporal shifts without losing track and without the story's losing continuity. But we still have an inherited loyalty to peculiar versions of the Unity of Action, and we still have trouble understanding how the value it was meant to protect can be secured without fairly tight naturalistic controls. Accordingly, we tend either to contrive ways of reading Shakespeare that keep him within the bounds of a central plan to which everything is subordinated, or (more rarely) we acknowledge that he did not stay within those bounds and pardon him for his inconsistencies on the grounds that he wrote in a precritical, presophisticated, pre-Enlightenment time.

I want to make a case for the following propositions: (1) *our* sense of the aesthetics of unity is in many respects as provincial as the old Unities of Time and Space, and misses the point of an equally respectable Shakespearean sense of that value; (2) *our* tolerance for, and even our sense of, inconsistency in Shakespeare is accordingly as faulty as the Restoration critics' botherment about the legitimacy of Shakespeare's distributing a play's action over an arbitrary amount of space and time according to the needs of the play rather than according to the rules; and (3) *our* sense of what Shakespeare should be trying to achieve in characterization, thematics, poetic effects, realism, and the overall experience of the audience or reader is misguided and needs serious correction. Implicit in all of this, though not on the agenda for separate discussion, is (4) *our* sense of Shakespeare's achievement tends to fall far short of what is available to us through the texts (which have fortunately been preserved from a place close to his own mind and hand but which have rarely been read appropriately since the Restoration), and may be recovered through what the same texts show us about how they are meant to be understood and appreciated.

1. Respectful writings on Shakespeare's plays often strain to show that there is a governing idea or a central image or a key meaning that guides the organization of the play in question, and that all the dramaturgical planning of the play was in the service of this point of unity, subordinating everything to the task of its realization. Some writers suppose that this was a conscious program; others seem to presume it a function of his instinctive genius. But the assumption that there must be a Unifying Principle in there somewhere inspires a considerable proportion of the interpretive ingenuity applied to the plays.

Why should one make such an assumption?

It is, I think, instinctive to modern interpreters, who have inherited a version of the aesthetics of Immanuel Kant (who is regularly regarded in philosophical circles as the watershed thinker whose critiques have formed the continental divide between modern and premodern thought), mediated especially through the English critic and theorist who argued more successfully and articulately than anyone else the independent intellectual dignity and privilege of literary art, Samuel Coleridge. Coleridge is not often cited in modern theoretical and critical discussions, and his observations on Shakespeare are relatively uninfluential in current critical work, though they remain respected. But I think that this is where the tide turned.

Such literary theorizing as there was in Shakespeare's own time leaned especially on the authority of Plato and Aristotle. Aristotle, as interpreted by sixteenth- and seventeenth-century thinkers, dominated theoretical and critical writings on plays (as well as other literary forms) well into the eighteenth century, but mainly in the form of compositional rules (the Unities of Time, Place, and Action being among the most important rules rather than constituting a total unitary aesthetics). Horace's *Ars Poetica* was a major guide to literary practice in the same period of time, but its promotion of literary unity is not particularly strong, and the poetical epistle in which he presents his views was (and is) notoriously sprawling and un-unified. The seventeenth-century rediscovery of *Longinus on the Sublime* gave rise to an eighteenth-century attention to Great Moments in literary art, which tended to distract from the value of overall unity. In the meantime, plays (and, by extrapolation, other literary forms) on the quasi-Aristotelian model and lyric poetry based on both classical and modern precedents were probably more influential than anything else in promoting the *practice* of Unitary Principle literature, which still waited for an adequate theorist.

In England, Coleridge was that theorist. Whether or not he was well understood, or even read, he provided the philosophical basis for a set of notions that had long been present in the flow of literary history: literary art had its own independent dignity, quite apart from whether it was morally edifying or a successful purveyor of the kind of truth sought by philosophers, and that dignity rested especially on its capacity to gather its materials into an organization that released an experience of beauty—and that was all that could be asked. Beauty, said Coleridge, is especially the experience of unity transcending variety, the ordering of the stuff of human knowledge and feeling into a construct in which everything participates in the mutual creation of a point, or a vanishing-point, of unifying satisfaction.

From Coleridge on, there seemed to be little need to fight the skirmishes of the previous two centuries over whether successfully satisfying art is its own justification. It was no longer necessary to contrive arguments to say that art makes people morally better, or more enlightened, in order to legitimate its place in culture. Other theorists continued to argue that *great* art will always do that sort of thing, but their basic cause had already been lost in the emancipation of art from morals and philosophical understanding. Its job was now to deliver beauty, and the best delivery of beauty was the manifestation of what but nearly everyone agreed was rooted in *form*, which is a more digestible word for the same idea: a oneness made up of many parts, a harmonized shape confected from carefully organized subordinate components, a dynamic complex of moments under the effective governance of a unifying principle.

All of this is rather attractive, and may be thought importantly liberating. So why *shouldn't* one make such an assumption?

The main reason is that it is not the only assumption that can be made; the close-running second reason is that it is not the only assumption on which major literary and dramatic works were built; and the strongly contending third reason is that, whatever virtues it may have as a grounding for new works of art, as a principle of *interpretation* it is bound to distort the proper appreciation of artworks that were not put together that way. A glance around the world through recent history may suggest that the essential purpose of government is the creation of wealth, but that insight is more likely to retard than to advance one's capacity to understand ancient Sparta, or the Indian Six Nations in eighteenth-century America, or modern Maoist China. The notion, not uncommon among seventeenth-century students of religion, that all known (sometimes extended to all knowable) religions are either deformations of or faltering aspirations toward the worship of an essentially Christian God, is not useful as a procedural principle in the attempt to understand religions. Kantian and Coleridgean aesthetic principles do not map what Shakespeare was doing.

Elizabethan writings on art in general are almost nonexistent, and writings on literary/dramatic art (with the spectacular exception of Sidney's) are neither richer nor deeper than modern general theorizings about sports. They tend to pay homage to the received pieties about moral improvement and deeper insight, often without conveying a great deal of conviction, adding that literary examples are more vivid and unambiguous than those from life, and that meter and rhyme make good maxims easier to remember.

Jaques' argument with the Duke about the value of satire in *As You Like It* 2.7 is a representative example of late Elizabethan literary theory, with Jaques claiming that if he were given free rein, his impersonal fictions representing types of vicious and virtuous behavior would inspire a general reformation as good citizens scrambled to dissociate themselves from the former and emulate the latter. The Duke's *ad hominem* reply, arguing that Jaques' jaded libertine background, the putative inspiration of his bitterness as a reformer, would lead to an unedifying disgorgement of unsavory stuff that would be better left unsaid, is left unanswered because of the interruption of Orlando's aggressive entrance. But there was not, in fact, much more to be said. The Duke's specific charge is lame and unfair; the strength of his counterposition is acted out rather than spoken, and it roughly amounts to saying that Jaques' ideal of literature is not nice, not humane, not really *appropriate*.

Appropriateness is the key category. Writers of Shakespeare's time were as aware that they were *supposed* to be doing high social service as modern corporations are clear that their essential purpose is to serve the common good. But when they were thinking about what makes a good play, Shakespeare and his contemporaries were probably concentrated more on what seems functionally appropriate to their audiences and to themselves, simultaneously taking care of an undefined moral responsibility while keeping a keen eye on effective box-office results.

I have touched on some of the more specific values in earlier chapters. An engaging story, populated by aptly drawn personages who say lovely and grand and witty and amusingly silly things in the course of the story's working-out (these various effects being, of course, decorouly distributed among the roles according to station and situation), with some exciting confrontations and if possible some good swordplay (only two of our seven plays lack it, and they both remind us of it), all resolved in an ending that knits up everything appropriately—this is the real task, the real calling.

Appropriateness is, of course, a slippery critical category. Right now, I want to do two things with it. The first is to suggest that in the sense of appropriateness that governed the aesthetics of Shakespeare's plays, which was a function of the sense of appropriateness generally prevailing when he wrote, the modern received notion of unitary principles did not much figure, and that we are therefore approaching the plays misleadingly if we search for it, and doing them no favor if we find a way of interpreting them to conform to it. The second project is to suggest some of the differences between the modern bias for unitary principles and the Elizabethan/Jacobean sense of what is satisfactorily appropriate.

Classical standards, whether we consult Aristotle on poems and plays, or Palladio on architecture, or Plato on philosophy, tended to simplify, streamline, and abstract in order to produce a harmonized and unified effect. The revival of these standards was already strong in Shakespeare's time, and became dominant not long after his death. When the old landmark Gothic cathedral of St. Paul's perished in the devastating London fire of 1666, Christopher Wren designed its successor, which still stands, as a very un-Gothic, relatively unelaborate, structurally balanced and unified *classical* edifice, following in the classically revisionist tradition of Shakespeare's contemporary architect Inigo Jones.

That was a representative happening. When the theaters had been closed for eighteen years and then reopened (the theater-history equivalent of the London fire), late-seventeenth-century literary critics freely quoted the continental codifications of pseudo-Aristotelian principles as if they were both Aristotelian and definitive; but they had not been altogether so, even among their earlier and admired allies. Ben Jonson had a similar reverence for Aristotle, but was—doubtless unwittingly—old-fashioned enough to misread him by importing the traditional English bias toward edification and enlightenment.

The tension between these two tendencies in the Constitution of thought was registered well before the great clearing of the dramatic stage between 1642 and 1660. Thomas Blundeville's 1574 treatise on writing and reading history follows the "Methodicall" rationalism of Francisco Patricio through the first task, which occasionally reads as if the writing of history is like the designing of an utterly true play, and then suddenly switches to the *reading* of history, with an emphasis on the appreciation of divine providence and the chances of appropriating the moral lessons for which his model for its *writing* leaves no appreciable room, without ever giving a sign that he sees how different these two approaches are.[1+] William Baldwin's Elizabethan book entitled *Moral Philosophy* is not an analytic treatise, probing the essential principles of moral behavior and demonstrating how they unify the subject (which is what could be expected from such a title if offered a century later), but rather a rambling set of maxims and life observations of the sort we get from Friar Laurence and Polonius.

Like the British Constitution itself, the aesthetic that can be inferred from the received habits of mind that obtained in Shakespearean England had a large and accepting tolerance for unrationalized multiplicity. Londoners walked from place to place through lanes and streets that were often indirect, but which got them there. The coins in circulation came from various lands, but people knew how to evaluate and spend (or receive) them appropriately, and dramatists refer to a wild variety of currencies as a result. They were teased by their dramatists for the way they dressed, combining the fashions of all Europe in their various upper and lower garments—but the same dramatists' plays were produced by companies that had in their wardrobes costumes identified as Spanish doublets, French hose, Italian trousers. They not only lived with unrationalized variety, but apparently preferred it, seeing nothing in it nearly as inappropriate as the notion that all streets should be straight, merchants should be free to refuse a good Venetian ducat in payment, and the rationally coherent Puritan Basic Black should be the fashion.

Rather than multiply examples (which can only suggest, and cannot prove, no matter how many there may be), I will simply aver that the aesthetics, the taste, the sense of appropriateness that prevailed popularly in Shakespeare's time, did not share the subsequent (and still lively) bias toward rationalization and unifying principles. I add one more image, not as proof but as illustration.

At the time of Shakespeare's birth, England's top-level financial market was centered on London's Lombard Street, and was conducted in what seemed to Thomas Gresham an unsophisticatedly random way, by comparison with Antwerp's renowned Bourse. In addition to helping to regularize the way the Crown borrowed money and to rationalize its treatment of foreign merchants, Gresham founded a Bourse in London in 1568 (gratefully consecrated by Queen Elizabeth as The Royal Exchange) where financial transactions could be made in a centralized and uniform and regulable fashion. London soon replaced Antwerp as the financial center of Europe.[2]

Shortly before Shakespeare's death, Robert Cecil built an upscale and rival New Exchange, governed by strict corporate rules that excluded the marketing of ordinary perishables and provided sanctions against violations of the deliberate high tone of "civility and refinement."[3]

These projects seem to me significant as cultural artifacts as well as financial reforms: they are symptomatic of a profound change in overall aesthetics, a shift in the sense of appropriateness for which reverberations and resulting analogues can be found, during approximately the same period, in all the arts and in religion, philosophy, politics, and clothing fashions as well.

This did not happen with smooth regularity, nor all at once, but it changed the perception of values permanently, requiring reconsiderations and reassessments and revisions and reformations and restructurings and reconstitutions in almost every phase of life. In most cases, we have forgotten what had been there before this massive readjustment, or we dismiss it as an evolution into something more mature, or we just assume that double negatives always made a logical positive and that maximizing the gross national product was always a preoccupation of governments and find a way to reinterpret the evidences of the past. But the mentality that created the Royal Exchange and the New Exchange was new; and before it came to be, the dominant image that preceded it, the image that tended especially to express that earlier sense of how life works, was the fair.

The fair was an effective image because it was a familiar practical reality. The fair was the quintessentially various, decentralized, nonrationalized, and disunified great social and economic occasion. From a popular point of view, the fair was social life at the summit and at its most ample manifestation. The fair was (and had been from a long time before) the great metaphor for how life sprawled out in its self-determining variety, excitement, and disordered opportunity, combining nearly all walks of life and all manner of projects, from buying a bit of ribbon to selling the year's produce, from watching acrobats to setting up a great congame. From Langland's field full of folk[4] through Ben Jonson's Bartholomew Fair to Bunyan's Vanity Fair, *this* was the summation of the gorgeous multiplicity within which people could seek and sometimes find what they want, have a various good time among the jugglers and mountebanks and hawkers and general abundance, and hope that everything turns out appropriately. The fair was a metaphor of the world, and often of life itself.

The carefully regulated market eventually streamlined, simplified, and abstracted the process of business. But that was apparently not what Shakespeare's early contemporaries were most busy about, or in the market for. He wanted, as they wanted, a satisfying end to the day's adventure at the fair; but he knew, as they knew, that it could not be nearly as satisfying or appropriate if he had not in the meantime provided something more like the fair's burgeoning variety than like the pruned and efficient style that was beginning to take over.[5+]

I do not in the least mean to imply that Shakespeare or his audiences could have been satisfied with a a dramaturgy of wild abandon. The alternative to unity is not chaos, nor even disorder. There are various alternatives, and the most important one is, in the case of Shakespeare and the fading Elizabethan aesthetics to which he remained partisan, something more like *connected multiplicity*. Shakespearean dramaturgy takes pains to make sure that nearly everything in a given play has some sort of continuity with everything else (often a linkage above and beyond the call of dutiful coherence, often quite artificial and otherwise nonfunctional), but does not carry this to the extent of organizing the play around a central principle to which everything else is subordinated.

I have dealt with many of the specifics in earlier chapters. Shakespeare usually sees to it that we have a sense that a given action is temporally continuous with what precedes and what follows, but there is no central clock: time may be expanded or contracted, the linkages may be artificial (even literally impossible), and he may omit specific links altogether—but his management of the illusion of time is such that he nearly always leaves us with the sense that there are no blank spots, no temporal discontinuities (positive continuities often being overtly reinforced, sometimes quite unrealistically, as in the movement from *King Lear* 1.3 to 1.4) in the action. Space may likewise be contracted or expanded within a single scene, but even relocations as we shift from one scene to another are evidently grounded in the assumption that space is imaginatively continuous beyond the limits of any given scene's use of it, and therefore that an abrupt shift between forest and court in *As You Like It* or between Verona and Mantua in *Romeo and Juliet* is not significantly different from what the audience may do at will as they shift their attention between the marching masquers and the Capulet mansion after the opening words of *Romeo and Juliet* 1.5.

Arbitrary and unnecessary personal linkages abound: Edgar is Lear's godson, and partied with his knights; Rosalind's father loved Orlando's father, though their children apparently never met until it was time to fall in love (and Rosalind makes no effort whatever to be recognizable to her father before the play's last scene); Paris is related to Mercutio, and both of them to the Prince. Multiple actions are cemented together similarly: Theseus and Hippolyta have dallied with Titania and Oberon and owe them one on the occasion of their wedding, but the woods outside Athens also happens to be one of Titania's favorite haunts—and when the lovers have got properly sorted out, why not make the ducal wedding a threesome of couples, as if this were socially obvious? And what could be more unlogically logical than to bring Jaques de Boys into the last scene of *As You Like It*, impressively well informed about relevant recent events, to share in the joy of his brothers' weddings (which are inevitably conjoined with those of such peers as Silvius and Phoebe, Touchstone and Audrey)?

No need to lengthen the list or stuff the tongue farther into the cheek. Shakespeare makes things belong together, and demonstrates by his care in doing so that this was an important point of dramaturgy to him—but he regularly does so simply by connecting them (sometimes with wonderful impertinence), not by building a unitary construct that automatically defines a set of inevitable relatednesses. Connection, linkages, continuities were his usual mode of unification. And although such unification was important in his dramaturgy, it did not have to devolve centrally from a unifying principle: local managements were quite sufficient to create the sense of collective unity within the multiplicity that was a competing, but governable, dramaturgical value.

2. Those who approach Shakespeare's plays with a bias for consistency can easily fault them for their carelessness on that front. Alternatively, they can usually find ingenious ways of explaining the inconsistencies away. There is at least one other way of dealing with this phenomenon: appreciate the dramatic appropriateness of the original definition of the situation, and allow Shakespeare to change the rules when it becomes dramatically appropriate to do so—i.e., change your sense of what consistency is.

A Midsummer Night's Dream opens with Theseus lamenting to Hippolyta that their wedding is four days away; but the thrust of the action thereafter gives us only one long and adventuresome night before the wedding day. Why not have Theseus say that it is a long time until tomorrow (which in the circumstances is true enough) if that is the way things are going to be?

One good reason appears in Theseus' next speech: he sends Philostrate to stir up some celebration among his subjects. Shakespeare wants the Pyramus and Thisby play for the last act. He prefers to let us in on the beginnings of things, as evidenced in Capulet's sending out his invitations on the morning of his accustomed feast. But it is one thing to squeeze guests into a foreshortened brief notice, and quite another to expect Philostrate's invitation to be answered by the next night: the Athenian mechanicals need time to get their act together, including rehearsal time, and a token four days will serve as a foreshortened allowance analogous (given what they have to do) to telling guests in the morning that they are expected in the evening.

But once Theseus has established that he is giving some room for act 5 to be put together, there is no particular need to hold him, or the play, to it. *Pyramus and Thisby* can be hustled into place in four days according to the same sort of foreshortened timetable Capulet is using—neither is realistic, but both are tolerable in a dramaturgical idiom that obeys realism only when it pleases to do so—and Theseus' duty is done. If the wedding entertainment is ready when act 5 comes around, the next evening, we are no more entitled then Peter Quince to say that it can't be. It is. The question about whether it realistically could be is therefore irrelevant, and is not asked.

The changes in the text and cast of *Pyramus and Thisby* are of another order. We heard the plans, we saw the rehearsal, and the performance is significantly different—almost *absolutely* different—from both. There is no way to charge this off to a shifted finesse (four days to put it together is, within a Shakespearean play, an initial allowance with token reasonableness; further token representations of initial organization and raw rehearsal allow us to accept that it is ready at the end of the next day; but roles and lines cannot be mutated with foreshortening alone).

The inconsistency in this case is more closely analogous to Shakespeare's representation of the understanding of the Athenian lovers in 4.1 (where they know only that it has all worked out, without any overt inkling that fairies were involved) and the very different understanding reported by Hippolyta at the beginning of 5.1 (where it is plain that the lovers have told her about the fairies, thus setting off Theseus' most memorable—only memorable?—speech). In the latter case, it is simply better for *A Midsummer Night's Dream* to change the state of the lovers' information. It is good for them to be totally ignorant of what we have seen through act 4; it is also good for Theseus to be in a position to dismiss testimony about fairies at the start of act 5. The contradiction is utterly blatant, mediated only by the fuzzy-mindedness of the lovers as they are newly wakened; but it is good for the play, and therefore appropriate enough to embrace if Shakespeare can get by with it.

He gets by with it. He knew that *our* state of information contained both an awareness that the fairies were importantly there as organizers of a happy ending, and that the lovers thought that they were on their own. With an interim passage that registers the lovers' dreamy puzzlement and confusion, it was easy enough to pretend that somehow they now, in act 5, know what they had not known when we last saw them, and it is rare for even careful readers of the play to notice the contradiction.

That is as it should be. It is a contradiction only from a Total Coherence point of view. From the perspective of Shakespearean-style dramaturgical management, it is merely an appropriate (and well-engineered) rearrangement.

By the time we get to the end of the first scene of *Henry IV, Part 1*, we are no longer thinking of the conditions that obtained at the beginning: a new development and a more immediate problem has distracted our attention. That (also fairly, though not rationally, well engineered) shift allows King Henry to produce new information without our adverting to the fact that no messenger has delivered it. Theoretically, he must have known from the start of the scene; dramaturgically, he didn't. And that makes enough difference to allow Shakespeare to finesse another technical contradiction well enough to foreshorten the scene's movement as well as (or better than) he could have done by the literal introduction of news.

Lear sends Kent to Gloucester in 1.5, obviously expecting that Regan will be there. And of course there she is when Lear himself arrives in 2.4. But Goneril in the meantime has sent Oswald to the Regan–Cornwall home base (which obviously makes more sense), and this turns out to be the occasion of Regan's abrupt move to Gloucester's place—as the stocked Kent confirms, with his story of having arrived *chez* Regan just after Oswald's embassy had somehow messed up Lear's reception by Regan and Cornwall. That is, Shakespeare lays out both the logical sequence of having Lear move before the appointed time from Goneril to Regan, with abrupt notice given, *and* the dramatic sequence of having Lear's confrontation with Goneril followed by a further confrontation with Regan *chez* Gloucester. Lear's sending Kent to Gloucester in order to inform Regan of his coming is the direct line to the next major stage of the play, though it otherwise makes no sense; Kent's superficially insubordinate trip to Regan's is the logical tack, and Shakespeare arranges that we know why it results in a general flight to Gloucester, where the major roles converge for a showdown. Shakespeare, in short, is playing two games at once, and very inconsistently: game #1 is the pursuit of what is eventually going to happen, the Shakespearean shortcut; game #2 is the more painstaking logical setting-up of why it turns out to happen that way.

I list the games in that order because it seems to me that Shakespeare, while interested in giving us both a dramaturgy of logical progression and a dramaturgy of cut-to-the-chase, preferred the latter. The former often comes off as dutiful tokenism. But rearrange the order if you like: the main point is that he offers *both*, even though they are technically inconsistent with one another. The net result is that the action develops in the most *dramatically* efficient way, while he acknowledges that he hasn't forgotten that he ought to make the rational connections. Faced with an either/or of plotting, he skirts it by providing a both/and.

One may argue that this is not proper procedural justice: but Shakespeare was more interested in being fair than in being just. *Justice*, in this sense, is the avoidance of contradiction, the even-handed measuring-out of all happenings in accordance with a consistent set of rules, the observance of the rational order that governs space and time and all human limitations. *Fairness* is making things happen effectively within a play that owes more allegiance to effective happening than to the rules that obtain in the world the play only imitates and is free to reflect in somewhat distorted mirrors if they bring things off more effectively. Token acknowledgement of the distortion is not really necessary, but more fair in that it displays simultaneously an awareness of the world's rules and the candid admission that a play need not observe them and is free to take shortcuts. The contradictions thus generated are not faults in dramaturgy but strategies. Shakespeare does not try to lull his audiences into thinking that they are watching life rather than a play: on the contrary, his texts are seasoned with little occasional reminders that the play is the thing we're doing, and that it's fair to take advantage of the difference.

A dramaturgy of both/and is troublesome to systematic rationality, but the latter was not the medium in which Shakespeare worked. He worked in participatory imagination. What is a blemish to the former is a liberated and liberating efficiency to the latter. And on the whole, one may say that Shakespeare never did dramaturgical injustice but with fair cause.

3. Shakespeare's stories are enacted through the parts that his actors played, and as long as these parts carry their share of the burden, there is no necessity of their being endowed with anything like personality or independently motivating psychology. We understand this well enough in modern situation comedy, where the project may be launched by something extraneous like needing to come up with the rent payment, or something quite routine like wanting to make a new dress for a forthcoming party, and as the plot moves along it is often enough for the principal roles to act and react as virtually anyone would. It is often useful to introduce *types* in some of the parts, roles that carry familiar clusters of attitudes or traits (the impatient and suspicious landlord who wants to get grounds for eviction and will allow no extensions; the scatterbrained blonde who mislays things and misunderstands instructions and gets dates wrong), since they are efficient ways of creating expectations and setting up amusing situations. But we have a different set of rules for what we think of as "serious drama," where we tend to insist on personalized motivation, psychological depth and coherence, and the sharp individuation of characters.

Shakespeare did not share this double standard. For all the serious drama of *Romeo and Juliet*, he gives us a Lady Montague who has little to do but express concerned puzzlement over Romeo's obvious symptoms, a Prince who does merely what any firm prince would do, and a Lady Capulet whose most potentially interesting psychological moment (a notion of having Romeo poisoned in Mantua) is a straight man's throwaway with no more realistic life or substance than the seed that falls accidentally upon the rock. Even in *King Lear*, after Shakespeare's dramaturgy has shifted more toward modern preferences, there is virtually no attempt to account for Cornwall's vicious tyranny, to endow the prominent Fool with personality or motivation, or to give even Cordelia much more to know her by than forthrightness, compassionate kindness, and heroic loyalty.

Shakespeare invests in the various parts the functional characteristics necessary to make the plot work well. He will often elaborate such functional characteristics, making them (and the role endowed with them) more vivid and personalized than is altogether necessary for the execution of the functions. If he goes well beyond dramatic necessity in this—and he does, even bestowing touching personality traits upon roles that have no leverage in building the action—he nevertheless remains dramaturgically purposeful in controlling our affections and our loyalties, taking advantage in what seems to have been a dramatically unrivaled skill in making us concerned about what happens to the least of the major roles' brethren in getting us to notice and care about how we regard the outcome of the principals. That is, he *humanized* his dramaturgy to make it work at a more engaged level of involvement.

What Shakespeare does in the formation of his *characters* (as distinguished from his types or his mere roles) is not a general endowment but a set of specific investments, not a gratuitous enhancement of our sense of a role's personality but a strategic provision of what the play will need.

Consider Capulet. First appearing in 1.1 as an irascible and hotheaded opponent of Montague, he is rapidly more humanized and personalized in 1.2, as he acknowledges that he can keep the peace comfortably enough and then turns to a thoughtful consideration of Paris' suit for Juliet's hand, concluding that despite her youth, the match is fine with him if she finds it good, and that Paris can take Juliet through the next step at his customary feast that evening. This is considerably more personal amplitude than is given to Lady Capulet in the folowing scene, where she raises the matter with her daughter in a rather stiffly stylized way.

Are we to conclude that Lady Capulet is simply a more drab personality than her husband? Not at all. Personalities are not in question. Capulet simply has a larger set of responsibilities in the play, and Shakespeare lays the groundwork early. Capulet's relaxed attitude toward the feud as he chats with Paris, and his hostly manner in celebrating his feast pay off in 1.5, where he amplifies the latter in his effusive welcome to the masquers and his banter with the ladies and his warm and casual reminiscences with his cousin—and again when he responds to Tybalt's indignation at Romeo's presence with a generous recognition of Romeo's good reputation and a genial willingness to let the party proceed untroubled by the now-trivial feud. Tybalt's momentary insubordination awakens a sputtering authoritarianism in him, vaguely related to his angry first appearance (but amusingly mixed with hostly asides to the guests and servants), and his performance closes in his genial mode after Romeo's match with Juliet has been founded.

The whole Capulet performance in act 1 is a fine cameo of an amiable but excitable father, host, and substantial citizen, marginally involved in an ancient grudge but mainly considerate even while being insistently authoritative. He is a memorable character—but that is not the point of the way Shakespeare has defined him.

He is, much more importantly, a character who has the (unrealized and never tested, but no less poignant for all of that) potential of being understanding about Juliet's dedication to Romeo and solicitous of her happiness, and simultaneously a character with the potential to change his solicitousness abruptly to a furious authoritarianism when he meets Juliet's tearful rejection of the Paris match in 3.5. Shakespeare has set it up so that we know enough about Capulet to feel that we are deliciously close to a happy turn of events, but also know enough to recognize that he is acting characteristically when he turns the situation in the opposite direction.

Capulet's two sets of traits are compatible, but there is a small (yet crucial) inconsistency in his makeup. In 1.2, he tells Paris that it's up to Juliet: "My will, to her assent, is but a part." In 3.5 this is forgotten: Juliet will do what he wants or starve in the street. Shakespeare can get by with this because he has made us understand how furious Capulet can be when his will is temporarily crossed over a relatively trivial matter: we are ready for how much more may come forth when his careful and advantaging plans for his only child are wantonly rejected. He is not as careful with Friar Laurence, whose unprepared (and rather obviously uncharacteristic) moment of cowardice in the final scene brings about Juliet's dramatically necessary desertion at the tomb. The show must go on, even at the expense (temporary: he is soon generally reaffirmed as a characteristically "Holy man" as he confesses all to the Prince) of a major dignified personage's moral standing.

Enough other examples have been dealt with to allow this point to be closed perfunctorily. The conclusion is this: the modern serious-drama habit of looking for psychological studies in principal characters was for the most part not present in Shakespearean dramaturgy. Characters were built outwardly, toward the needs of the play, rather than inwardly, toward the disclosure of personal depths. Hamlet's soliloquies are, like Jaques' satirical sallies in *As You Like It*, designed more to give us a glimpse of how the outer world may be seen if we look more closely (even if only one character is invested with that way of seeing) than to allow us to peer into the heart of his personal mystery. The *play's* the thing, not the character: and the play can afford to encompass a variety of representations and evaluations of life without being obliged to obey a unitary principle in presenting them or to resolve them definitively in the ending.

The thematic dimensions of Shakespearean dramaturgy are not an exception to this general pattern. The plays *beget* thoughts rather than being *derived from* them. If we must ask what a given play is about, the best first answer is to turn to the story. *Romeo and Juliet* is not about love, nor is it about what Shakespeare's source-book called "a coople of unfurtunate lovers, thralling themselved to unhonest desire"[6]—it is about Juliet and Romeo. Their adventures generate a variety of thematic notions, some through Friar Laurence (too rash, too unadvised, too sudden), others through Capulet and his wife (outrageous insubordination), still others from their dramatically and poetically compelling self-representation (which the play, isolating them at this level, affords no outside commentary until the summations of the final scene, when everyone gratuitously joins the dramatic and poetic compulsion to say with us that it was somehow very beautiful, which generously supplants, but does not cancel, the earlier reasonable evaluations).

Similarly, *Henry IV, Part 1* is not about rebellion or reformation or the integrity of England as a nation, but rather about a crisis in obligation and trust between two powerful forces, and especially about how Hotspur and Hal respond to the crisis. *Richard II* raises serious questions about the sources of a king's right to govern because there is a problem that forces this to be an issue: the fact that competing explicit or implicit ideologies are brought to bear on the matter is a function of Shakespeare's elaboration of the dilemma, not a way of thinking it through to a philosophical resolution. *A Midsummer Night's Dream* offers little thematizing about the fickleness of men and the jealousy of women, but is content simply to represent it, along with a showing of the craziness of love at all levels. *As You Like It* burgeons into explorations of the pastoral and satirical modes of literature, and various dramatically and literarily conventional and unconventional ways of representing love, as well as received notions about true nature with its multiple manifestations and powers and fanciful vs. real distinctions between court and pasture or forest. But this is because Shakespeare chose to make it rich and various in action, and allowed the resulting episodes (which are linked but not systematically integrated) to churn up interesting thoughts (which are engaged with one another but not resolved).

A lingering modern taste for thematics, parallel to the taste for psychological studies of characters, pushes readers of Shakespeare to look for a theoretical principle of unity in a given play—a search that still sometimes comes to rest in the dead end of appearance and reality (can anyone imagine a duller basis for a play, or a play that does not manage to touch on some version of it?). This, I suggest, is looking in the wrong place.

Shakespeare was a theorist in something of the same fashion that Friar Laurence was, able to reflect interestingly on the flowers he picked but doing so only after he had picked them, for purposes other than philosophizing. Laurence's moral philosophy was not a systematic theory of human nature but (like that of Thomas Baldwin, and in the general style of Shakespeare's time) an appreciation of concrete situations and an ability to rouse the locally appropriate generalizing proverb—or competing proverbs. Shakespearean thematics are a by-product of the unfolding of his dramatic action, not a blueprint for it.

And thus also his "imagery," which has often in modern times been elevated to the status of a unifying principle. But it too is local, an outpouring of metaphors and similes that express his gift for making specific verbal connections that illuminate an insight, a state of mind, an emotional turn, a judgment, and then moving on—not accumulating in a catalogue of references to clothing or animals or light or things that can be bought in an average market, but disappearing once they have made their point, "quick bright things" in Lysander's phrase, "brief as the lightning in the collied night, / That (in a spleen) unfolds both heaven and earth; / And ere a man hath power to say, 'Behold,' / The jaws of darkness do devour it up." Whether it be the slow elaboration of a complex comparison or the quick bright phrase that catches a moment on the wing, Shakespeare's specific uses of language are to be appreciated as the temporary objectifications of the dramatic moments they express, without prejudice to what may be appropriate a few lines, or scenes, down the way. In language as in other aspects of dramaturgy, his individual artistic decisions are neither legal precedents that he is bound to keep the rest of the play conformed to, nor hints of a unitary vision to which the play will be consciously or unconsciously conformed through what used to be called the alembic of his imagination. They are individual artistic decisions with no necessary or nonprovisional implications, opening new opportunities rather than further restricting potentialities that had been available.

In summary, the coherence of a Shakespearean play rests not upon a principle, or a set of principles, of centralized unity, but upon a connectedness that is usually achieved locally and a continuity that arises from and serves the unfolding of the story through dramatic action and reaction. It does not exclude inconsistencies, which Shakespeare is quite prepared to introduce if the continuity may be better served thereby (especially if they are sufficiently finessed not to be noticed, or sufficiently useful to be readily charged up to the privileges of dramatic illusion). It does not even exclude contradictions (especially when they take place within the then-traditional manipulability of space or time) or abrupt changes that seem inadequately prepared at a realistic level (especially when they are, at some other level, appropriate). Shakespearean dramaturgy is the way in which Shakespeare held his artful and versatile mirror up to nature—*our* nature still, even if not necessarily our taste, or our sense of dramatic propriety—in order to give us satisfactions and realizations that unaided and inartistic reality rarely gives.

4. If Shakespeare was not in pursuit of a unifying (or vanishing) point, but rather served a different aesthetic that permitted inconsistency and incoherence and downright contradiction (which seem to have been sufficiently expiated by the mere provision of connections, no matter how insubstantial, artificial, local, and inessential they may be)—and if he aspired neither to be a modern psychologist before his time, nor a pioneering philosopher, nor the anticipator of the ideals of modern poetry—then just what *was* he doing? What was he attempting to accomplish?

The strong critical bias that looks to tragedies for profundity and considers comedies relatively frivolous—and doesn't quite know what to do with histories at all[7!]—will get in the way of attempts to pursue such a question unless we are careful not to project it on Shakespeare. I think it works for an approach to classical Greek drama: Aristotle's clear preference for tragic form as the most accomplished type of dramatic poetry had something to do with Aristotle's own philosophical taste, but it had more to do with how the circumstances of Greek dramatic productions conditioned the general sense of appropriateness, the ways in which the great Athenian dramatists had risen to the occasion, and the resulting body of achievement that served as Aristotle's point of critical departure (his available database was actually rather limited).

The Elizabethan critical landscape presented more Latin, and less Greek, than the one that has prevailed for the last several generations of Western thought. Francis Meres compared Shakespeare with Seneca and Plautus, not with Sophocles and Aristophanes, because that was what he and his readers knew. Neither Aristotle's *Poetics* nor Aeschylus' *Oresteia* formed part of their Bureau of Standards. Tragedy was, for them, an alternative form of drama, not a clearly superior one. They had their sad songs and their joyous songs, and their ballads recounting great historical events; I think they had their tragedies, comedies, and histories in much the same way, without much prejudice about which might be considered more significant or more important or more worthy of appreciation.

In general, I propose that Shakespeare thought his primary task to be the delivery of sad stories, delightful stories, and historically formative stories in a dramatic mode that permitted his audiences to engage imaginatively in a maximally effective taste of their sadness, delight, and exciting struggle—and that he subordinated his dramaturgical strategies to the end of meeting his experienced audiences halfway and guiding them through the rest of the journey to the appropriate type of dramatic satisfaction. There will be qualifications offered in my subsequent book, to take account of changes in how he went about his task over the years, but this will do for the moment. But it is still too abstract.

More concretely, as Shakespeare worked through the medium of dramatically presented stories, he established expectations and created loyalties. He was careful about letting his audience in on what the personages in his stories were after and how they proposed to bring about the results they sought; at the same time, he endowed these personages and projects with qualities that were calculated to induce our taking sides, to make us want these to succeed, those to fail, and often as many as possible to be reconciled.

To be sure, this more detailed tinkering with our attitudes often involved a process of qualifying our support by refining our judgment—the ones that are to lose out are often made more sympathetic than they had been at the outset, and those destined to be successful as often have their deserving questioned. He sets up and reinforces the main systems of expectation and audience loyalty, but thoughtfully desimplifies most of them as the action moves along, creating degrees of ambivalence and ambiguity that give him a wider range of dramatic possibilities for what may appropriately follow from any given state of affairs.

It is his careful creation of this matrix of definite expectation and sympathy, partially destabilized by his qualifications of what we should expect and where our sympathies should lie, that permits him to do what perhaps he does best, and what no other dramatist has ever done as well. And that is his constant manipulation of the story, the projects, the personages, and the concomitant expectations and loyalties of the audience, in what may be called—and will hereafter be called—a dramaturgy of *surprise*.

The superficial dramatic effectiveness of surprise is well known. In nearly all times and places, dramatists have thrilled audiences by establishing impediments to what they want that seem frustratingly insuperable—and then providing, usually very suddenly, the wherewithal to overcome them (the notorious *deus ex machina*, the unexpected divine intervention, being the proverbial example).[8+] Or the reverse: just when everything seems under control, the disruptive introduction of a new element or character or turn of events is dramatically exciting, even if farfetched.

This is not Shakespeare's type of surprise. Nor is the sudden revelation of information or identities that have been withheld until the crucial moment, things that obviously must have been known to key personages from the beginning (or are unnecessarily withheld from them) but are guarded from us until the moment is ripe for them to change everything. Shakespeare occasionally uses devices like this (e.g., Paris as Mercutio's kinsman) but not for substantial purposes. He is in fact unusual among dramatists of his time (and of subsequent times as well) in keeping the audience more informed than any of the characters about important matters.

It is not the cheap (however effective) surprise of *withholding and then releasing* discoveries that constitutes the Shakespearean dramaturgy of surprise, but rather the consistent building of situations that *seem* destined to go one way but can as readily take a turn in the opposite direction on the basis of what has already been set up, without any faltering in our sense of the consistent appropriateness with which the action moves from step to step, for better or for worse. Shakespeare's surprises, that is, are normally not like the hilarious new revelations that resolve the final scene of *The Importance of Being Earnest* nor like the sudden animation of the Commodore's statue at the end of *Don Giovanni*,[9+] but rather like the punch-line of a well-constructed joke, where we feel drawn to anticipate one sort of result only to be given a very different one which we recognize to have been equally well prepared, as if we have been lulled into expecting the lady (or enthralled with dread of the tiger) and are suddenly, but fairly, visited with the alternative. Shakespeare would doubtless have appreciated and approved of what Aristotle had to say about dramatic reversal, however he might have regarded the rest of the *Poetics*.

As You Like It provides a helpful way of illustrating this value at work in Shakespearean dramaturgy, in that it is a play drawn almost extensively from a single skillfully written literary source, permitting us to watch Shakespeare at work altering Lodge's *Rosalynde* for dramatic effect. I do not suppose that Shakespeare assumed that his audience had an intimate knowledge of his source-text and was scoring points by being deliberately different from Lodge: that is not the way his alterations seem to work. I merely suppose that he had before him a well-wrought story and that we can learn something about his own dramaturgical values by noticing how he selected and adjusted. Let me count the ways.

If we break the loose term "surprise" into varieties of the not-quite-expected, one of the simplest and lowest-grade varieties is *abruptness*. The provision of smooth connections, intelligible motivations, rationalized coherences, and explanatory backgrounding is a graceful way of assisting a story to make good comfortable sense, and one may normally expect that the revision of a story will diminish its abruptnesses and polish the texture of its internal continuities.

What is perhaps most striking about Shakespeare's handling of the Lodge original is that he does the opposite. He increases the abruptness, abandons established connections, and generally roughs up the texture of the opening material.

Thus Oliver's abuse of Orlando is explained by Lodge as being rooted in his covetousness of his brother's share of the inheritance, which he schemes to acquire. Shakespeare, by contrast, not only offers no motive but underlines its absence through a soliloquy in which Oliver confesses that it makes no sense for him to hate Orlando, he doesn't know why it is the case, and he will nevertheless pursue it. Lodge's Oliver, as part of his nasty scheming, notes that the usurping Duke has set up a wrestling to get courtiers' minds off politics, talks Orlando into showing his valor by answering the challenge, and bribes the Duke's wrestler to do his brother serious harm; Shakespeare's wrestling has no stated purpose, Orlando responds for no stated reason, and Oliver finds out only because Charles comes to warn him that Orlando plans to come in disguise (!) to try his mettle. The whole ensemble is almost aggressively abrupt, and the interview in which it takes place further emphasizes the crude once-upon-a-time atmosphere by having Charles rather arbitrarily describe the happy life of the exiled Duke and by having Oliver even more arbitrarily (and pointlessly) inquire as to whether "Rosalind, the Duke's daughter" is exiled too—both of these bits adding useful background to the play but in a curiously mechanical and abrupt way.

And so it continues. Lodge has the girls brought in to grace the tournament, in keeping with received courtly custom, which leads to a discussion of love and valor. Shakespeare has the wrestling brought to *them* as they chat with LeBeau, and underlines their relative uninterest in it: there is no coy playfulness about love and valor to create the atmosphere for Rosalind and Orlando to be smitten with one another, and Orlando does not enter the ring newly motivated by love, as in Lodge—the conventional love token is bestowed upon Orlando after the match rather than before.

In the opening sequences, that is, Shakespeare has taken a well-designed fratricidal foundation (analogous to Edmund's against Edgar) and a richly conventional mediating foundation for romance (analogous to Romeo's privileges and obligations as a masquer) and dismantled them rather than making them even more smooth and complete—in the meantime, stuffing in some background information with a notable lack of finesse. I can only conclude that the punch of abruptness was a more important value to his dramaturgy than the usually preferred rationalized coherence, so much so that he virtually advertises his preference for it. Is it that abruptness is stronger or more memorable, or that it establishes his right to neglect smooth coherence in more important aspects of the play's design? It is impossible to be sure. But the procedural fact is undeniable.

The play accomplishes Orlando's exile by exaggerating Oliver's scheming (he plans to torch Orlando's lodgings, and Orlando with them, and has backup plans if this one fails—all of which Adam just happens to have overheard). Orlando links up with the exiled Duke rather coincidentally—neither Lodge nor Shakespeare has Orlando deliberately seek out the Duke's company—and Orlando is then free to forget his earlier preoccupations and concentrate on his romantic side (which Lodge had kept more visible through this transition than Shakespeare does). The scene is now set for exiled Orlando to get together with exiled Rosalind/Ganymede.

Here Shakespeare moves into a more ambitious level of surprise: playing out a situation in a way that is counterintuitive to audience expectation. That Lodge's Rosalynde stays in disguise is one pleasant variety of that strategy. Lodge might well have had her resume her true identity once she is safe in the forest and free to cast off both the traveler's masculine disguise and the Duke's daughter's aristocratic sophistication. Playing out in her own real person the romance that had begun in courtly playfulness would provide a charming and wholesome alternative both to her earlier artifice and to the proud and conventional Phebe. Lodge keeps her embedded in something like that initial courtly game of romantic playfulness in which she had first addressed Orlando, and Orlando plays along by wooing her as if she were Rosalind. The result is a variant on the flirting game: a portrayal of true romance at one remove, a kind of rehearsal that both is and is not the real thing, much in the spirit of Romeo and Juliet within the conventional embrace of the masque that both conceals and reveals.

One might call this a strategy of partial dissociation, just oblique enough to what we might well expect as to capture and hold our attention usefully. But whether or not the audience had read Lodge, Shakespeare's tack is a surprise of a different order. He takes Rosalind a large counterintuitive step beyond the sustaining of the partially dissociative disguise and the expected teasing-out of Orlando's wooing that goes with it: Rosalind as Ganymede will play the game not to allow them both to wallow in romance, but exactly the opposite. On the pretext of curing Orlando of the malady that is romantic love, she will satirize, criticize, and enact the sillinesses that conventionally belong to that state, deflating its conventional pretensions and attitudinizings from within the state itself. This not only gets our attention but disrupts our expectations.

That Rosalind is working from within romance rather than from something like Jaques' critical distance is emphasized in the Ganymede–Jaques encounter at the beginning of 4.1; but it is of course far more vivid in the moments in which she is caught off-guard, as when, after she mocks the foolish love verses she had plucked from the tree, her discovery that they are Orlando's demolishes her composure—or when she whimpers, alone with Celia, or when she swoons at the sight of Orlando's blood and then tries to cover up with a veneer of swagger. These sudden departures from the established Mercutioesque poise of her Ganymede role are surprises without precedent in Lodge. They not only emphatically point to who she really is beneath the surface of critical self-possession, but create an impact of character definition that is far more thorough and efficient than Lodge's more coherent and consistent disclosure. In the meantime, Shakespeare introduces two related types of surprise that may help bring us closer to his purposes.

The first is that he turns Orlando the other way around. In act 1, Orlando is about as dizzy with his love-at-first-sight as Rosalind ever gets: when at the end of 1.2 he turns from the Duke's ominous displeasure to face his plight vis-à-vis the cruel brother who is plotting ever more extravagantly against his life, he concludes with the punch line "But heavenly Rosalind!"—which is not different in kind from Silvius' breaking from Corin's company with "O Phebe, Phebe, Phebe!" in 2.4.

Once his situation in the forest is stabilized, his dedication to the project of carving and writing verses to his absent love seems to culminate in the lines Rosalind is reading as she enters in 3.2, which are nearly as bad as Hamlet's pitiably inept verses to Ophelia. We are ready for another moonstruck Romeo, without the concomitant sympathy, now that Orlando is free to concentrate on his principal preoccupation. But that is not what we get.

He has none of the conventional marks of the deranged lovesick swain, as Rosalind/Ganymede reminds us; his manner is rather matter-of-fact, even when he mouths the romantic pieties ("Then in my own person, I die" [4.1] is charmingly lacking in sincerity, just another stage of playing the courting game in the way that *she* is supposed to be conventionally entitled to). He takes on Ganymede's therapeutic project of wooing him committedly as Rosalind not defiantly, as Romeo accepts Benvolio's challenge to compare his Rosalind with others, but as a sort of interesting sport; and he is casually late for a tryst with his artificial beloved, for no good reason and with no abject apology. In short, just when we were prepared for unusually histrionic extravagance that could out-Silvius Silvius, Shakespeare gives us an Orlando who loves not too well but wisely.

The second major surprise is a deepening of one already provided by Lodge. Phebe falls in love with Ganymede. Lodge's occasion is Ganymede's tasking Phebe for her aloofness to Silvius: she is too coy, too disdainful, too unappreciative—all of which stays within the convention and within the complaints traditionally made by the unrequited wooer. Shakespeare adds an unexpected twist: "Mistress, know thyself," says chiding Ganymede, pushing Phebe beyond the bounds of the convention as firmly as "My mistress' eyes are nothing like the sun" does in another mode. Be realistic, and the appropriateness of the conventional stance simply dissolves. The Ganymede with whom Shakespeare's Phebe falls in love is not a more eloquent attorney for the disdained and abject wooer, but an insightful critic of the whole artificial pose. It is this ungilded truth that starts Phebe toward a happy ending for her part of the play.

The common denominator of these examples can now be named more adequately. It is not a mere attention-getting abruptness, though that is a component part of each instance. It is not just a twist against what the audience was readily prepared to expect, though that too is an ingredient in each case. It is an abrupt disruption of expectation that is achieved not by the simple effrontery of imposed change, nor by Shakespeare's shifting to other established vectors in the plot or properties in the characters, but by *an appeal to more elemental truths and values* than those that had seemed in charge of the play in general or the situation in particular. Shakespeare's dramaturgy of surprise is simultaneously a dramaturgy of arrestingly pointed reminders— reminders about what life is really like, about the superiority of nature to art, about the power of the ultimately real over temporary deflection and distortion. The governing aesthetic is not confined to organizing the stuff of the play itself, but constantly includes the legitimacy of overruling the play's provisionalities through a higher court of realism with which the unfolding of the action is always constitutionally in touch.

This does not amount to a philosophy. It is still a dramaturgical matrix. The realism to which Shakespeare could appeal for these striking and memorable surprises, both small-scale and large-, was more like a system of proverbs than a system of metaphysics. In *As You Like It*, he works with a world in which every dog may have his day, the truth will out, and all's well that ends well. It is not in the long run surprising that Oliver and Duke Frederick are thwarted and then converted; it is not even surprising that these turns of events are brought about in surprising ways. But a governing pattern of proverbial truths may be realistic without being definitive. For a telling example, let us return to another play whose source materials are fairly well known, *King Lear*.

The opening of *King Lear* exhibits the same sort of derationalizing as we see in Shakespeare's reworking of Lodge for the beginning of *As You Like It*. The unknown author of *The Chronicle History of King Leir* had taken pains to make genuine sense of the traditional arbitrary way in which Lear had divided his kingdom. A substantial part of the business of the opening scenes is given over to Leir's concern to arrange a marriage for the reluctant Cordella. The contrivance of a plan to have his daughters declare their love for him is neither grandiose egoism nor senile foolishness: it is a clever scheme to induce Cordelia to make a public declaration that she loves him enough to be willing to do whatever he asks of her—whereupon Lear plans to call her to account by asking her to marry the King of Gaul. Whatever one may think of this strategy, it at least makes sense and relieves Leir of the irascible arbitrariness of the traditional story. Shakespeare simply scraps this rational improvement and restores the fairy-tale abruptness that his source had finally overcome through this rather clever revision.

From this beginning, Shakespeare proceeds to exploit his dramaturgy of surprise as thoroughly as in any other play he ever wrote. Far from being the most metaphysically philosophical of his plays, it is quite possibly the most proverbial, owing no loyalty to any consistent principle by which life might be thought organized, guided, contained, or symbolized. He takes us off balance at the start, and keeps us there until we no longer know what to expect, however aware we may be of what we want. The governing proverbial notions are as legitimate and realistic as those of *As You Like It*, but the selection is so totally different that it is hard to find popular proverbs (which are not hospitable to such pessimistic insight) to echo them: the Latin *homo homini lupus*—man is a wolf to man—never got denizenized in English, Sophocles' "call no man happy until he is dead" still feels like the alien quotation it is, Hobbes' characterization of human life in the state of nature as "solitary, poor, nasty, brutish, and short" was not popularly accepted, and the nearly universal terror of death became a problem to combat proverbially rather than to formulate. *King Lear* was, and is, against the grain of popular sensibilities, and the history of its critical reception has mainly been a history of efforts to ignore, bypass, countermand, explain away, or sublimate what it is and does.

The surprises of *King Lear* accordingly tend to thrust in the opposite direction from those of *As You Like It*. There are no healing conversions, but there is corruption and degradation in the willfullness of the initially dutiful Goneril and Regan that ultimately takes them to the grip of the "canker death" more terribly than even wise Friar Laurence's proverbial philosophy envisioned. Coincidences specialize in the unhappy rather than the happy, which is equally realistic. The notion of virtue being its own reward, usually reinforced in plays like *As You Like It* by the provision of a bundle of other more tangible rewards, becomes more economically (and disappointingly) true in *King Lear*. And the glib and comforting theories of evil and of providence voiced by the characters are blown out one by one, like candles, and there is no illusion left about getting one's wish when they are all extinguished.

But that is generalization, and the play arises from the concrete dramaturgical decisions by which Shakespeare engages our loyalties, expectations, and sense of appropriateness. Rather than attempt a detailed exposition of the latter, I will simply point to a couple of substantial instances that show Shakespeare's adjustments of his sources in the direction of surprise that I have indicated, while promising a return in a later book to some of the larger issues raised through this brief comparison of two very dissimilar—yet dramaturgically similar—plays.

First, a simple scene that powerfully illustrates the continuity of Shakespeare's technique along with the reversal of its impact.

Scene 5.2 is the penultimate scene, and although we have no programs we can tell by the time of day and the structure of the action that the play is almost over. After Lear's terrible ordeal over the last few acts, he has recovered his sanity under the tender auspices of faithful Cordelia, whose gradual progress toward the rescue of her father, under way since 3.1, has now reached its culmination. The time for showdown has come. We know from previous indications, and especially from the preceding scene, that the British forces, under Edmund/Regan/Goneril/Albany (the first three being moral derelicts, the fourth an indecisive weakling), are strained with internal dissension, and things are beginning to fall apart on that front, with a plot on Albany's life and a wild jealousy between Regan and Goneril for possession of Edmund: in 5.1, it was touch and go as to whether they could manage to put an army into the field, let alone hold their own against the ordered and purposeful attack of the Lear/Cordelia forces. It is not necessary to have heard or read any previous version of the Lear story to know what to expect, though it is likely that most of Shakespeare's audience had done so. In every known version before Shakespeare, Lear and Cordelia are victorious and Lear is restored to the throne, just as any decent audience would desire. In the way that Shakespeare has loaded the situation now, it is more obvious than ever that this is the only appropriate way for things to turn out.

Scene 5.2 opens with Lear and Cordelia, both of them more dignified and regal than ever before, processing over the stage with their army and with drum and colors. No glimpse is given of the disordered enemy. When this obviously significant pageant is over, in which Edgar leads the blind Gloucester (who still does not know that his guide is his abused son) to a shelter in the vicinity of the final battle, and, after a quick exchange of some five lines, goes off to observe from some other unnecessarily separate, and unexplained, place.

The bulk of the scene is apparently in offstage sound effects. We see blind Gloucester waiting, and we know that Edgar is offstage watching. It is unnecessary for us to be put through a routine series of alarms and excursions representing the thick of battle: a more abstract representation, created by the trumpet calls that mean attack and then, eventually, retreat (perhaps punctuated by shouts and groans, perhaps not), is sufficient to register what is going

on, and when Edgar rushes back onstage we have every reason—*every* reason—to presume that he will announce the foregone conclusion, that Lear
and Cordelia have defeated the wretched coalition and justice is restored.

That is, of course, not what he says. Without rhetorical elaboration he announces simply that "King Lear hath lost, he and his daughter ta'en," and in
some seven lines the scene is over.

What sort of aesthetic can embrace this abrupt and outrageous surprise?
On every ground—morality, poetic justice, patterned buildup, propriety, previous versions of the story, audience loyalty, plausibility, quality of leadership,
cosmic righteousness—there is only one appropriate outcome. But no, on second thought: it is the only appropriate outcome on every ground but one.

The exception is sheer reality. Things can always go wrong just as easily as they can go right. Violating every other canon of appropriateness,
Shakespeare has reached into the bottom of his repertoire of resources and
come up with the undeniably admissible truth that things can go terribly
wrong. And so, with a lame proverbial summary, "Ripeness is all" (which
here must mean neither more nor less than "You have to be ready to accept
absolutely *anything*, since *anything* can happen"),[10] Edgar, echoed still
more lamely by his father's "And that's true too," closes this brief and devastating scene and takes Gloucester off, intent on the next practical piece
of business. Brief, concise, largely wordless, somewhat eerie, and utterly
decisive, this strategically situated scene is perhaps the best example in all
of Shakespeare's work of the authority of the reality principle in his aesthetic design, and the importance of disruptive surprise in his dramaturgical principles.

From the detailed engineering of this small passage, I turn now to the overall shape of *King Lear* to remark that the same dramaturgical principles are at
work here as in *As You Like It*, despite the nearly total difference in effect.

King Lear 5.3, the final scene, was certainly as open to manipulation as
5.2. Shakespeare could easily have followed through with the self- and mutu-
ally destructive patterns he had established among the victors of 5.2 to effect
a collapse that would place Lear on the throne after all, rewarding faithful
Cordelia with a perpetual pact of peace between Britain and France (and perhaps contriving to marry her to Edgar, as Nahum Tate's revision of the play,
which drove Shakespeare's off the stage for over a century, managed to suggest). Gloucester could have become Duke of Cornwall, and Kent might have
been constituted titular Prince of Wales with an abundance of ancillary hon-
ors. It would still have been a stark and sobering play, reminding us how
closely ruin can lurk within the coziest of commonweals, and Shakespeare
would not have had to violate any established dramaturgical principles to
carry it all off.

In fact, he comes close to doing exactly that. Edmund is on the brink of taking over definitively when Shakespeare blows the whistle he had been designing all along, and within less than fifty lines Goneril and Regan are dead and Edmund is dying, weakened to the point that morality creeps in sufficiently to effect the rescue of Lear and Cordelia a little later than the conventional eleventh hour. We could have been instantly back to the spirit of the scene's beginning, with ripened Lear and noble Cordelia ready to face anything, and now discovering that this means total restoration. But unfortunately, the timing is off.

It is not off by much, as the urgency on stage reminds us: perhaps something like a minute earlier, we might have had our happy and traditional ending after all. The audience—never before disappointed in other versions of the story—doubtless continues to expect that it will be so. Why soften Edmund at the end ("Some good I mean to do, / Despight of mine own nature") except to take advantage of the malleability of Shakespeare's rules in order to pull it all out of the fire at the last possible moment? The answer to that question comes quickly. It is in order to galvanize one last twitch of hope so that it may be thwarted. The reality is that a minute here or there makes a difference, and Shakespeare dips once again into a truth beyond propriety in order to redouble the devastation he has already perpetrated.

Lear enters mad, carrying Cordelia dead. Shakespeare rubs our noses in that fact until everyone has lost everything important and the play can collapse upon itself with hollow formal sentiments. We are left with a smouldering ruin, despite critical attempts to ignore or evade the design. Sometimes *everything* goes wrong. This is a taste of what that is like. Reality comes in two prominent flavors, which are not systematically connected but rather discrete, the way proverbs sort them out into alternatives. However one may label them from a philosophically detached viewpoint like that of Friar Laurence with the poisonous/medicinal flower, from the perspective of participatory imagination one is named *Yes!*, and the other is named *No!*

The heart of Shakespearean dramaturgy is, I think, based on this fundamental truth. He chose stories that could carry the weight of side-trips, multiplicities, explorations; he endowed his roles with traits that made them versatile as well as often arrestingly memorable, always keeping open the option of lively surprise at every level from the turn of a phrase to the total shape of the plot, keeping a satisfying continuity without being pulled into a restricting unitary continuum. He took advantage of loose spatial, temporal, characterizational, and expectational rules in a way that kept his audience in the game but slightly off-balance, obliged to recognize the legitimacy of his deft reorderings of things toward or away from what they wanted. There was almost always something going on that was beyond expectation, requiring attention and readjustment. The surface texture was almost always deliberately rough—often rougher than his sources had achieved in their pursuit of different values—and this assisted his gradual building of the groundwork for larger surprises, sometimes delightful good news, sometimes dishearteningly bad, but always within the reach of a dramaturgy that could claim a birthright to incorporate any set of established internal strands or conventional liberties to effect an abrupt left or right turn whenever one or the other might be more dramatically effective.

In *Romeo and Juliet*, he played around with notions of fate, providence, astral determinism, even a touch of heavenly envy at earthly happiness. In *King Lear*, where the temporal setting left his dramatic personages technically free of any obligations that might be attached to Christian thought, he entertained ideas about demons, determining astrology, malevolent deities, and the utter emptiness of guiding principles. Nothing systematic can be extracted from this decorative flailing about the imponderable truth. In *Romeo and Juliet*, nothing important happens except through the intermix of moral decision and sheer chance. In *King Lear*, nothing important happens except through the intermix of chance and moral decision. In *As You Like It*, chance and moral decision cooperate to bring about a delightful result. Again and again, the matrix of happening delivers the realistic realization that I am the mistress of my fate (read: fortune), and I am the lieutenant (j.g.) of my soul. There are these three: plot, character, and reflective thought—and greater than these is the dramaturgy that reminds us that anything can happen appropriately, if we admit reality to the equation.

Notes

PREFACE

1. If the terms are puzzling, I promise an explanation in chapter 3.

2. Examples may be easily found randomly distributed among the subsequent notes.

3+. You may not agree afterward that a given footnote was worth looking up, but I have tried to reserve the plus-signs for notes that at least have a good chance of being worth it. Besides, the page-numbers in the notes section make things easier: even if you don't tuck a bookmark into the notes section, it's easy to zero in.

4*. You may find this system annoying, but at least please consider that I'm trying to make it easier for you. Try to remember the last time you attempted to hunt down, say note 27, and then discovered merely the title of a book you weren't interested in. I'm really saving you considerable time and frustration, if you will work with me on this.

5!. I intend to follow this book with another, built according to the same principles and preoccupations (with improvements gleaned from the reception of this one) but taking in the entire Shakespeare canon, and fortified as much as possible by parallel evidence from the non-Shakespearean plays of the same period. If it works out, it will be a fairly comprehensive handbook of Shakespearean dramaturgy, relying on this book as a general introduction to the subject but going well beyond it. If you like what happens in this book, you may look forward to a more thorough followthrough; and if you don't, you will know not to bother with the sequel.

1. IF WE OFFEND, IT IS WITH OUR GOOD WILL

1*. This convention usually seems odd to the inexperienced, but it is in fact no odder than the modern convention of using capital letters at the beginning of sentences and proper nouns, and lower-case letters elsewhere, even though their shapes may be quite different and their sounds may vary. *Gill* and *gill* are to us obviously the same word, though the initial letters are quite different in form, and their pronunciation may take either of two strikingly different sounds, depending on whether we are dealing with scaling fish or measuring Scotch whisky.

2. Colons were sometimes used to indicate a pause in the speaker's delivery, and an absent period occasionally signaled an interrupted line. If the editor repunctuates in these cases, she may add a note to indicate that the change could be slightly misleading.

3+. This is not a systematic trait—Jaques does speak verse in later scenes—but it nevertheless has dramatic value in this first meeting with him, and is an aspect of his characterization as contrasting with his romantic and musical colleagues: cf. his overt unmusicality in this scene, reinforced by the Duke at the beginning of 2.7. There will be more said about Shakespeare's significant use of prose in a later chapter, and more said about his unsystematic treatment of character in the meantime.

4. A quick trip through the Variorum edition of this play will perhaps startle a reader who recognizes that this made-up verse must be rhythmically and metrically parallel to the original refrain. Various commentators have asserted arbitrarily that there must be emphasis on the last syllable, and some have failed to notice that the musical line to which it is adapted requires a trisyllabic pronunciation.

5. The editions available to me occasionally (but very rarely) remark that productions of the play have sometimes constructed such a circular gathering. None of them suggests that this was in fact what Shakespeare had in mind. I admire their reporting of potentially significant information about directorial interpretation, but I regret that none of them seems to have twigged to this having been Shakespeare's idea for the climax of an otherwise unclimactic scene.

2. How Long Is't Now Since Last Your Self and I Were in a Masque

1. See Gerald Eades Bentley, *Shakespeare & Jonson: Their Reputations in the Seventeenth Century Compared* (2 vols.: Chicago: University of Chicago Press, 1945). After gathering considerable new evidence, Bentley's study overturned the usual supposition, concluding that: "The evidence is emphatic that only in the third, ninth, and tenth decades of the century did Shakespeare seriously rival Jonson's reputation as the great dramatist of England" (vol. 1, p. 134), and that "Not only was Jonson generally more admired and more familiar than Shakespeare, but Jonson's plays individually were more frequently discussed than Shakespeare's" (p. 135), and that notwithstanding Shakespeare's considerable reputation for drawing dramatic characters (the one category in which his reputation outstripped Jonson's in the seventeenth century) "Clearly, Jonson, and not Shakespeare, was the dramatist of the seventeenth century" (p. 139), especially among the educated and cultivated.

2. The basic work on this industry of Shakespearean revision is still Hazelton Spencer's *Shakespeare Improved* (Cambridge: Harvard University Press, 1927).

3. "Harriett Hawkins, in part 1 of "The Year's Contributions to Shakespearian Study," *Shakespeare Survey* 34 (1981), p. 177.

4. Interpretation might argue that King Hamlet did not return to mortal life, and that this is what Hamlet is saying—but that is hardly what the lines mean. The speech depends not on the question of traffic from the afterworld, but on this world's impenetrable ignorance of what the next one is like. Hamlet, Sr. had already given his son some pointed indications, however incomplete.

5. E. K. Chambers, *William Shakespeare: A Study of Facts and Problems*, vol. 2 (Oxford: The Clarendon Press, 1930), p. 210 (quoting Jonson's *Timber*,

printed in his Second Folio of 1641). The quoted line does not appear in *Julius Caesar*; the closest we can come is in 3.1, where Caesar says "Know, Caesar doth not wrong, nor without cause / Will he be satisfied." It is of course possible that this is a corrected version, made either by Shakespeare himself or by his editors after Jonson had raised his objection in person (though not yet in print).

3. A LOCAL HABITATION, AND A NAME

1*. The First Quarto's parallel statement about its having been played at Oxford does not necessarily imply that it was there played by Shakespeare's company. It is not at all implausible that it had been staged there by students who got their text by conning speeches at London performances and suborning the assistance of minor actors.

2. It is difficult to give a page reference, in that the Folio starts *The Tempest* at sig. A1r, page no. 1, but has several pages of unnumbered prefatory material, with irregular signaturing. The quotation occurs on the recto of the leaf preceding *The Tempest*: call it p. -2 or sig. B1r -14.

3+. Shakespeare has fun with a parallel situation in *Love's Labours Lost*, and solid (not to mention amusing) historical evidence of the practice is available in contemporary descriptions of such entertainments, notably those produced by the local folks for Queen Elizabeth on the occasion of her visit to the Earl of Leicester at Kenilworth in 1575.

4+. This is what both Q1 and Q2 say, though I have modernized the spelling. The Folio's reading, "pray you if be," is an apt example of the minor corruptions of the printing-house: the compositor's eye (apparently looking at an annotated copy of Q2) has evidently skipped over the "it" that obviously belongs between "if" and "be." It doesn't cause much of a problem.

5. For more about this practice, see Bernard Beckerman, *Shakespeare at the Globe*, p. 132, and Peter Holland, *Ornament of Action*, p. 65.

6. Further detail may be found in, and through, M. M. Mahood, *Bit Parts in Shakespeare's Plays* (Cambridge: Cambridge University Press, 1992), p. 10, Michael Hattaway, *Elizabethan Popular Theatre: Plays in Performance* (London: Routledge and Kegan Paul, 1982), and especially T. J. King, *Casting Shakespeare's Plays: London Actors and Their Roles, 1590–1642* (Cambridge: Cambridge University Press, 1992).

7+. There is an anomaly in the text: Quince says that Flute/Thisbe has spoken "all his part at once, cues and all"; yet his penultimate line is obviously the cue to Pyramus, and the line following is just as obviously Thisby's response: where, then, is the cuing phrase from Pyramus that should sponsor Thisby's final "I'll meet thee, Pyramus, at Ninus' tomb"? Has Quince made a false accusation about Flute's reading "cues and all?" Not quite. I will return later to this very minor point in conjunction with a more important general consideration.

8+. Warren D. Smith, *Shakespeare's Playhouse Practice: A Handbook* (Hanover, NH: University Press of New England for the University of Rhode Island, 1975), mentions in chapter 2, "Stage Business in the Dialogue," that he has counted nearly three thousand implicit directions for stage business in the dialogue, as compared with only 320 "marginal notations" (i.e., explicit business directions), and observes that the great majority of the implicit directions appear after the piece of business rather than before it. This alone would obviously make it more difficult for whoever copied out the "parts" to insert such actions explicitly into them, especially when the dramatic point of the action (and therefore the most appropriate way of executing it) would be unclear without the full context; and of course some such actions apply to several characters at once, such as the suggested gathering in a circle at the end of *As You Like It* 2.5, and would need to be recopied into several parts: if there were a better way, it would surely be taken.

9+. We have good evidence that rehearsals were at least sometimes available to observers: they liked the fencing matches, and would likely have been somewhat intrigued by the more routine ways of putting the play together—not least their being in position to tell pals that the devices of the company were known to insiders.

10. Alfred Hart, "Did Shakespeare Produce His Own Plays?," *Modern Language Review* 36 (1941), pp. 173–83.

11. David Klein, "Did Shakespeare Produce His Own Plays?," *Modern Language Review* 57 (1962), pp. 556–60.

12. The date seems fairly secure: its grounds may be found through E. K. Chambers, *The Elizabethan Stage*, vol. 3, p. 498.

13. The translation is the one given by Klein in the aforementioned article, p. 556. The original is from a manuscript preface to a translation of *Lingua*, an academic play written around 1602 and published in 1607, which Rheinanus made for Maurice of Hesse Cassel in 1613, entitling it *speculum aistheticum* (according to W. Creizenach, *Die Shauspiele der englischen Komödianten* (Berlin u. Stuttgart: Verlag von W. Spemann, ND [1889]) pp. 327; other sources spell it *Speculum Aestheticum*. The original text, as transcribed by Creizenach, p. 328, reads "Was aber die *actores* antrifft, werden solche (wie ich in England in Acht genommen) gleichsam in einer Schule täglich *instituiret*, dass auch die vernembsten *actores* deren order sich von den Pöeten müssen vnder wayssen lassen, welches dann einer wolgeschriebenen *Comoedien* das leben vnd Zierde gibt vnd bringet; Dass also kein wunder ist, warumb die Engländische *Comoedianten* (Ich rede von geübten) andern vorgehen vnd den Vorzug haben." Klein's version of the original differs only in two capitalizations and a joining of *vnderwayssen*.

14*. I am quite aware that those who have published my books have final authority on their titles, the design of their dust jackets, and many other aspects of their presentation. For many of these matters, I need not even be consulted. But I daresay that the situation would be different if I were a major shareholder in the publishing house, held the post of vice president in charge of editorial matters, and were the author of three or four of the house's previous best-sellers—none of which, alas, has been the case.

15!. There has been some disagreement about what should be meant by "produced" or "directed." I consider the latter less misleading, and will use it in a general fashion, meaning that Shakespeare in some way largely determined how his plays were to be acted out. It is immaterial to my argument whether or not he ever asked an actor to make a speech sound more lofty or condoling, or whether he blocked the actors' movements in a highly precise way, or whether he was always regarded as the definitive authority on how something should be done. He was working with advanced professionals, after all. I claim only that he had particular elements of design in mind, communicated them mainly during rehearsals, was undoubtedly regarded as the one who best understood the play in question and whose advice would usually secure the most effective performance, and that he instructed his colleagues (and was usually deferred to) in a routinized way when the company was putting on something he had written.

16. See especially Ann Pasternak Slater: *Shakespeare the Director* (Brighton: The Harvester Press), 1982.

17. Andrew Gurr, *The Shakespearean Stage, 1574–1642*, 3d ed. (Cambridge: Cambridge University Press, 1992), p. 209.

18. See Neil Carson, *A Companion to Henslowe's "Diary"* (Cambridge: Cambridge University Press, 1988), p. 56. The Diary itself is readily accessible in an excellent edition, *Henslowe's Diary*, ed. R. A. Foakes and R. T. Rickert (Cambridge: Cambridge University Press, 1961).

19. Gurr, *The Shakespearean Stage*.

20. See Andrew Gurr, *The Shakespearean Stage, 1574–1642* (original edn., Cambridge: Cambridge University Press, 1970), p 48; 3d ed., p. 69.

21+. The modern version of the Man in the Moon is a face; but in Shakespeare's time, it was regularly construed as a full-sized man with a bush (or a bundle of sticks) and a dog. I have no idea yet about how either interpretation arose, or how the earlier one, which was well established, gave way to the later.

22+. A fairly exhaustive treatment of the nature of the stage as assumed in 276 plays produced between the fall of 1599 and the closing of the theaters in 1642 may be found in T. J. King, *Shakespearean Staging, 1599–1642* (Cambridge, Mass.: Harvard University Press, 1971). But note that King is surveying evidence for all the playhouses, and they differed from one another. During the period he covers, Shakespeare's company played at the Globe, which they owned, and Shakespeare had no reason to write into his plays anything that the features of the Globe couldn't handle. His pre-Globe plays were produced in various playhouses, and could involve a different range of physical features—e.g., *Romeo and Juliet* requires at least a window's worth of upper playing area, which does not seem to have been available at the Globe—see Bernard Beckerman, *Shakespeare at the Globe, 1599–1609* (New York: Macmillan, 1962). There will be more on this subject in the next chapter.

23*. This may not in fact be a whimsical variant: a final *e* and a final *d* were often virtually indistinguishable in the standard Elizabethan handwriting, and we may be dealing with a mere compositorial misreading in the few instances of "Rosaline."

24*. Mercutio's fantasy about Queen Mab in *Romeo and Juliet* 1.4 similarly diminutizes fairies, in a way that suggests that there was already well-established popular lore to that effect. The surviving evidence is insufficient to tell us how popular imagination made them tiny, while at the same time sustaining the notion that they were (at least sometimes) so indistinguishable from ordinary mortals that a fairy "changeling" could be substituted for a stolen mortal child without leaving any clues other than "fey" mannerisms. (The boy over whom Theseus and Oberon contend is referred to as a "changeling" in Oberon's first speech in 4.1, but that is of course from the fairy viewpoint: it is a mortal child, as Titania explains midway through 2.1.)

25+. There is a minor problem with the time scheme, which I will attend to later. But there can be no question about the drift of Bottom's message: they are to stage the play right away.

26+. His not actually having done that in 3.1, despite Peter Quince's accusation, is just another instance of a localized and provisional double-value: it's funny to think of him doing so, and it doesn't have to happen literally in order to be imagined as having happened, especially if (as must certainly have been the case) he delivers the lines in such a thoroughly incompetent way as to make such a further blunder plausible.

27*. That is, he has *at least* established the chink as localized at his crotch, possibly by using the same 3.1 finger-made chink in that position (though Bottom doubtless did not hold it there when offering this solution originally). In any event, the lines ask for the chink to be made there, however. It was certainly handled so as to catch the audience by surprise—one of the many setup gags (cf. Jaques's *ducdame*) that Shakespeare obliquely referred to through Peter Quince as he counseled the advisability of rehearsing in the woods: "for if we meet in the city, we shall be dogg'd with company, and our devises known." Such strategic withholding and change of plan is typically Shakespearean: witness the change in the casting and text of the *Pyramus and Thisby* play itself, which is utterly unrealistic and entirely unexplained but therefore more dramatically effective. For the record, it was Skip Shand who originally drew this "devise" to my attention ca. 1967; he backed down when he rediscovered the finger-direction in 3.1, but took heart again when I pointed out that the text and cast changed, and the original chink might obviously have been overruled as well. I mentioned it to Ron Bryden at Stratford in 1972, and he (as delighted with it as I had been when Shand pointed it out) later told me that he had promptly cabled Peter Brook, whose production of the play was showing in London at the time, and that Brook had adopted it for subsequent performances. Clfford Leech had been somehow involved in the discovery of this bit, along with Shand (both were in Toronto at the time) and published something along these lines. In short, I neither poached the deer nor brought it down in the first place: I take credit only for cooking it nicely.

28+. Q1 reads "antique," but Q2 (and F, which regularly follows Q2) read as I have quoted, and should be followed by modernizing as *antic*. Although sometimes confused with "antique," "antic" (and its variant spellings) entered English as a fully independent word, meaning *grotesque* or *fantastic*: Theseus is categorically dismissing the lovers' stories as incredibly bizarre, not merely patronizing them as old-fashioned.

4. IN SHORT SPACE, IT RAIN'D DOWN FORTUNE

1. The contract has often been reproduced in full, e.g., in Andrew Gurr, *The Shakespearean Stage, 1574–1642* (3d ed., Cambridge: Cambridge University Press, 1992), pp. 137–38.

2+. All of these are attested for plays of the period, along with beds, hearses, bodies, an altar, an arbor, a canopy, a monument, a seat, a sedan, a State, stocks, a throne, a tree, a trunk: see T. J. King, *Shakespearean Staging, 1599–1642* (Cambridge, Mass.: Harvard University Press, 1971), pp. 18ff. The inventory of properties belonging to the Lord Admiral's Men, taken by Philip Henslowe early in 1598, begins, memorably, with "1 rock, 1 tomb, 1 Hellmouth" (*Henslowe's Diary*, ed. R. A. Foakes and R. T. Rickert [Cambridge: Cambridge University Press, 1961], p. 319). It is possible that large properties like these were introduced on stage through a larger central door that was not normally used for regular stage traffic.

3. With respect to this and other features of Shakespeare's principal theater, a deft survey of the relevant evidence and its implications may be found in J. W. Saunders, "Staging at the Globe, 1599–1613," *Shakespeare Quarterly* 11 (1960), pp. 402–25; Gerald Eades Bentley, ed., *The Seventeenth-Century Stage: A Collection of Critical Essays* (Chicago: University of Chicago Press, 1968), pp. 235–66.

4. See Bernard Beckerman, *Shakespeare at the Globe, 1599–1609* (New York: Macmillan, 1962), p. 92. T. J. King, *Shakespearean Staging, 1599–1642* (Cambridge, Mass.: Harvard University Press, 1971), offers a more comprehensive and minute study of stage phenomena, and is worth consulting on any question bearing on stage features.

5+. That is, he might have dramatized this battle as effectively as the one in *Henry IV, Part 1*, but it was not dramatically expedient to do so, since in *King Lear* he was dealing with a battle designed to have a very different sort of dramatic effect. The technique he chose was decidedly more dramaturgically appropriate to the design of the final stages of *King Lear* than representative excursions would have been.

6+. "Over the stage" is not a silly redundancy, but evidently a cue for a procession that moves not from one door directly to the other, but rather downstage and around the platform. J. W. Saunders, "Staging at the Globe, 1599–1613," *Shakespeare Quarterly* 11 (1960), pp. 402–25 (reprinted in Gerald Eades Bentley, ed.: *The Seventeenth-Century Stage: A Collection of Critical Essays* [Chicago: University of Chicago Press, 1968], pp. 235–66) estimates that the average time required for this maneuver is ca. twenty-five seconds (presuming a dialogue rate of twenty lines per minute, which is a fairly common hypothetical rate, though perhaps too fast). In that time, a brisk (and short) procession could move from a stage entrance almost to the front edge of the platform, loop around, and leave by the other door. Of course, not all processions are constrained to conclude within someone's eight to ten lines: one that takes place in total stage silence (as seems to be the case in *King Lear* 5.2), or begins in such silence, could be more slow and stately. The absence of speech makes it the more dramatic, as well as creating a potentially useful ambiguity about how much time is being represented.

7+. The logistics of 1.3 also suggest that we are at the gate, since Capulet has evidently just been walked home by Paris and "the Clown," and the latter is not provided with any indication of travelling before he encounters the stolling Romeo and Benvolio; 2.5 begins with the expectant Juliet, and the Nurse's entrance with Peter is immediately followed by her instruction "Peter, stay at the gate," thus apparently defining the other side of the door they have just entered. Shakespeare does not *require* that we imagine this way, as it is not particularly important; but it strikes me as dramatically pleasant that he evidently had Juliet waiting at the gate rather than in her chamber, and he reinforced this setting by having Juliet subsequently answer the Nurse's "Where is your mother?" with "Why, she is within."

5. DEVISE THE FITTEST TIME, AND SAFEST WAY

1. The motivation for accepting them was perhaps primarily a patriotic interest in having a deep and heroic antiquity; the founding evidence rested on the authority of Geoffrey of Monmouth's chronicle of earliest days in Britain, reinforced by various subsequent chronicles as well as poems and plays, but the resulting sense of their historicity was more literary than antiquarian. A modern near-equivalent may perhaps be found in William Tell, a longstanding hero who—according to more recent research—probably never existed; his story may nevertheless be effectively told or dramatized, whether or not it ever happened in history, and without the author or audience having to take a stand on the matter.

2. See AYLI, Arden edition, and parallel discussions on the marriage issue in *Measure for Measure*.

3. *The Whole Prophecies of Scotland, England, France, Ireland and Denmarke* (Edinburgh: STC 17842) is a 1617 re-edition of a book with nearly the same title that appeared in 1603 (STC 17841.7) and again in 1615 (STC 17841.9), all of which are related to the *lytel treatyse of ye byrth & prophecye of Marlyn* published in 1510 and 1529 (STC 17841 and 17841.3). Shakespeare's imitation is not close, only generally evocative. (A sample of Merlin from STC 17842: "Yet this wicked world shall last but a while:/ While a Chiftane vnchosen choose foorth himselfe, / And ride over the Region, and for Roy holden: / Then his scutifiers shal skale al the fair South, / From Dumbarton to Douer, and deal al the Lands" &c. (sig A7–A7v).

4+. This might be called *condensed time* from another perspective, insofar as a larger time frame has been compressed into a relatively short stage happening; but I think it better procedure to start with what is immediately exhibited and look toward what is ultimately represented than the other way around.

5+. Capulet does say that he has "invited many a guest, / Such as I love," and it would be possible to construe the servant's mission as a mere reminder; but I think the design is more temporally intricate. Shakespeare often offers two different time schemes for a happening, a localized projection of earlier developments that gives it a more realistically adequate context and an enacted version that recapitulates the whole process. Thus the scene begins with Paris alluding to earlier stages of his suit, seconded by Capulet's offering his reluctance as "saying o're what I have said before," but then treats Paris' suit as if it were new and entirely welcome—1.3 has Lady Capulet obviously breaking the first news to Juliet (and the Nurse) that Paris (whom Juliet has evidently never seen) has asked for her hand, and neither of Juliet's parents ever again shows signs of anything but delighted surprise at the good fortune of such a catch, so suddenly presented. After 1.2, it is as if there were no earlier attempts by Paris, and certainly no reluctance in Capulet. The feast is similarly dealt with. Capulet speaks in 1.2 as if he has already issued the invitations, and then acts as if he had not yet done so. Looked at in one way, this is utterly incoherent; looked at in terms of Shakespearean dramaturgy, it is rather clever.

6. The country feast in *The Winter's Tale* 4.4 includes two such dances explicitly, as entertainments; but they take place in a more relaxed and expansive atmosphere than Capulet's feast can provide, given our expectations, and evidently with a separate cast of dancers.

7!. There is no reason to suppose that we can rely on the conventional way of dividing up the play. None of Shakespeare's plays was published with scene divisions during his lifetime, and only some of the Folio's texts are so presented (*King Lear* being one of them); the Folio scene divisions, like those of later editors who subdivided the acts of the remaining plays (and imposed both acts and scenes on the six plays that have neither in the Folio, which include *Romeo and Juliet*) are often made with questionable judgment. In this case, we cannot assume that the procession of the army belongs more closely with the Edgar–Gloucester passage than either does with what we are given as 5.1 and 5.3. If we *must* have scene divisions, 5.2 would be better divided into two scenes.

8+. We are not told where we are in 1.4, but the nature of the conversation evokes the default sense of Richard's palace, which would be less than an hour's journey from Ely House, just north of St. Paul's Cathedral in London.

9*. His report, of course, turns out to be true, but that is not the point. Shakespeare normally warns us about a report that is not to be believed, and the nature of this one makes misrepresentation almost unthinkable. (Admittedly, Shakespeare leaves unresolved the conflicting reports of Mowbray and Bolingbroke in the first act of the same play, when it is clear that at least one of them must be importantly inaccurate; but resolution turns out not to matter dramatically, and the conflicting reports amount to a dramatization of the sort of irresolvable accusations and counteraccusations that had once seemed to make sense of the trial by combat that then ensues. That is, the uncertainty about whether we should trust Mowbray or Bolingbroke is made dramatically functional rather than problematic.

10+. Shakespeare, of course, could have Bottom rejoin the others and induce them to get ready to perform just in case. But that would reduce the eagerness and urgency with which 4.2 ends, which is worth a compromise in rationality, just as the swiftness of the movement from Theseus' choice to the performance itself is worth what it costs in realistic plausibilitty.

11!. The Folio and Second Quarto texts duplicate the first four lines of the Friar's soliloquy as being also part of Romeo's exit speech. I do not think that the duplication is Shakespeare's intent (that would be implausible on various grounds), but the lines' suitability to either character has raised some question about to whom they should be assigned: I take this as a nice demonstration of how well Shakespeare established the sense of direct continuity. I also suspect that the duplication arose from a revision by Shakespeare, made substantially to fortify the sense of temporal continuity. I suggest that he transferred to Romeo's conclusion the lines originally assigned to the Friar (as they are in Q1), precisely in order to expand the time of 2.2 until dawn (the internal references are otherwise to night, looking forward to the morning) so that it might link more directly with the Friar's "Now ere the sun advance his burning eye," which become the beginning of his speech once the previous lines have been given over to Romeo. The way in which cancellations were indicated in manuscripts of the time makes this theory more plausible than it may otherwise seem: a simple vertical line in the margin, easily overlooked. The text of these four lines varies interestingly in their three different forms (one in Q1, two differing from it and each other in Q2 and identically in F), and I suggest that the Q2 Romeo form might be argued as the final version, and place, on stylistic grounds alone.

12*. The routine insertions of the stage direction "Exit an attendant" obviously indicate that the editors suppose that Lear's demands for his dinner and his fool are being obeyed, and that Shakespeare was merely careless, as he often was, in failing to prescribe the obedient responses. But these directions are emendations by editors who failed to catch the design and force of 1.3: as emendations, they are normally placed in square brackets to indicate the absence of early textual authority, and where they are *not* thus identified as the editor's guess, they are less than honest. See John C. Meagher, " *King Lear* I.iv: 'Exit an Attendant'," *Notes and Queries* 12 (1965) pp. 97–98.

13+. An exception occurs in *The Tempest*, where Prospero exits at the end of the fourth act and immediately reenters to begin the fifth: that is frequently argued to imply that the production of that play included a break between acts, so that Prospero actually reenters after an interval of absence. (A more complex case in the transition between 5.3 and 5.4 in *Cymbeline* is probably only an internal locational change, mislabeled by an editor who imposed a scene break along with a reentry that was accordingly demanded: remove both, and it flows satisfactorily according to usual Shakespearean dramaturgical principles.)

14!. Shakespeare's craftsmanship is not always as subtle and successful as this last example. Two odd and only marginally relevant scenes in *As You Like It* can serve to illustrate a cruder fashion of inserting an intervening scene to supply a necessary suspension in a continuing action. 4.2, an inexplicably curious bit of brief byplay involving a slain deer and some conversation and song about presenting the successful hunter to the Duke, seems to have little to do with the play's more purposeful actions. It is mildly entertaining and was doubtless pleasantly musical, but offers little by way of substantive dramaturgical function other than supplying an interval between the exit of Rosalind and Celia at the end of

4.1 and their reentry, with a remark about the intervening passage of time, at the beginning of 4.3. There is no attempt to construct 4.2 in such a way as to suggest an interval anything like the approximately two hours that we are asked to imagine between 4.1 and 4.3; in terms of time continuity, 4.2 seems to establish only a token notice that some time is passing. 5.3 introduces another song, sung to Touchstone and Audrey by two previously (and subsequently) unknown and unexplained "Pages." An interval is needed here as well, since 5.2 concludes with Rosalind (as Ganymede) promising to resolve the various romantic relationships with a wedding "tomorrow," and 5.4 takes place on the designated day. It would have been more typical of Shakespeare's time management to have 5.2 promise the resolution for later the same day, but in fact 5.3 actually emphasizes that a time gap occurs between it and the next scene, by having Touchstone remind Audrey that they will be married tomorrow. I confess that I am helpless to explain these rather flagrant counterexamples to Shakespeare's usual care to keep up the constant momentum, and am very hesitant (although not altogether unwilling) to speculate that these may be instance of his occasional practice of reminding us that this is a play that is susceptible to arbitrary manipulations of the author (cf. Lear's Fool's saucy reference to the still-future Merlin). For now, I will settle apologetically for remarking that this sort of slapdash treatment of time is rather rare in Shakespeare's plays.

15+. The pivot of his decision is nicely arranged: it comes on the heels of Paris' remark that the circumstances allow no wooing, and his goodnight to Lady Capulet together with the request that he be commended to her daughter. The stage direction in the generally untrustworthy first Quarto reads "Paris offers to goe in, and Capolet calles him againe," which is doubtless correct (and might be inferred from the lines alone). Capulet, eager to place his daughter well, can hardly be expected to like things being left so indefinite, and responds by making a desperate deal on his own authority—inconsistent with his earlier assurance to Paris that "My will, to her consent is but a part" (1.2), but certainly typical of Capulet's take-charge mode, to which we have been amply exposed.

16+. This particular discrepancy doubtless points to the difference between Juliet's still-vague intentions to thwart the parental scheme and her mother's acceptance of her husband's arrangements. I guess that Shakespeare was here relying on his audience's general familiarity with the story rather than employing what is commonly called "foreshadowing," a word that usually signals the author's failure to understand how Shakespearean dramaturgy actually works. But I admit that I may be overreacting.

6. AND I MAY HIDE MY FACE, LET ME PLAY THISBY TOO

1+. Though advertising that six is enough, *King Darius* seems in fact to require seven: on sig. D3, "Aethiopia, Percia, Iuda, and Media enter" to where Darius is waiting along with the characters Perplexitie and Curiositie, and each of the seven makes a brief speech before they sit down together.

2. "mit ohngefahr 15 personen . . agieren," quoted in E. K. Chambers, *The Elizabethan Stage*, vol. 2, 364f.

3. "The Number of Actors in Shakespeare's Early Plays," in *The Seventeenth-Century Stage: A Collection of Critical Essays*, ed. Gerald Eades Bentley (Chicago: University of Chicago Press, 1968), pp. 110–34.

4+. The Lord Chamberlain's Men first emerged as such during the plague-troubled year of 1594 and changed to the King's Men during the plague of 1603. In the meantime, plague-suspensions occurred in 1596, and other inhibitions of playing in 1597 (over a theatrical scandal) and 1603 (at the death of Queen Elizabeth): there are some records of the company's touring during those times, and they appear to have traveled every year from 1604 to the end of Shakespeare's life. For more detail, E. K. Chambers, *The Elizabethan Stage*, vol. 2, pp. 192–220 for a brief history of Shakespeare's company and vol. 4, pp. 345–51 for plague records.

5. The corruptions and incompletenesses in question may originate in Shakespeare's manuscript (omitted exits, illegible words, skipped lines, and the like) or (in the case of the "Bad Quartos") they could be the by-product of memorial reconstruction, or they might be introduced in the process of composing and printing the text. Virtually no one doubts that textual interference took place at all three levels. Contemporary scholarship tends to be much more careful than before, however, about the possibility that what seems to be an incompleteness may be a deliberate omission by Shakespeare, and what may look like a corruption could be an authentic alternative version.

6+. Some skeptical voices have been raised against scholarly work on doubled roles on the grounds that such a practice would ask too much of the cast. I have already hinted at the economic arguments that support doing it this way. I regret that I can't recall who it was that pointed out gently, against this objection, that some actors really love acting, and would probably not feel burdened by a chance to do more of it.

7*. Dominick Grace, who first suggested this nice piece of dramatic doubling to me, wrote a succinct and persuasive argument for it, but to the best of my knowledge it has not yet been published. It should be acknowledged that if Shakespeare is using such a design, it follows that Friar Laurence must be transformable into a gaunt apothecary who must be able to don a friar's robes swiftly: between the apothecary's exit and the friar's entrance we have only Romeo's resolute exit couplet, his exit, and the entrance of Friar John together with his call to Friar Laurence. It could be done. It requires only that the actor playing Friar Laurence be gaunt in the first place (he is often presented as rotund, but on no textual authority; the convention of plump friars has no more standing than the more ascetic look, and we know that Shakespeare's company included at least one notably skinny actor) and that his ragged costume as the impoverished apothecary, which he has plenty of time to put on, be susceptible of quick masking by donning the friar's robes over it—which could be accomplished in a few seconds.

8!. My best guesses so far are as follows: (1) Earlier versions of the King Lear story, including the play that seems to have been Shakespeare's chief resource, bring Cordelia's royal husband with her in the invasion of Britain. Shakespeare may initially have deployed France's actor in another role that made it

seriously inconvenient to him to be brought back on stage, and thought it indecorous for the King of France to leave her on her own for such an undertaking, and
thus provided him with an unseen arrival and an explanation for an early departure to cover the problem that his actor was otherwise employed—and then decided that this was either unnecessary or too artificial, or both, when he revised
the play. (2) Egeus' overruling by Theseus may not have left him disgruntled, but
we have no further lines or entrances for him to clear things up explicitly. It could
have been done by stage business, but Shakespeare apparently thought better of
this skimpy treatment and wrote him into the final act comfortably by taking over
the bulk of Philostrate's part—except for one apparently uncorrected F line,
which is still assigned to Philostrate. Philostrate has no lines before act 5 in either
version, only a momentary appearance at the play's opening before Theseus instructs him briefly and sends him off. I suspect that he was originally intended to
double with Egeus, even if the handling of his exit and Egeus' entrance in 1.1
presents some problems in quick costume shift, and that the revised version essentially changed the name of his role in act 5 in order to reintegrate Egeus, perhaps resulting in his original appearance being given to a one-shot mute who is to
be forgotten or (more likely) given to the same actor who played Egeus, requiring
only the tossing-off of his Master-of-the-Revels robe in the few lines before he
reenters. (3) Adam's dramaturgical functions are not extensive, and after he has
been so warmly received into the Duke's company—and the attention to Orlando
has completely changed from his previous sorrows to his new romance—he is
conveniently absorbed into another character—Corin would be appropriate, as
such a doubling would provide us with advance notice as well as a comfortable
way of making Adam pseudo-present even after his particular usefulness has
ended. This sort of strategy is, I believe, used more often in Shakespeare's plays
than is recognized: see "Economy and Recognition: Thirteen Shakespearean
Puzzles," *Shakespeare Quarterly*, v. 35, n. 1 (Spring, 1984), pp. 7–21. and if possible, "The Least Time I Saw Paris: With Much Ado about the Metamorphosis of
Jack Wilson," which at this writing is still under editorial consideration but will
eventually be published somewhere.

9+. The Folio omits the Chorus's Prologue to the play as it appears in the
Second Quarto. Since the Chorus's second sonnet appears at the beginning of
act 2 in both F and Q2, we may plausibly assume that the omission of the Prologue was accidental. F was evidently set from a corrected copy of Q2, and the
omission was probably the by-product of the Prologue's having been presented
on a separate preliminary page and followed two pages later by the play's title
and the opening dialogue. It was either torn away from the copy used for setting F or understandably overlooked by a compositor who took the title as his
starting cue.

10+. Shakespeare was apparently one of the pioneers in making fairies
diminutive, though (as I suggested in an earlier note) he was probably not the ini-
tiator. Elizabethan popular notions tended to assume that they were, like the Irish
sidhe, otherworld replications of full-sized human beings—hence the lore of the
changeling, a child whose oddity is to be explained by its being a fairy child

substituted in exchange for the human original. See Kathleen M. Briggs, *The Anatomy of Puck* (1959, 13–16)

11. William A. Ringler, Jr.: "The Number of Actors in Shakespeare's Early Plays," in *The Seventeenth-Century Stage: A Collection of Critical Essays*, ed. Gerald Eades Bentley (Chicago: University of Chicago Press, 1968), pp. 110–34.

12+. The same atmosphere, with its emphasis on expansive natural harmonies, serves well for the resolution that takes place with the awakening of the Athenian lovers, but it may also be part of a further original design. An entertainment for Elizabeth's visit to Oxford in 1566 included a bay of hounds in the outside courtyard; and if the first production of *A Midsummer Night's Dream* was in the context of an aristocratic wedding, as seems likely, there may well have been a similar incorporation of the festive sound of a hunting pack as background music. The hunt itself was dispensable. Since it is dispensed with, Shakespeare could afford to keep the rich lines about the music of the hounds without literally producing it for subsequent performances in public theaters, since he has Theseus speak only of what Hippolyta is *going* to hear when the hunt begins.

13+. Ringler expressly rejects the doubling of Theseus and Hippolyta with Titania and Oberon without explanation. It seems to me obvious that this is the way Shakespeare designed the play, from start to finish.

14+. Lear retires into the hovel, and is unseen by Gloucester, who enters immediately afterward and asks for him. The Fool may accompany Lear into the hovel, and be left there when Kent, at Gloucester's insistence, retrieves Lear in order to shift him to a safer place. I suppose it more likely, however, that Gloucester's "take up thy master" is spoken to the Fool as a supplement to, rather than a redundancy with, his previous direction to Kent to "take him in thy arms," and that Gloucester's later "take up, take up" is directed to both Kent and the Fool. Shakespeare's strategy, that is, probably gives the Fool his last exit, though without warning us that we will not see him again: cf. Benvolio at the end of 3.1.

15*. The greatest impediment to this hypothetical doubling is the movement from 2.3 (ending with Friar Laurence escorting Romeo to further assistance in his project to pursue Juliet) to 2.4 (which begins with the entrance of Mercutio and Benvolio). It would be distinctly problematic to transform the Friar to Benvolio on such short notice. But not impossible. Consider that (a) the Friar's exit line, "Wisely and slow, they stumble that run fast," makes a slight pause before the next entrance dramatically appropriate, as does the change in tone and focus of concern; (b) if Juliet and Romeo heed this admonition enough to follow the Friar offstage at his slower pace, the actor playing the Friar gains a little lead time; and (c) doffing the Friar's robe to reveal Benvolio's costume under it need not take more than five seconds, with a little help. It could be made to work. There may be a better way to explain Benvolio's disappearance, or perhaps it need not be explained at all; but in the meantime, this is at least worth considering.

16+. The relevant page of F was reset during the printing of the book, and the corrected version changes this heading to "Boy," perhaps because of a confusion with the nearby speech of Paris's page, which is headed "Boy" in Q2, and changed to "Page" in F. The uncorrected F page is reproduced at the back of

Hinman's Norton Facsimile of the folio. Its *Balt* speech heading is doubtless derived from the corresponding heading in Q2, from which it was set; the corrected version was probably reset from Q2, with a slip of the compositor's eye resulting in "Boy" and a subsequent change of the page's "Boy" to "Page" in order to distinguish them.

17*. Henry Swinburne, author of *A Treatise of Spousals or Matrimonial Contracts: wherein All the Questions relating to that Subject are ingeniously Debated and Resolved* (London, 1686), actually wrote his treatise around 1600, as the prefatory remarks of its 1686 publication observe and excuse. An eminent jurist in the York Prerogative Court, and author of what everyone seemed to regard as the definitive work on wills and testaments, his partially finished work on spousals got a late publication but an enormous respect, and may safely be considered the best source for the legal understanding of the tricky modes of matrimonial self-commitment in Shakespeare's day. This must have been a matter for popular gossip, in that it was far easier to commit marriage in those days than in these: Swinburne makes it pedantically clear that words such as are uttered between Orlando and Rosalind in 4.1 are quite enough to constitute the "kind of Spousals (as I have often foretold) [that] are in Truth and Substance very Matrimony indissouluble" (sig. L1v). The dramatic scene in question is virtually (and perhaps exactly) as if Shakespeare is impishly pushing the legal limits: on Swinburne's terms, which must have been available in discussions of the time in one form or other (Swinburne was an interpreter of law rather than a legislator, and his particular opinion need not be assumed to be in question) would make this a genuine marriage, *except* for the fact that Orlando, although accepting Ganymede as Rosalind and as his wife, does not know that this fiction is in fact true.

7. A GOOD PLOT, GOOD FRIENDS, AND FULL OF EXPECTATION

1. *The True Order and Methode of Wryting and Reading Hystories* . . . By Thomas Blundeuill [STC 3161]. Blundeville acknowledges that he is mainly translating the work of two Italian theorists, but a comparison of his own treatise with that of Francesco Patricio will show that it is precisely in the special moralizing dimension that Blundeville makes his rare departures from the source that he otherwise rather slavishly follows.

2*. But these entertainments are within the boundaries of what Shakespeare's contemporaries could have called a "play." In various sixteenth-century texts, "stage-plays" are distinguished from, say, "comedies," because "stage-play" (or just "play") encompassed things like fencing-displays, tumbling, and the like: any performance staged as entertainment. Many a scholar has said misleading things as a result of misinterpreting these terms.

3. Both Quartos use this title on their title pages, though in the running headers through the body of the book, both abbreviate it to the same form as used by F. (The running headers in the *King Lear* Quarto abbreviate to *The Historie of King Lear.*)

4!. We inherit and share something of these obviously inconsistent biases (as contemporary controversy about docudrama shows), even though it is fashionable for literary people to maintain that historicity is of indifferent value. We also share the Shakespearean casualness about embroidering and reorganizing the truth of history when it comes to entertainment: books on "newsworthy" happenings often imaginatively reconstruct whole unrecorded and unwitnessed conversations, quotation marks and all, without being expected to admit to taking liberties; and "true-story" films regularly revise their documentary sources extensively without apology or notice. In these respects, the general psychology to which Shakespeare addressed his history plays does not seem to have changed much. Vividness and aesthetic/moral satisfaction remain a high priority for eager audiences, even when the subject is ostensibly what really happened. History evidently tastes better cooked than raw!

5+. Q1 reads almost identically: "can you not play the murder of *Gonsago?*" A very random check of modern editions shows that the first seven I came upon all print the last four words in italics or quotations marks as if it were a title—including, to my surprise, the Variorum edition, which renders it in italics without a note indicating this editorial change or registering the readings of the original texts. The typographical conventions used in the original text are unambiguous; cf. Polonius' reference in 3.2 to his own acting days in the university: "I did enact *Julius Caesar*, I was kill'd i'th'Capitol: *Brutus* kill'd me." Here, *Julius Caesar* is not the title of a play but the name of a historical personage. All proper names are italicized in the original texts; when Gertrude, a few lines later, says "Come hither my good *Hamlet*, sit by me," she is addressing her son, not the play. The modern editors appropriately eliminate the italicizations in these two passages.

6*. In all of this, there is an inadequately recognized dramaturgical shift that needs to be explicitly addressed. Shakespeare has Hamlet set up a special interpolated speech that initially seems to be the thing that will catch Claudius' conscientious notice, but a careful attention to the text will register that Shakespeare subsequently has Hamlet revise his plan. After his histrionic soliloquy about the Player's tears for the fictional Hecuba, he returns to practicality *as if he had never thought of a dramatic entrapment before*, and this time he thinks in terms of a larger story:

> Fie upon it! Foh! About, my brain.
> I have heard that guilty creatures, sitting at a play,
> Have by the very cunning of the scene
> Been struck so to the soul that presently
> They have proclaim'd their malefactions.
> . . . I'll have these players
> Play something like the murder of my father
> Before mine uncle.

The beginning of 3.2 seems to return to the original plan, in that it refers to "the" speech, but it is useless to attempt to identify Hamlet's twelve to fourteen lines in the production of *The Mousetrap*—the remainder of this episode reverts to the secondary plan. I do not think it necessary to suppose that Shakespeare's final production of *Hamlet* excised either one or the other: alternative competing understandings, each locally exploited for potential dramatic effectiveness, are fairly common in Shakespeare's designs.

7*. In a way, it backhandedly reveals something about those who watch it, in that their wisecracking commentary displays the shallowness of their patronizing toleration, but it seems impossible to calculate what sort of attitude toward them Shakespeare expected to elicit from *his* audience. I suspect that he had in fact stolen a march on the putative aristocratic witnesses of the conjectural first performance, forcing them into an uncomfortable self-recognition about their own random witty putdowns that would predictably have been voiced about "these fairy toys" earlier in the performance. But in the long run, Shakespeare is rather kind to the onstage audience of *Pyramus and Thisby*: the cast shows no hurt feelings, and Theseus concludes with a graciousness that evidently conceals from them (though not from us, or from his companions) the last rude digs at this fiasco.

8+. This is the Quarto reading. The Folio substitutes "Heaven's" for "God's," in keeping with a 1606 ordinance against oaths in stage plays that required texts to be purged of careless references to God before they could be staged or published: see E. K. Chambers, *The Elizabethan Stage*, vol. 4, pp. 338–39. The Quarto also has Carlisle reply to this speech with "My Lord, wise men ne'er sit and wail their woes," which the Folio changes to "My Lord, wise men ne'er wail their present woes." I have no doubt that the Quarto reading in this case too represents the original design, and that Shakespeare had Richard sit on the stage as he spoke of doing so. The Folio change may mean that Shakespeare later dropped this piece of stage business: perhaps it looked too indecorous, or drew laughs.

9*. W. W. Greg pointed out long ago (in *The Review of English Studies* 4 [1928], pp. 152–58) that act division is common to nearly all extant academic and boy's company plays from 1591 to 1610, but that less than 20 percent of the public theater plays (19 of 102) of the same period are given act divisions. Wilfred T. Jewkes found that of the 74 adult company plays printed from 1591 to 1607, only five (and all by Ben Jonson!) are act-divided (*Act Division* [Hamden, Conn.: Shoe String Press, 1958], pp. 98–99). *None* of the Shakespeare plays printed within his lifetime is act-divided. The scene divisions have a better case, which James E. Hirsh has prosecuted in detail, in *The Structure of Shakespearean Scenes* (New Haven: Yale University Press, 1981), as "the most important common structural denominator found in all his plays, the individual scene" (p. 210). But even in the matter of scenes, the question is dicey.

10*. Reprinted in John C. Meagher, "The London Lord Mayor's Show of 1590" (*English Literary Renaissance*, vol. 3, n. 1 (1973), pp. 94–104). This show is quite typical of such public entertainments, but it also contains some interesting and atypical dramatic strategies, notably a shift in which characters who are first presented simply as the moral abstractions Dignity and Rebellion suddenly become representations of the corresponding historical personages William Walworth and Jack Straw, and briefly act out the scene for which Walworth became especially famous. This is worth remembering when we turn to the subject of character in the next chapter, in that this close relationship between historical personages and moral abstractions was a dramaturgical presupposition that Shakespeare partially shared.

11. For the general subject of dumb show "pageants" in the drama of this period, see Dieter Mehl, *The Elizabethan Dumb Show: The History of a Dramatic Convention* (London: Methuen & Co Ltd, 1965).

12. Geoffrey Bullough, *Narrative and Dramatic Sources of Shakespeare* (London: Routledge and Kegan Paul, 1961), lists six texts as unqualified "Sources" for *King Lear*, plus one additional probable source and four possible beyond that. For *Richard II*, he offers three sources, a probable source, two possible sources, and an analogue.

13. The story was most generally known from Ovid's *Metamorphoses*, bk. 4, where the wall and its chink are rather more important to the tale than Peter Quince's version make them. The ballad version that appears in *A Handefull of Pleasant Delites* (1584) does not explicitly mention the wall, but nevertheless assumes it: the lovers have carried out their wooing for "long tract of time" without seeing each other's faces. (This version is reprinted in Geoffrey Bullough, *Narrative and Dramatic Sources of Shakespeare*, vol. 1 [London: Routledge and Kegan Paul, 1961], pp. 409–11; the five-sentence version, printed in 1573, is reprinted in the same volume on pp. 404–5.)

14*. The chronicles offered this order: (1) the articles against Richard are drawn up; (2) Richard is advised to resign; (3) Richard is persuaded to renounce his crown; (4) the renunciation, together with the adoption of Henry as his successor, is reported to Parliament; (5) Parliament calls for a formal confession of Richard's crimes; (6) Henry claims and assumes the throne; (7) accusations are made against Aumerle and others; (8) Parliament requests the publication of Richard's crimes; (9) the Bishop of Carlisle protests the impropriety of the proceedings against Richard, and is attained; (10) the Abbot of Westminster conspires with others to overthrow King Henry. Shakespeare made significant changes in about half of them, and presented them, within a single scene, in the order 7, 4, 6, 9, 1, 5, 8, 2, 3, 4, 10. He could hardly be accused of following his sources slavishly.

15. Bullough lists four sources as certain (Holinshed, Spenser, the King Leir play, and Higgins' poem in *The Mirror for Magistrates*) and adds one additional "probable" and three "possible" sources (vol. 7, pp. 269–420).

16+. Shakespeare routinely places such ceremonies offstage; the mock (and potentially valid) wedding of *As You Like It* 4.1, and Hymen's quasi-solemnization of the four marriages of the play's final scene are to some extent deliberately playful partial exceptions.

17. Thomas Fenne, *Fennes Frutes* (London, 1590: STC 10763), sig. O4v–P1. Fenne's version, incidentally, is that "Leyr" doted on the older daughters and had never fancied the youngest, who had therefore received nothing from him and stayed out of the kingdom. The gradual denials of Leyr's needs by his ungrateful older daughters finally drive him to seek (and find) relief and remedy from his kinder youngest. It is, for Fenne, a lesson in "what miseries, calamaties,

enmormities, infinit troubles and dayly vexations, consequently doo fall to man by that fond conceipt in doating folly, inordinately louing and immoderately fonding ouer wife, sonne, daughter, or others whosoeuer." That was not quite the way Shakespeare saw it.

18. *Henslowe's Diary*, f3.9; Foakes and Rickert edn., p. 21.

19+. Some modern editors place Romeo's entrance eight lines later, presumably influenced by the fact that he does not speak until then: that is indeed where the entry is placed in the Quarto editions. I think it likely that F's prescription of an earlier entrance represents Shakespeare's deliberate, probably revisionary, dramatic design.

20+. This is the Q1 reading, and is probably correct. Q2 reads "And fier end furie," an obvious error that is corrected by Q3 as "And fier and fury," (ditto Q4 except for the comma), which in turn resulted in the Folio's "And fire and Fury." The intrinsic superiority of the Q1 phrase (as well as the progressive stages of its corruption) come clear once it becomes clear that Q1 has Romeo vividly apostrophize two personified moral qualities, while the deteriorated version weakens and dilutes this effect in shifting the focus.

21+. The most conspicuous awkwardness in the plot is the apparently arbitrary invention of a plague to prevent the Friar's letter from getting through to Romeo. Why didn't Shakespeare at least have the Prince mention the plague as a further reason for discouraging public assemblies of Capulets and Montagues? This was a common enough phenomenon in the lives of Shakespeare's audience, frequently resulting in closing the playhouses until the epidemic had run its course. It is at least imaginable that Shakespeare deliberately failed to make it seem to fit, so as to deliver another irrational and inexplicable impediment to a happy ending, as a bolt from the blue. But I don't think so: careless, for a change.

22*. There is, of course, a little more to it than this. The first scene's emphatic attention to *naturalness*, applied especially to Orlando's resemblance to his beloved father Sir Rowland de Boys and Oliver's gross lack of resemblance, sets up the conditions for a recovery much as a similar treatment of Demetrius' early unnaturalness in *A Midsummer Night's Dream* prepares the way for his homecoming to Helena. Oliver's lack of motivation—in Lodge, the youngest brother is the major heir, and Oliver is after the money—is underlined by his explicit puzzlement about why he hates a lad whom everyone else esteems, and leaves a vacuum that can be filled with a later rush of natural feeling, rescuing him from his moral deformity and restoring him to who he much more truly is, rather like the moral recovery of Demetrius.

8. STUFFED, AS THEY SAY, WITH HONORABLE PARTS

1+. He enters 1.3 as "Hereford," and 2.3 as "the Duke of Hereford," but otherwise is some version of "Bolingbroke" in all speech headings and stage directions from first to last.

2+. In 1.2, by the clown who at that point has no name (more on that later), and in the final scene, by "Second Brother," who apparently no longer has one (he introduces himself merely as "the second son of old Sir Rowland"

and his speech-headings are simply "2. Bro."). Referred to as "Jaques" by Orlando in the play's opening speech, this middle brother is never again mentioned until his sudden appearance seventy lines before the end; by that time, we may suspect that Shakespeare's assignment of the same name to quite a different character has canceled out that initial identification, even though it remains in the received text. Shakespeare's source called him Fernandyne, and gave him more presence in the story; "2. Bro." is quite sufficient for what Shakespeare eventually enlisted him to accomplish for the play.

3+. The speeches of Dogberry and Verges in *Much Ado About Nothing* are for a brief while headed *Kemp* and *Cowley*. Sometimes there is an occupational name: *Constable*, or some abbreviation thereof, heads more speeches in *Much Ado About Nothing* than *Dogberry* (or *Kemp*). The use of Kemp's name is confined to 4.2, and is not consistent even within that short scene. When the local constabulary are first introduced, in 3.3, it is as "Dogbery and his compartner with the watch," and their speech headings remain abbreviations of Dogberry and Verges thereafter—unless I am right in supposing that in the textual confusions at the end of the scene, Dogberry is referred to as some abbreviated version of *Constable* and gets mixed up with *Conrad*—see John C. Meagher, "Conrade Conned: Or, the Career of Hugh Oatcake" (*Shakespeare Quarterly*, v. 24, n. 1, 1973, pp. 90–92). In 3.5, Dogberry enters as "the Constable," and his speech headings are abbreviated versions of "Constable Dogberry" for something less than fifty lines, after which he becomes first merely *Const.* and then merely *Dogb.* In his last appearance, 5.1, Dogberry enters as "Constable" and remains *Const.* throughout. Constables and clowns have an affinity in Shakespearean dramaturgy. Town constables were amateur appointed peacekeepers, and it was easy (as well as fun) to play them as a species of Keystone Kops. When Shakespare shifts from the comic name Dogberry to the occupational title Constable, he is not moving very far.

4+. Kent's "This is not altogether fool, my lord" appears only in the Quarto text, and has no parallels even there—and amounts to little more than Polonius' musing in *Hamlet* that the title character seems sometimes to make rather good sense, even though he is quite out of his wits.

5+. When the costume-identifiable workmen enter 3.4, it is difficult to imagine that Shakespeare did not suppose that his audience would expect to be in for an interval of ribaldry. Their comportment is one of the quieter surprises of the play: labeled at their entrance as "a Gardener, and two Servants," they conduct themselves with what must have been unanticipated dignity, and their speech headings sustain the respectful titles that Shakespeare silently accorded them. One of the "Servants"—surely an unusual title for such a role—does not speak, and I cannot account for his presence, unless he is needfully involved in transforming the walls of Flint Castle into the chair of state for the next scene (which I think plausible), apart from the sort of in-house training that is so nicely suggested by Molly Mahood in *Bit Parts in Shakespeare's Plays* (Cambridge: Cambridge University Press, 1992).

6+. That is in fact one of the minor points of Shakespeare's agenda in Edmund's opening soliloquy in 1.2: we are temporarily teased by his argument that the legal disadvantage of bastards does not make sense. While he is at it, Shakespeare has Edmund add that the legal advantage of elder brothers does not make sense either, but that theme is never brought to our attention again, even within Edmund's soliloquy: legitimacy is the sole question as he concludes. Such localized happenings are routine in Shakespeare's dramaturgy, and do not obligate him to follow through in any systematic way.

7+. On a larger scale of practicality, as Molly Mahood's excellent study of bit parts reminds us, this personalized differentiation also provided a good opportunity for giving some significant stage experience to apprentice actors.

8*. Well, almost enough: I have often noticed that Juliet's final speech in 3.5, dismissing the just-exited Nurse from her trust and confidence, is regularly thought entirely justified. I suggest that what is really happening dramaturgically is that Shakespeare gives the Nurse—in verse, not prose—a lovely speech that bumblingly (and entirely in established character) tries to make things best for her beloved Juliet, and that Juliet reacts with feigned appropriate deference at first and then slams into a self-willed fury (not unlike Romeo's unfortunate reevaluation of Mercutio's death in 3.1) that (unjustly, but effectively) does the job of cutting the Nurse off from any further confidence and therefore from any further importance to the plot.

9. See Gerald Eades Bentley, *Shakespeare & Jonson: Their Reputations in the Seventeenth Century Compared* (2 vols.: Chicago: University of Chicago Press, 1945).

10. "The Vice" is used explicitly to typify such a character in, e.g., *The Trial of Treasure* (1567), *The Life and Repentance of Mary Magdalene* (1567), *The Tide Tarrieth No Man* (1576), *Like Will to Like* (1587). Where the label is not expressly used, the type would surely have been as easily recognized as Hamlet's "adventurous Knight," or even his "Clown."

11. E.g., in *Like Will to Like*, or the better-known example in Marlowe's *Doctor Faustus*.

12. See Ulpian Fulwell's *Like Will to Like*, Lewis Wager's *Enough Is as Good as a Feast*—and cf. Wager's *The Longer Thou Livest*, and George Wapull's *The Tide Tarrieth No Man*. Apropos of Falstaff as Vice, it may be noted that in *King Darius* (1577), the Vice type is named Iniquity and overtly provided with a temporarily threatening dagger.

13+. So Lear's speech is divided and capitalized in F, but it is likely to be intended as prose, that being more appropriately indecorous: Q1 reads "nay and you get it you shall get it with running," properly set as prose.

14+. Shakespeare shows little interest in lower-class social climbers who affect eloquent Latinate "inkhorn" words. This type is common enough in plays by his contemporaries, and is no less amusing than what Shakespeare often settles for. I suspect that his apparent distaste for it may have had something to do with its unresolved unclarity about social place: a self-disqualifying bumbler of ordinary language is socially unambiguous, but a pretentious commoner who flaunts some real education might create a social dislocation that Shakespeare—unlike, say, Anthony Munday in his depiction of Rafe in *The Downfall of Robert, Earl of Huntingdon*—might feel obliged to resolve dramatically before everything could be settled.

15!. It is perhaps notable that Shakespeare passes up the chance to have one of them brag that he has caroused with the Prince of Wales, which would have been easy enough and would have provided better grounding for Hal's boast, at the beginning of 2.4, that he has won the esteem of the local tapsters and "can drink with any Tinker in his own language during my life"—not to mention that when he is King of England, he "shall command all the good lads in Eastcheap." I do not know how to account for Shakespeare's not having exploited the opportunity. I am reluctant to suppose that it never occurred to him, though that might be the case, and I am uneasy about suggesting that he didn't want to manifest any such popular pretension that Hal could not directly control. But in any case, we need to ask what is the function of this brief interlude. I can only register what I find to be its successful effect: on the heels of serious and ominous business, it (like the beginning of *Romeo and Juliet* 1.5) opens briefly a refreshing window that enlarges our perspective and reminds us how much of the world carries on as usual, unaware of the story that has been dominating our attention—a dramatic analogue to Brueghel's "Fall of Icarus" as appreciated in Auden's "Musée de Beaux Arts." That may possibly be what was intended.

16!. One of the unhappy failures that occurred as the Restoration mentality disdained the "unsophisticated" work of its predecessors is that Sidney's *An Apologie for Poetrie* (alias *The Defence of Poesie*: it was published under both titles in 1595) was not integrated into the English critical tradition, which leaned rather on Continental commentators after 1660. Sidney's distinction between the comedy of scorn and the comedy of delight strikes me as one of the most important distinctions in the history of criticism; as far as I know (I have looked, but my ignorance should not be taken as definitive), it was never pursued in an adequate way. Of course, we still have time.

17!. Cordelia's critique is unfair. Neither of her sisters have said anything incompatible with their marriages. Her snitty remark that, if she should wed, her husband would get half her love, does not call the marriages of Goneril and Regan legitimately into question against their protestations of love for Lear nearly so much as it calls into question Cordelia's judgment and motives. But this is a momentary happening, and Shakespeare does not allow us enough time to reflect. The truth that lingers is that Goneril and Regan have said appropriately extravagant things, and that Cordelia has undermined their sayings by arguing that they can't live up to them if we take them literally, and that Cordelia—by her earlier conscientious asides as well as by her refusal to play Lear's self-indulgent and phony game—has won our confidence, and that therefore she gets to say what is appropriate. We therefore see more sense in her argument than it deserves, and do not notice that she has distorted what her sisters have said (because from our sympathy with Cordelia's perspective, the whole thing was distorted in the first place), and the beloved youngest daughter has automatically acquired our sympathy in a tentative way before it is definitively established by Lear's disappointed and furious reaction which makes her a martyr for the truth. The engineering of this scene is wonderful, but consistent rationale is not one of its properties.

18+. The conversion of Proteus in the last scene of *Two Gentlemen of Verona* is probably the most conspicuous example of Shakespeare's reliance on what is appropriate at the expense of his taking care to make it credible. But that was perhaps his earliest play: at any rate, he never does such a crude piece of rehabilitation elsewhere.

19+. Laertes is the only example I can think of in our limited canon. Beyond it, there are cases like that of Enobarbus in *Anthony and Cleopatra*. Both of these are, I would say, very qualified; there are not many others elsewhere in Shakespeare.

9. A TASTE OF YOUR QUALITY: COME, A PASSIONATE SPEECH

1. That is the Quarto reading; F has him say "Wise men ne'er wail their present woes," which may well indicate a change in staging.

2+. The new King Henry's lines are presented as verse, but it is clearly a verse that approaches the condition of prose: the actors' manner of delivery doubtless reinforced the stark difference between Richard's aria and Bolingbroke's reply.

3+. Marion Trousdale, *Shakespeare and the Rhetoricians* (Chapel Hill: University of North Carolina Press), 1982, p. 61. On the following page, she remarks that "*Hamlet* remains a supreme accomplishment because of the copiousness with which Shakespeare finds topoi in the story itself and the skill with which he varies them." Difficult as it is to account for the accomplishment of *Hamlet*, I doubt that this judgment would prevail on the first balloting.

4+. Those to whom rhetorical facility comes easily will recognize that I am making a rhetorical point and will spare me letters of testimony to confute my allegation. I will not feel obliged to answer any rebuttals that are not decidedly fun.

5!. Ben Jonson's remark that the players commended Shakespeare for delivering texts with scarecely a blot (i.e., a correction) in them is a lead-in for Jonson's critical suggestion that Shakespeare's plays needed more correction than they got. The assumption seems to be that both Jonson and Shakespeare's colleagues thought that he composed without much self-correction. I suppose that we can probably trust that he brought clean copy to his company, on the basis of this evidence, and that he was assumed to be bringing something like first drafts. But that assumption grows increasingly doubtful as current scholarship attends to evidence of Shakespeare's rewriting (it is worth noting that the gaffe that Jonson especially picks on, "Caesar never does wrong but with just cause" does not appear in the published text of *Julius Caesar*, or any other play). I fancy that Shakespeare's conversation probably displayed an inventiveness that made him seem capable of writing *As You Like It* in a few intensive sittings over a long weekend, and I can imagine that he might have enjoyed giving that impression. But his playwrighting was slow-paced by comparison with many of his contemporaries, some of whom were regularly churning out plays on two or three weeks' notice, and it seems to me plausible that he did far more rewriting than his company, or Jonson, or a large body of modern commentators, have supposed, and made fair copies of the results before turning them in, without feeling obliged to correct the impression that it had all come easily. Nevertheless, the impression of unstudied fluency that his plays still give suggests that much of the text did come rather spontaneously; we will never know how much, or how little, effort he dedicated to refining it before offering it for production.

6+. Neither is it accidental that Polonius, who despite being often a tedious old fool has apparently earned a reputation for being notably astute as an adviser of kings, speaks his best wisdom to his son in maxims that have become proverbial, some of them perhaps having already been in circulation before Shakespeare put them in his mouth. Commentators who see them as inflated truisms or pompous pontifications seem to be making their judgments on the basis of Shakespeare's more usual portrayal of Polonius as a bumbling meddler who dithers in empty rhetoric, and assuming that his advice to Laertes must therefore be self-disqualifying. I suggest that anyone who reads the lines without such prejudgment, even if ignorant of the place they have won in subsequent folk wisdom, will make no such mistake. This time Shakespeare lets Polonius be wise.

7. See, for instance, Bryan A. Gartner, "Shakespeare's Latinate Neologisms," *Shakespeare Studies 15* (1983), pp. 149–70.

8. G. L. Brook, in his excellent study of *The Language of Shakespeare* (London: Andre Deutsch, 1976), remarks on p. 11 that "The reader, and even more the editor, of Shakespeare can profit from a knowledge of the ways in which the language of Shakespeare, while differing from that of today, follows its own rules which make one reading or interpretation possible while another is virtually inconceivable."

9. Albert C. Baugh, *A History of the English Language*, 2d ed., p. 273.

10+. The last factor was dramatically emphasized with the publication of the Third Edition of the great *Webster's Dictionary*, in which the traditional labeling of some words as "colloquial" was entirely dropped. I consider this an editorial mistake, as a major dictionary should be prepared to supply such information to readers interested in shades of tone and meaning (just as it should satisfy readers' curiosity about etymologies), but what the decision symptomatizes is far more significant than the limitation it imposed on the usefulness of Webster's Third.

11*. That, of course, is a way of putting it that I would probably not have been permitted by the editor fifty years ago, and would doubtless never have occurred to me to try fifty years still earlier.

10. THE PURPOSE OF PLAYING . . . AT THE FIRST AND NOW

1+. *The true order and Methode of wryting and reading Hystories, according to the precepts of Francisco Patricio, and Accontio Tridentino, two Italian writers, no less plainly than briefly, set forth in our vulgar speach, to the great profite and commoditye of all those that delight in Hystories.* By Thomas Blundeuill (London, 1574: STC 3161). When he departs from the guidance of Patricio on how to write history (in which there is an assiduous insistance to deal only with the facts, well told), and moves into how to read it, he tells us that the object is "First that we may learne thereby to acknowledge the prouidence of God, whereby all things are ordered and directed. Secondly, that by the examples of the wise, we maye learne wisedome wysely to behaue our selues in all our actions . . . Thirdly, that we maye be stirred by example of the good to follow the good, and by example of the euill to flee the euill" (sig. F2v–F3). He never implies that he even sees the difference between his advice about writing and his advice about reading, but it is clear that he is more enthusiastic about the latter, however correct he may suppose the former to be in its place.

2. S. J. Teague, *Sir Thomas Gresham* (Bromley, Kent: SynJon Books, 1974). Teague actually says financial center "of the world," but Europe is at least sufficient for the point.

3. Alan Haynes, *Robert Cecil, Earl of Salisbury* (London: Peter Owen, 1989), p. 180. Haynes thinks that the great classical architect Inigo Jones may have been involved in the planning of the New Exchange (which opened in 1609), but does not offer evidence: it certainly would have been appropriate to the overall conception of the project.

4. I don't want to lean very hard on this reading, but I suggest that it would be both likely and appropriate if the "fair field full of folk" at the beginning of *Piers Plowman* had been intended to be understood not as a lovely meadow that happened to be well populated, but rather as a crowded fairground.

5+. It is perhaps worth noting that in the many uses of the life-is-like-a-stage topos in Shakespeare's time, the various roles and actions being played are virtually always treated as detached pageants rather than as subordinate components of a preordained larger design. It was easy enough to employ the pious Christian notion of Providence, or the rather impious but familiar classical notion of Fate, in order to show how everything fits into a larger scheme—but Shakespeare, while prepared to play with either or both, tends to invest his allegiance rather in the more concrete decisions and specific pageants, linking them in a satisfying resolution rather than coordinating them into a metaphysical scheme.

6. Brooke's Prologue, "To the Reader," Bullough v. 1, p. 284.

7!. I have scamped this question, except to the extent that I have draw attention to the way in which the titles of Shakespeare's plays, in their various editions, alternate easily between history and tragedy as their major categorizations. The collection of 1623 divided his plays into three categories, but it is not altogether clear that this was apt. *King Lear* is a legitimate history play as much as *Richard II* is a tragedy: so the history (and perhaps tragedy) of their titles implicitly admit. Subsequent criticism asked for new categories: Romance, Tragicomedies, Romantic Comedies, Dark Comedies, and so forth. This is critically useful as a way of apprehending real differences, but the classifications have no claim on what Shakespeare thought he was doing. I hope eventually to spell out the following sentence more adequately, but at the moment I will settle for it: Shakespeare set about to tell effective stories dramatically, and deliberately wrote some that were happy and some that were sad, knowing that this distinction was conventional and important and did not amount to much more than that; he also knew that this distinction was unreal with respect to life, and qualified it in both directions; and when he thought his essential dramatic task included the assimilation